TRUTH

New Rules for Marketing in a Skeptical World

Lynn Upshaw

American Management Association
New York · Atlanta · Brussels · Chicago · Mexico City · San Francisco
Shanghai · Tokyo · Toronto · Washington, D.C.

Special discounts on bulk quantities of AMACOM books are available to corporations, professional associations, and other organizations. For details, contact Special Sales Department, AMACOM, a division of American Management Association, 1601 Broadway, New York, NY 10019.
Tel: 212-903-8316. Fax: 212-903-8083.
E-mail: specialsls@amanet.org
Website: www.amacombooks.org/go/specialsales
To view all AMACOM titles go to: www.amacombooks.org

This publication is designed to provide accurate and authoritative information in regard to the subject matter covered. It is sold with the understanding that the publisher is not engaged in rendering legal, accounting, or other professional service. If legal advice or other expert assistance is required, the services of a competent professional person should be sought.

All registered company, brand, and product names, and copyrighted slogans, are the sole property of their respective owners and the parent companies noted in the text. The term "practical integrity" is not related to any product or service provided by any company other than Upshaw Marketing.

Library of Congress Cataloging-in-Publication Data

Upshaw, Lynn B.
    Truth : the new rules for marketing in a skeptical world / Lynn B. Upshaw.—1st ed.
       p.   cm.
    Includes bibliographical references and index.
    ISBN-13: 978-0-8144-7376-4
    ISBN-10: 0-8144-7376-8
    1. Marketing.   2. Marketing—Decision making.   3. Integrity.   I. Title.

HF5415.U67   2007
658.8' 02—dc22   *2007001114*

Printing number

10   9   8   7   6   5   4   3   2   1

With love, to Maurine Elizabeth and Molly Elizabeth—

two women of great integrity.

Contents

Acknowledgments

Book writing will never become a team sport, but it's a lot easier with support from friends and loved ones. My many thanks to all those who helped me fill in the blanks.

To Gary Klien, Jeff Jacobs, Thom Miller, Ron Nahser, Jason Pitts, Lauren Pitts, Jan Soderstrom, Dianne Snedaker, Earl Taylor, and Jennifer Upshaw, for reading drafts and for their encouragement and steady stream of good thoughts.

To Aditya Jha of Infosys; Rick Ridgeway, Eve Bould, and Jane Sievert of Patagonia; Kate King and David Aznavorian of Timberland; Mark Schurman and Kris Manos of Herman Miller; Shannon Cooney and Cammie Cannela of Kiehl's Since 1851; Dan Henkle, Michele Banks, and Marcus Chung of Gap, Inc; and several other key contributors in other companies.

To many present and former associates who provided real world stories of marketing missteps.

To my AMACOM editors, Ellen Kadin, with thanks for her support and sound advice, and Mike Sivilli, for his helpful guidance. And special thanks to Niels Buessem, for his thoughtful and insightful editing.

To all of my family, who feed me support and sustenance when I need them most.

And above all, to Susan, a peerless editor and researcher extraordinaire, and my patient and loving wife of many beautiful years.

What Was Naive Is Now Necessary

Marketing is rolling through one of the most exciting eras in its long history. Marketing is also about to get even tougher to pull off, and it was never all that easy.

While it is far from a science, marketing will soon be experiencing Newton's Third Law of Physics, the one about actions and opposite and equal reactions. The harder we sell, the less likely buyers will listen. The more we try to slide around their filters, the more quickly they will raise their shields. The more buyers wonder if we're telling them the truth, the more likely they will turn to another brand to find out what they've been missing.

If skeptical consumers and cynical business buyers don't believe what marketers promise, why will they be convinced by questionable claims shouted in higher decibels? If they don't think a brand is a good value at any price, why will they change their minds if the price is lowered? If they are bone-weary of being peppered with marketing messages, why will they be happy about marketers finding more invasive ways to get acquainted?

Now that skepticism and doubt have come home to roost in the marketplace, we in marketing are going to have to change the way we market. That change starts with recognizing that skepticism and doubt can best be trumped by marketing that is more honest than loud.

Unfortunately, many marketers do not consider integrity to be operable in their world. Integrity is all too often seen as a backdrop to daily work rather than its bone structure, a lofty standard instead of a necessary tool. And, by placing that standard on the wall as a guideline—and inevitably on the shelf as an afterthought—it immediately becomes *inoperable*.

How We Sell Is Now What We Sell

The world is full of segments, and some of those segments, albeit a dwindling lot, may blissfully sit still for a while longer as media machines sandblast them with messages, or they may meekly wait for marketers to tell them what they need to buy next.

But the rest of us want to know what marketers have done for us lately, and can they prove it? Buyers are beginning to judge a brand or company by the way it acts, not just by the product or service it offers. More than 75 percent of those responding to a 2006 Opinion Research survey said they preferred to buy from a company that operates ethically, even if they have to pay more.[1] Even if a large percentage of those respondents do not actually do what they say they will do, that's far too high a number to ignore.

While more and more business leaders are being indicted, it is buyers who are asking the prosecutorial questions: Has this company that keeps asking me to buy something also convinced me that I can trust it to deliver what it promises? Do they offer me a better value or just a lower price? Do I like their brand enough to want to be seen with it? Am I turned off by how they sell no matter how well their product or service performs? Are they telling me the truth?

Sooner or later, the brands and companies that hope to prevail in this marketplace of skeptics will have to demonstrate that they operate and market with integrity. Happily, there should be no need for them to sacrifice revenue or profit to do so. On the contrary, they may find that their integrity will become their strongest competitive advantage.

Convincing Them Instead of Selling Them

We talk about companies wanting to compete on a level playing field, but that's also what buyers want. If buyers feel they are being treated equitably by a brand or company and are provided with sound products that are priced fairly, they reward the marketers involved. If they see that the company has tipped the field against them, they are more likely than ever to steer clear. And once gone, they are less likely than ever to return.

Two-thirds of the respondents in a 2004 Yankelovich Partners poll agreed that, "if the opportunity arises, most businesses will take advantage of the public if they feel they are not likely to be found out." A total of 61 percent said that marketers did not respect them and one-third said that they would be willing to slightly lower their standard of living to live in a world free of marketing and advertising.[2] When was the last time you heard people *even claim* they would be willing to lower their standard of living?

Yankelovich's president J. Walker Smith once told a group of advertisers that buyers felt the way they did because they saw a marketplace blighted with too much clutter, filled with overly intrusive marketing techniques, and because of inappropriate targeting.[3]

The response of some marketers to these challenges is to throw more money at the problem or to find more inventive ways to slide into a prospect's back door like a professional party-crasher. There must be a better way, since more buyers are making it clear that they are not crazy about being "targeted," brand-ambushed, stealth-sold, guerilla-marketed, or commercially buzzed.

Money and intrusive messaging may work as a stopgap solution for a while yet, but both are likely to fail in the end. That's because our job as marketers is no longer to relentlessly sell until buyers buy; it is to convince buyers that they can trust us to tell them the truth, in the hope that they might consider buying from us. There's a world of difference between those two job descriptions.

Systematizing Integrity

The state, federal, and industry laws, regulations, and guidelines that are now in place theoretically prevent deceptive or misleading marketing. Yet consumers and business buyers are increasingly voting with their feet as they abandon companies that they perceive aren't being honest with them. That includes otherwise upright, well-meaning organizations, such as any number of food, automotive, and pharmaceutical companies.

In addition, product and marketing integrity problems can create serious revenue and brand equity declines, not to mention attracting unwelcome attention from federal and state regulators and the news media.

It was once considered naïve to believe that integrity was even relevant to marketing effectiveness. Soon, it may be considered the price of entry. When that happens, the companies that have strategically systematized their approach to marketing integrity will hold significant advantages over those that are reluctant to believe that integrity could ever be a driver of choice.

The book you are about to read explains why integrity needs to be integrated as a key working component directly into the very mechanism of marketing. *Truth* calls for retrofitting marketing practices with "practical integrity," a broad-based, integrated marketing methodology that systematizes integrity across the entire marketing mix. The "rules" from this book are revolutionary in that they call for a return to the original fundamentals that strong companies and strong brands were built upon. They are "new" because they have been forgotten by too many, too often.

The book will also explain the strategies and stories of some companies that have rigorously applied various forms of practical integrity to their full array of marketing and selling programs. These companies and others like them have learned that it is no longer enough to produce good products or services and expect that customers will trust you. It may not even be enough to hold the right corporate values and always try to do the right thing. The future may very well require an ordered application of integrity in all ways that the company and its brands are marketed.

Truth is set out in three parts:

- ❏ *Part One* (Practical Integrity) details some of the challenges and strategic solutions for business in general and marketing in particular in this age of skepticism and doubt. This part also examines the critical lessons learned from five companies that are driven by company-wide integrity that dictates their approach to marketing.

- ❏ *Part Two* (True Strategies) describes powerful marketing strategies derived from broad-based integrity. These strategy chapters also include brief sections called "A Conversation," which are fictional dialogues inspired by real experiences. Other sidebars, boxes, and "What if?" sections briefly spotlight some relevant subjects. Also, most chapters end with a series of recommendations, questions, and "Turn-Offs" to avoid at all cost.

- ❏ *Part Three* (Making It Happen) continues with additional integrity strategies, suggesting some internal marketing, benchmarking, marketing planning, and training that will help put practical integrity strategies into practice.

Truth does not focus on corporate social responsibility (CSR) or cause marketing. However, these have become frequent tools of companies that market with integrity. Mostly we focus on how selected companies create stronger marketing programs through their practice of integrity, and how those programs help achieve business goals.

One personal note: This author has worked in and around marketing for many years. On more than one occasion, I have been privy to, or part of, some actions that, in retrospect, could have been accomplished with more integrity. Nothing egregious, but questionable integrity rarely is. The point is, my house has as much glass as anyone's. This is not a book designed to throw stones, but simply to help marketers rethink what they do before they do it.

The Business We're All In

Marketing challenges have to be tackled on multiple levels. The right product or service, the right value proposition, the right marketing communications, the right pricing, the right channel strategies—all of these factors and many more must come together in perfect synchronization to achieve in-market goals. It now appears likely that, from this point forward, all of these building blocks will be significantly enhanced if they make use of some form of practical integrity.

In a 2005 interview, social scientist and researcher Daniel Yankelovich pointed out that those companies that forfeit the public's trust are losing a critical advantage they can't afford to lose, namely the benefit of the doubt.[4] No one needs the benefit of the doubt in these doubt-filled times more than the marketer.

Integrity is no longer just the business of prosecutors, preachers, and congressional committees. It is the business in which all marketers must now be engaged.

PART ONE

PRACTICAL INTEGRITY

CHAPTER 1

Convincing the Unconvinced

Practical Integrity and a Better Way to Market

Marketing can take credit for billions of transactions annually that keep economies humming around the globe. But if marketers keep selling as if the world wants nothing more than to be sold, the world may not always show its appreciation.

We marketers are doggedly finding new ways of parachuting into the lives of people who are frantically trying to close the skylight. Once there, far too many of us are routinely stretching the facts, or omitting some critical information, or obsessing on irresistible ends to justify any means, and considering it all to be harmless because they expect people to expect it.

What people expect today is just a fair chance to find the truth and buy it. That's become an even bigger challenge than it used to be, thanks to the real world we all call home.

Life As We Know It, If Not Love It

Here are some of the life changes that are making marketing more difficult:

❏ *We May Be Lonely, But We're Never Alone.* The Earth, according to Thomas Friedman, is flattening, and we're getting flattened right along with it. Friedman points to the public offering of Netscape stock on August 9, 1995 as a tipping point because it ultimately made it possible for us to navigate the Web.[1] Netscape and its successors proceeded to open up the floodgates before any of us realized we lived near water.

More than 700 million men, women, and children worldwide were online by the end of 2006,[2] which explains the nine trillion emails that they have to read every year and the billion searches

Google happily makes happen each day.³ For better or worse, we're never alone—least of all with our own thoughts.

❑ *Clockless and Clueless.* Americans spend about twice the amount of time with media as we think we do—a total of 11.5 hours a day—and that's probably at much higher levels for younger people.⁴ The number of messages piercing our lives results in a splicing of our attention spans and the degrading of our ability to focus. Time, which Professor Einstein always said was relative, is now becoming difficult to even gauge. Often we seem to stagger through our days like a gambling addict in a casino with no clocks.

With time slipping away, we are being forced to assess options faster than we may understand them, to make decisions more quickly than we want to, and often to buy before we are ready. It's a formula for more aggravation and less satisfaction among both marketers and their buyers, especially as information you can trust becomes harder to come by.

❑ *Walter Cronkite Doesn't Live Here Anymore.* In the good old days, say about 1990, you could count on your left hand how many "trusted sources" you needed to check with to be fully informed. Today, trusted centralized information sources are on a one-way trip to the Smithsonian, replaced by blogmasters and peer-to-peer mind melds.

We are becoming a world of sharers, which our kindergarten teacher always said was a good thing. In fact, we share more information during a day than other generations may have shared in a year. But what kept peace in the sandbox is complicating life for communicators.

Information is no longer distributed so much as released into the air. Facts have become negotiable. Messages that stick have to be sliced and diced to make them edible to audiences that want their information cooked with the same precision as their eggs. Marketers are forced to rely on more intermediaries to transmit their messages, and then must hope that the telephone game ends with a message remotely similar to the one they sent out. The only answer, of course, must be to just send out more messages. Right?

❑ *Thank You, Sir, May I Have Another?* It may be a pillar of free markets, but commercialism has become a synaptic cholesterol that clogs every waking hour. Depending on whom you talk to, the typical American is exposed to hundreds—and more likely thousands—of commercial impressions every day.

The term "commercial clutter" has become laughingly redundant. So-called *ad creep* is now at a decided gallop. Brazen commercial messages are cropping up in toilet stalls, inside taxi cabs, on the outside of private vehicles, in almost every scene of almost every feature film, all over football uniforms, throughout elementary schools, in Broadway musicals, draped over Monopoly game tokens, and even on some human foreheads, to name just a few venues.

Not that everyone is opposed to the commercial onslaught; there are some—for example, the urban hip—who wear badge brands to spotlight their cool or to show that they belong. But most of us are scrambling to at least filter the flow a bit.

❑ *Defending Our Lives.* In 1975, we had relatively few ways to receive, process, and store information. Thirty years later, our lives are a blur of cross-communications (see Figure 1-1).

Digital video recorders (DVRs), security software, personalized news services, spam filters, and many other defensive gadgets are finding their way into the welcoming arms of harassed consumers and overworked business buyers. The crush of information alternately stimulates us and drives us back into our cocoons. We spend a growing percentage of our energy checking to make sure the coast is clear.

More than half of the respondents (54 percent) in a 2005 Yankelovich study reported that they actively resist marketing; 69 percent said they are interested in products that can block advertising, and 56 percent said they resist products whose marketing tends to overwhelm them. Even more telling, the manner in which marketing is practiced is more important to these people than seeing marketing in new media outlets.[5]

Naturally, the more consumers push back the more marketers pour it on, like some unrelenting form of torture aimed at breaking buyers if it cannot convert them. Much of the marketing industry is now employing embedded messaging under the theory that, if audiences won't let us come to the party, we'll surprise them with a counter-party while they're in the shower. What some marketers get in return is an audience of annoyed, if not angry, people who thought they were gaining control of one part of their lives, only to find that they were losing it in another.

None of this sounds like fertile ground for business building. It certainly wouldn't be a great time for marketers to be held even more accountable for their end-products. Oops, too late.

Figure 1-1. Content/delivery options: a. 1976. b. 2006.

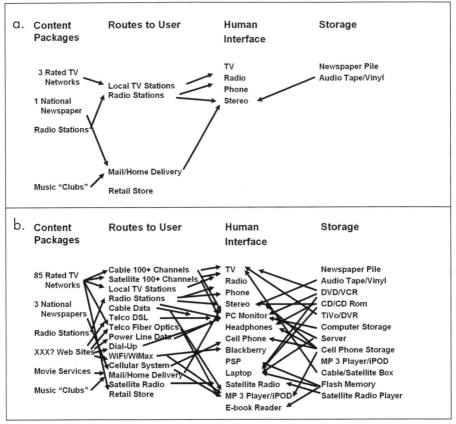

SOURCE: Adapted from Tom Wolzien, Sanford C. Bernstein & Co. Used with permission of Wolzien L.L.C.

❏ *The Accountability Crunch.* In a 2005 survey, 74 percent of several hundred marketing and management executives polled said that marketing accountability was either "extremely" or "very" important.[6] They didn't poll their CEOs, but we can guess the results.

More than ever, marketing spending is positioned as an investment by marketers but seen as a necessary cost by management. Marketing budgets are the first to be cut because their impact is the most ephemeral and the least quantifiable. That is slowly changing, but even refined return-on-marketing-investment tools will only bring marketing closer to parity with more highly valued cost centers, such as product development or sales.

On the other end of transactions, buyers are also making marketers more accountable for what they market. Put another way, buyers do not want to deal with businesses that are less than straightforward with them. And why should they? They almost always face an over-choice of options so, when a marketer loses their trust, it makes it easier for buyers to overcome their inertia and switch to a more trust-worthy provider.

Thus, marketers are caught in a squeeze to deliver more to demanding management by asking for help from buyers who themselves are becoming more demanding.

The fastest route through this thicket of challenges is the integrity trail. Unfortunately, business is finding it more difficult than ever to find that particular trailhead.

Not Even the Beginning of the End

In 2002, as corporate scandals were beginning to rock a number of business centers around the globe, the Gallup International Association polled 36,000 people in forty-seven countries, statistically representing 1.3 billion souls. They were told by respondents that business executives from multinational companies are among the least trusted leaders when it comes to acting for the benefit of society.[7]

Three years later, Harris Interactive found that the overall reputation of American corporations had continued to slide. In 2005, 71 percent of respondents rated the reputations of U.S. businesses as either "not good" or "terrible," up from 68 percent the year before.[8]

That same year, the term "integrity" was the most frequently looked-up word in the Merriam-Webster online dictionary.[9] Was that because integrity was in the news? Or, because people wanted to understand integrity so they could test its limits? Or, possibly because more people are coming to grips with how and why integrity might be important in their lives, including when they buy things?

Some wishful thinkers have predicted that the current hand-wrenching about integrity in business will soon become just another passé topic of conversation. That is a dangerously short-sighted point of view, as the post-Enron stock options back-dating scandal has proven. Gretchen Morgenson of the *New York Times* pointed out after former top Enron execs were convicted in May 2006, "Enron verdicts were, at best, the end of the beginning of this dispiriting corporate crime wave. They were certainly not the beginning of its end."[10] Figure 1-2 shows the business integrity damage to date. For those of you keeping score at home, all of us are losing.[11]

So, has most of business really been operating outside the law, or are prosecutors just getting better at finding the bad apples? Are there that many alarmingly

Figure 1-2. Business Integrity Scorecard.

Business Executive Convictions		Executive Financial Penalties	
July 2002 – August 2006		July 2002 –June 2005	
Titles	Convictions	Penalties	Amounts
Chief Executive Officers and Corporate Presidents	More than 100	Restitution, fines and forfeitures	$226 million
Vice-Presidents	More than 100		
Chief Financial Officers	More than 30		

SOURCE: Based on U.S Department of Justice Fact Sheets: Corporate Fraud Task Force (August 9, 2006) and Corporate Fraud Task Force (August 29, 2005).

indictable executives on any given day, or just too many reporters with nothing better to write about?

Actually, it doesn't matter. Nowhere is perception more like reality than in politics and business. There have been too many scandals, too many angry shareholders, and far too many ethically challenged executives for us to expect the public to trust easily again any time soon. (Keep in mind that the second tenet in the Enron company values statement was "integrity.")

For marketers, this is about much more than fixing the mistakes of foolish businesspeople; it is about regaining customer faith, which happens to be the only absolutely indispensable ingredient of every successful marketing program.

Separated at Birth: *Laissez Faire* and *Caveat Emptor*

Marketing is business's most visible example of the *Star Wars* force. It can be used to fight for a great cause, wielded as a bullhorn to let the world know about something they need or want, or spread through a crowd as a one-on-one whisper about a sensational value at the store down the block. Or, when it's drawn to the dark side, it can be a deliberate or inadvertent weapon of pointless deception.

It's a good thing we're all capitalists here, otherwise we'd have something to worry about.

Adam Smith, the world's first economist, is best known for his book *The Wealth of Nations,* in which he essentially advocated *laissez faire* (although he never literally used that phrase) as the release of free market forces from unnecessarily stringent government control.

But Smith expected his thoughts on free markets to be read within the context of his first major work published seventeen years earlier, called *The Theory of Moral Sentiments.* In that book, which first made Smith famous, he explained that economics was part of a larger human enterprise to create a positive society, in which individuals actually acted as if they cared for one another. This is a very different picture from that usually drawn by Smith devotees, who believe that his only concern was for government to back away and let an "invisible hand" lead the market wherever it might go, regardless of whatever impact that market may have.

Selfless Self-Interest

Laissez faire may call for free markets that are driven mostly by self-interest, but it does not call for disregarding the consequences of those free markets. On the contrary, Smith argued that the entire purpose of an economic market is to provide for *all* players in the marketplace, both on the institutional and individual level.[12]

How would Adam Smith feel about the business world of today? It's hard to know for sure, but he might like what some companies are up to, such as Whole Foods. With revenue of more than $5 billion and consistent profitability the last five years, Whole Foods is the biggest reason yet to believe that organic foods are here to stay. More to the point here, it is one of the better examples of how integrity can happily cohabitate with success.

Founder and CEO John Mackey has made it very clear that his company's mission is to put the customer ahead of everyone else, including the shareholders. That stance alone should have buried Whole Foods long ago, based on the way Wall Street usually thinks about such things. But Whole Foods is actually succeeding with its mission to practice an extraordinary form of capitalism that, in Mackey's words, "more consciously works for the common good instead of depending solely on the 'invisible hand' to generate positive results for society."[13]

More skeptical customers—that would be all of us—are inclined to judge the worthiness of a brand or company by its ability to deliver what it promises. Buyers don't want to hear why a marginal claim was justifiable just because the competition was doing the same thing. They are growing more irritable about caveats, hedges, and restrictions to offers. Sure, they like to be entertained, wooed, catered to, and pampered, but they are probably even more interested in simple truths.

Caveat emptor (buyer beware) made good business sense—at least from business's point of view—when the marketplace was more of a free-for-all. But that attitude, which has been seen by some as potentially predatory to buyers, now could be equally harmful to marketers. How could it be otherwise in today's environment that spawns multiple watchdog groups for every industry, a growing band of take-no-prisoners regulators, politically motivated state attorneys general, and blogs called "*(fill-in-the-brand-name)sucks.com*"?

A 2006 Edelman study found that business opinion leaders see a loss of trust because of ethical misbehavior as having a debilitating impact on customer behavior, regardless of what country the marketer operates in.[14] (See Figure 1-3.)

A 2005 *Fast Company* survey revealed that many of the 1,665 businesspeople interviewed believe, "Good ethics is also good business. . . . It builds brands, draws customers, and saves money in the long run."[15] And in 2004, *CMO* magazine found that 42 percent of the 300 chief marketing officers polled believed that deceptive sales and marketing practices is a top ethical issue for their companies.[16]

It's an issue all right, but is it an action item?

Burying the Lead: How Integrity Gets Lost

What will help convert skeptical buyers is demonstrating that integrity—in all facets of that word's meaning—is as important to marketers as it is to their customers. Not just that a company has nice-sounding values, but that it consistently markets with the same integrity it touts in flowery values statements. Not just integrity with honesty, but a broad-based integrity that drives all of the marketing programs.

Figure 1-3. The importance of trust.

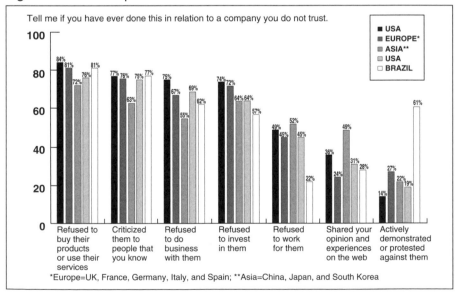

SOURCE: 2006 Annual Edelman Trust Barometer.

Before that can happen, marketers will have to incorporate integrity as an operative factor in their daily work. Typically, there are several reasons why that view has yet to gain traction:

❑ *There are other things to talk about.* In a 2006 poll, 1,800 communications professionals were asked about ethics in their organizations. Only half of them agreed that discussion of ethical/unethical conduct was encouraged.[17]

If you don't talk about ethical behavior, you can't expect people to give it much thought when it comes time for them to do their job. The problem may be that everyone knows that they are supposed to act ethically, and they don't have any problem with that. It's just that ethics seems faintly irrelevant compared to the hard realities of business. Which is like saying that Sarbanes-Oxley is faintly irrelevant to corporate boards of directors.

❑ *They didn't know it was loaded.* Some questionable marketing is launched because marketers just don't understand where the integrity line is, much less when they've crossed it. Inexperienced executives can approve dubious advertising or promotions that may have been cleared by legal but still mislead the company's marketing audiences. Lab technicians approve claims statements that are used out of context, and without their knowledge. Media experts may devise better ways to smother the customer in awareness-building brand contacts, not realizing that the avalanche is snuffing the life out of buyer interest.

❑ *Everyone's a Raider at heart.* The Oakland Raiders, one of the grittier American football teams, operate under a simple charge from their owner, Al Davis: "Just win, baby" (they haven't lately, by the way). Winning at all costs is the unspoken mantra at many, if not most, companies in a market-driven economy.

❑ *Those guys did it first.* Competitive pressures wrack the brains of most marketers every day of every month. It's what makes the system work but it would be nice to come to work and not have to worry about the other guy. Competitors earn varying degrees of share-of-market, but they always achieve a high share of their rival's mind. Consequently, nothing is more likely to tempt a marketer to stretch integrity than hearing that the competition did it the day before.

❑ *The Liars Club.* A 2005 psychology study discovered that 60 percent of their subjects lied at least once during a 10-minute conversation, and lied about an average of 2.92 things during that brief period.[18] Apparently, we most often lie to someone we know, usually for self-esteem reasons. But if we're all lying that much over routine things, it does make you wonder whether Seth Godin's book title, *All Marketers Are Liars,* should be considered all that tongue-in-cheek.[19]

❏ *Moving day is every day.* Personal integrity can sometimes take a backseat to the ever-present desire to move up. A marketer's supervisor, and that supervisor's supervisor, and up the chain-of-command, are all looking for results that will justify management's faith in them. And they are all more interested in those results than in wondering how they were obtained. That is why some marketers believe that questionable means are more than justified by a glorious end.

❏ *It's a labor of love.* Virtually all chief marketing officers are held personally accountable for driving revenue, and doing so with demonstrable return on marketing investment. That's as it should be unless it is accomplished in a way that compromises a company's or brand's integrity. Unfortunately, integrity is a soft measure and quarterly revenue stretch goals are as hard as it gets. So, when your 14-year-old tells you that she really digs the idea of the Ivy League, suddenly a little stretch here and a little fudge there doesn't seem all that out of line.

❏ *It's no big deal.* A 2002 UK study found that, while 75 percent of UK citizens had boycotted a brand because of the unethical way that a brand behaved, so-called ethical companies tend to have very small shares of their markets, and are not necessarily succeeding to any greater degree than their less ethics-driven competitors.[20] Separately, Professor David Vogel of the Haas School of Business at the University of California at Berkeley reviewed hundreds of studies and concluded that companies that are well known for their corporate social responsibility work have not necessarily delivered stronger profitability, nor has their market equity increased at a greater rate than that of other companies.[21]

It makes you wonder whether all of this is a lot closer to a mole hill than a mountain. But studies such as these deal largely with companies' social outreach programs. It's highly debatable whether a company that invests in local communities will be forgiven for questionable marketing to the citizens of those communities. After all, one of the most generous corporate givers in the world is Altria, Inc., formerly known as Philip Morris Companies.

"Moral Myopia" and "Moral Muteness"

In a 2004 study, more than fifty advertising agency executives from major U.S. business centers frequently demonstrated what researchers called "moral myopia," or the distorting of moral issues in a way that made them less relevant to business. Researchers also found what had been previously identified as "moral muteness," which meant that even those who saw ethical issues rarely talked about them in business settings.

The advertising executives generally didn't believe that the question of right or wrong was part of their business world; it rarely or never came up. When probed about why ethical issues weren't all that important, some of the executives tended to believe that the responsibility for ethics lay elsewhere (e.g., family, the law, regulators). They also passed along responsibility to society itself, blaming the media and culture for creating the conditions in which they worked. Advertising, after all, reflects the world—it does not create it.

This research and other such studies photograph an attitude that likely prevails in many companies. It's an attitude that can best be summed up by the well-known organized crime phrase, "It's just business." No one's killing anyone in the above-ground business world, but there are certainly some creative rationalizations being used to salve consciences.[22]

Marketing with Practical Integrity

We used to believe that business operated with a safety net below our high wire act: buyers would forgive the exaggerations and truth-stretching if we just didn't do anything really stupid. Don't look now, but that net is unraveling. Old-fashioned consumerism has returned in a new, more virulent strain, and this time it's being fed by virtually unlimited information.

So now, while we're still atop the wire, might be a good time to ask this question: Exactly why should *caveat emptor* be the tacit policy of free markets? Why should consumers and business buyers bear the primary responsibility for discerning what is being marketed truthfully and what isn't? Why is that not the joint responsibility of the buyer and the seller?

To put it more bluntly, what right do we in business have to put the burden on the party that is spending the money to figure out when that money is spent for something less than what is promised? Because we're all adults and no one ever promised that life was fair? That answer is not going to cut it in a world where buyer trust is hard to get and easy to lose.

These new times demand a new way to market, centering around what we will refer to from this point forward as "practical integrity." This is integrity that is much more than simply telling the truth; it is a broad spectrum of attitudes and actions that pragmatically meet both customer and marketer needs. Practical integrity can be defined as follows:

> *Practical integrity* is a systematized process of marketing planning and execution that drives multiple forms of integrity throughout the entire marketing mix, enabling customers and marketers to thrive in a high-integrity environment.

This is a marketing operating system that revolves around the central concept of sticking to systematized integrity, regardless of market changes. It starts with a more realistic way to treat marketing customers, drives through the major sectors of the marketing mix, and returns again to reinforce the customer-marketer partnership (see Figure 1-4).

How Integrity Can Strengthen Marketing

Practical integrity speaks to contemporary and future customer needs and provides marketers with a more trustworthy approach to building business. Here is a preview of the specifics we'll be discussing in the remainder of the book:

Figure 1-4. The practical integrity proposition.

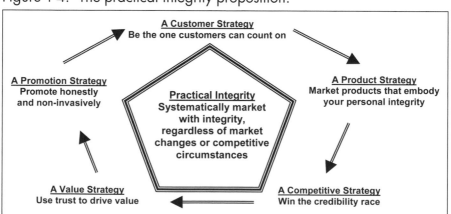

1. *Marketers need to build equitable partnerships with their customers, fused with integrity.* What buyers want from marketers is what marketers should seek from buyers—a partnership that delivers fairly earned and fairly received benefits to both.

   When that partnership is based on practical integrity, and marketers are catering to the needs of customers with particular interest in buying from companies with integrity, then the opportunities for business growth are unlimited. The companies you will see profiled in the next chapter have all succeeded because they are the companies and brands whose integrity their customers know they can count on.

2. *Forget product, think integrity.* Superior products have a way of creating their own marketing momentum. They require less support, and every dollar that is invested pays extraordinary dividends. But no matter how spectacularly they perform, ultimately they are less important than the integrity of the brand and company that they represent because no product can be protected from preemption.

   In the pages ahead, we will be exploring companies that succeed by making great products and services—because they consider the product to be a surrogate for their integrity.

3. *Prospective buyers want and deserve honest, noninvasive marketing.* Marketing communications and other promotional efforts that are less than honest—regardless of whether they may be adhering to the letter of the law—are the fastest way to communicate that the sponsoring company cannot be trusted. And invasive and intrusive promotional efforts are also likely to be avoided by shell-shocked marketing "targets."

   Buyers want something that is relevant to them wrapped in a message that they will find entertaining or intriguing or alluring. While it may run counter to conventional wisdom about the need for intrusiveness, persuasion by bludgeoning will soon result in more risk than payback.

4. *Value propositions should not be about lower pricing, but higher trust.* Part of being a high-integrity marketer is offering customers the greatest possible value, regardless of the price charged. How that value may be defined or delivered, and what pricing may accompany it, will depend on market circumstances.

   But while offering less value for parity or higher prices might be seen by some as smart marketing, it will be less effective from this point forward as skeptical buyers gain access to limitless information.

As that happens, they will begin to call questionable value into serious question.

High-value discount chains like Target and IKEA thrive because their low pricing is offered by a store that provides quality that people can trust. Economists define value as: "benefits minus price." Future marketers need to think of value as: "benefits plus trust."

If these strategies are part of a marketing plan's bone structure, they can lead to more stable businesses and greater growth opportunities at a time when customers are less likely to believe, and much less likely to patronize companies that market with questionable integrity.

Creating Sustainable Integrity[23]

Practical integrity can also help marketers to manage their efforts within the priorities of the greater world in which we all live. This is essential as more aware buyers are becoming more concerned that their world is being changed by what they buy. According to one 2004 study, 80 percent of U.S. consumers believe that American businesses are too concerned about making a profit and not concerned enough about their workers, consumers, and the environment.[24]

Today's purchasers of food products packaged in plastic or glass are more likely to think more about recycling such packaging even before they consume the contents (am I just adding to the landfill?). Shoppers for apparel are more sensitive than ever about the location of its manufacture (is it killing jobs by offshore outsourcing?) and the possible conditions in which the manufacturing takes place (are children or underpaid workers responsible for this garment?). Mass merchandisers are regularly put on the defensive about driving locally-owned shops out of business. And all businesses will sooner or later be affected by global warming that could drastically reduce water supplies, routinely prompt horrific climactic changes, and cost businesses billions in escalating insurance rates.

This customer-marketer-world triad raises questions about the integrity of marketers and the motives behind their companies' actions. Marketers are just now beginning to search for solutions that go beyond the customary buyer-seller relationships and toward delivering tri-mutual benefits through what could be called "sustainable integrity" (see Figure 1-5).

This interdependence means that the needs of buyer, seller, and the greater world of the buyer and seller must all be satisfied if an enterprise is to succeed. If a product is profitable for a business but not useful to its customers, it will not sell. If it is useful to customers but not profitable to the business, it cannot be marketed indefinitely. And if a product is profitable and useful to both parties,

Figure 1-5. The tri-mutual benefits of sustainable integrity.

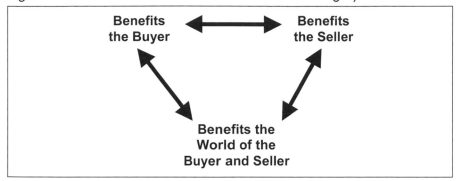

but it damages the world in which they live—economically, environmentally, socially—then its days, too, likely are numbered.

As more current and potential customers learn of a company's efforts to address these three needs, it can't help but have a positive influence on sales, just as it has had at such pioneering companies as Tom's of Maine and The Body Shop in the past, and is happening today at companies like Patagonia, Herman Miller, and Kiehl's Since 1851.

Practical Integrity and Net Brand Equity

Brand equity is (finally) being recognized as an extraordinarily important asset for most companies. In light of that, perhaps marketers should be looking at a more refined measure of that worth, what can be called "net brand equity," or the value of a brand after positive or negative forces in the marketplace have had an impact on it. When that happens, the result can be a rise or fall of a brand's "gross equity," leaving a dramatically changed net equity. This is usually a gradual change on the positive side, but can be precipitous in decline (see Figure 1-6, and also see Chapter 10 for a financial description of *net brand equity*).[25]

Brand equity can decline for any number of reasons, but decline has most commonly happened in the past when customers became disenchanted because of perceived product failures (e.g., Audi transmissions), marketing missteps (Nokia's late entry with clamshell cell phones and Samsung's late entry into low-end phones in developing countries), and unexpected marketplace events (Coca-Cola's tainted product in Belgium).

In the future, another major threat to net brand equity will be failures to maintain marketing integrity. Equity is based on the assumption that what cus-

Figure 1-6. Loss of net brand equity.

Gross Equity		Attrition Factors		Net Brand Equity
Total equities from all sources, including:	−	Product falls out-of-style	=	Net brand equity from all sources, overtime, including:
Initial loyalty		Customer base erosion		Ongoing core customers
Awareness		Clutter noise and negative awareness		Net positive awareness
Perceived quality		Product failures		Perceived net product quality
Brand associations		Declines in brand reputation		Net brand reputation
Other assets		Other equity declines		Net other assets

tomers see is what they get. Lose that trust and net brand equity will decline proportionately.

Integrity Without Sacrifice

Consumers and business customers are holding marketers more accountable because they are running short of patience with sellers who can't seem to shoot straight. If one company operates with practical integrity but its competition does not, isn't it likely that the constraints of practical integrity will result in a loss of competitive advantage? In this age of skepticism and distrust, just the opposite is more likely to happen.

Good intentions and sporadic initiatives won't create a reliable trust machine, unless you're dumb-lucky or unfairly blessed. But if marketers can establish a pragmatic, systematized approach to managing integrity, it will yield greater respect, credibility, and trust from the customer. That, in turn, should result in stronger revenue streams, strengthened brand loyalty, and a workforce that feels good about what they do for a living.

The companies you will read about in Chapter 2 demonstrate that every day.

CHAPTER 2

Practical Integrity Works

Five Companies with Something to Teach Us All

It's easy to spot the nonconformists in marketing. They're the ones that don't line up for network television up-front buys, or bury their customers in direct mail that looks like it comes from the IRS, or advertise when no one wants to be advertised at.

Some of them don't play the game because they can't afford to or because they've committed to other ways to promote their brands. But others rely less on conventional approaches because they rely more on the power of who they are.

These are impresarios of word-of-mouth that rarely launch massive buzz campaigns. They have devoted customers who return again and again, but they don't employ major CRM loyalty programs. They may sample generously but never try to fill up your mailbox. They often have the money to throw at massive marketing campaigns, but they spend it judiciously to encourage buyers without alienating them.

These are the masters of practical integrity that use it as the fuel for their businesses. Their marketing template is not right for all companies, but their belief systems and their enlightened approach to marketing have something to teach us all.

Uncommon Commonalities

This chapter profiles five companies: premier office systems and furniture maker Herman Miller; Infosys, a leading Indian technology consulting firm; Trader Joe's, the off-center grocery chain that has shoppers begging them to open stores in their communities; Patagonia, the outdoor apparel manufacturer and retailer that's out to save the world; and Kiehl's Since 1851, a beauty-care brand that is using practical integrity to market its way into the hearts of a small army of devoted followers.

Each of these companies has created a brand that is unique in the extreme. Differentiation is not a marketing problem for any of them. At the same time, they share traits that enable them to be more widely appreciated, accepted as significant players in their industries—if not outright leaders—and admired for the way they market as much as for how effectively they market.

Their products, services, marketing programs, and employee attitudes are all focused on retaining customers for a generation, if not a lifetime. For some, that may mean turning away prospects who want to change the company to fit their way of doing things. Some big money has been left on some big tables because these companies would not be bullied, coaxed, or nudged into a selling situation in which they did not feel comfortable.

They are selective about whom they sell to, or their way of working is self-selecting, because they are out to create mutually beneficial partnerships that, they believe, will yield more quality revenue in the long run.

The people within each company believe that there must be a reason for being in business beyond making money. The core of the Kiehl's mission statement would work for them all:

> A worthwhile firm must have a purpose for its existence. Not only the every-day work-a-day purpose to earn a just profit, but beyond that, to improve in some way the quality of the community to which it is committed.[1]

In all instances they are very sensitive about operating on a fragile planet and practice different forms of sustainable integrity. They may be actively involved as environmentalists, as is Patagonia, or strong supporters, as are Herman Miller and Kiehl's, or just generally trying to make the world a better place through their social consciousness, as are Infosys and Trader Joe's. In all cases, their beliefs about the world around them influence how they market to that world.

They don't feel the need for much conventional advertising, and often they rely on the spontaneous word-of-mouth momentum that is fueled by superior products and services. They refuse to become like their more ordinary competitors by unnecessarily contributing to the commercial clutter that exists in their industries.

Although these firms may market unconventionally, they are all very proficient marketers. Their products, partnerships with customers, value propositions, brand messaging and marketing promotions are all crafted by their own people—with honesty and transparency. Integrity is part of their DNA. They could no sooner extricate it from the way they market than they could withdraw quality from their products and services. Because of their integrity, they enjoy greater competitive advantage, not less.

They are each in business to win, but to win in their own way. All of them could probably be much bigger today than they are, but they want to grow on their own terms without losing what makes them exceptional. They are considered to be among the leaders in their fields, not necessarily because they are the largest, but because they are among the most admired. That admiration is as strong within their organizations as it is among their customers and external stakeholders.

Yet, make no mistake, the companies profiled in this chapter are not without their flaws. One company fell into Chapter 11 before turning the business around, and another lost money not that many years ago. The founder of one firm personally lost $100 million as his company fell victim to a worldwide recession. From time to time, one company has inadvertently carried a product that some of its customers believed did not reflect well on the store—then changed its offering if it believed the customers had a good point.

Throughout the periodic tough times that all of these companies have encountered, their focus on practical integrity has been their anchor. Their businesses are sound and successful because their businesses are customer-driven, yet also simultaneously beneficial to buyer, seller and the greater communities in which they all live.

Shared Differences

The five companies profiled are from very different industries and market a wide range of products and services. One is independent and privately owned, two are public, two are owned by large corporations but largely left to steer their own ships. Two are less than thirty years old, and three have long and storied histories. Two of the companies' parent corporations are headquartered in Europe, one in India, and two are based in different regions of the United States. Three market to consumers and two market to businesses.

While many companies are required to advertise heavily to compete in their industries, these five companies have something to teach us about how to replace some of that advertising with more grassroots marketing.

Other companies may sell adequate products or services, but these profiles may suggest how to deliberately build something better by assuming it will not be supported by significant marketing spending.

Although it may seem to make sense to market to as many segments as possible, these companies demonstrate how to make the most of a more manageable group of segments. Other companies may feel unfairly lured into price wars because they believe that their customers are primarily interested in price. These companies are priced all over the lot, but they successfully sell value over price.

Again, their specific business models vary greatly and are not presented here as others to emulate in that respect. It is their practical integrity that we are interested in understanding better, and how that has an impact on their full marketing mix.

Here, then, are five examples of fine companies that have adopted, adapted, and refined the business art of practical integrity, to their benefit and to the benefit of the rest of us who can learn from them.

Herman Miller: "The Truth Is Good Enough"

If you want to be a stickler about it, Herman Miller was not literally the founder of The Herman Miller Furniture Company. The company was founded in 1923 and managed by D.J. DePree in a venture funded largely by furniture maker Herman Miller, who happened to be DePree's father-in-law. DePree wanted the new company to get off to a good start and Herman Miller (the man) had a fine reputation in the furniture industry.

Herman Miller (the company) is an extraordinary provider of furniture and interior products and one of the great places to work. They are the recipient of so many design and corporate awards that it's a wonder some haven't been retired permanently. The company has been cited by *Fortune* magazine as the "Most Admired" company in its industry eighteen times in the last twenty years.

Herman Miller sells at the mid-level and high-end sectors of their industry, but in all cases their furniture and office and home living systems are superior in quality and value.

The company's product line reads like a what's-what of environmentally sound designs. That includes the Mirra chair, which is 96 percent recyclable and built with 34 percent recycled content, and the Cella chair, which is 99 percent recyclable. Both award-winning products are completely free of PVCs and assembled with 100 percent renewable energy. Herman Miller is the sole furniture maker that is included in the KLD Domini 400 Social Index and Global Climate 100 Index, two prestigious lists of organizations that are making a positive impact on the Earth's environment.

The local recycler of all the furniture companies' waste products in western Michigan once commented that the difference between Herman Miller and its competitors is that the competitors want something recycled only if it's profitable to do so. Herman Miller wants everything recycled until it is earth-neutral, regardless of cost. The company hopes someday to be "waste free." They are about 85 percent there.[2]

This is a company that markets and sells with practical integrity every day, and once in a while has to prove it. A major new customer prospect came to

Herman Miller a few years ago and asked for a very large order of furniture to be made with a certain veneer. The customer was ready to ante up seven figures for the job.

Unfortunately, the veneer the customer asked for was made from an endangered species, and so the Herman Miller designers presented some alternatives to consider. No, said the customer, I must have this veneer. Then, said the designers, we're afraid you'll have to find it somewhere else. The customer took his business and his seven figures and walked out the door. But when the door closed behind him, the Herman Miller integrity was safe inside.

A lot of companies want to work with Herman Miller because of who and what they are. Their eclectic but prestigious client list includes companies and organizations operating in more than forty countries. Some of their better known clientele are General Motors, BP, the U.S. government, Sara Lee, Time Warner, Cisco Systems, Cirque du Soleil, and the U.S. Olympic Committee, among many others.

The company grew steadily until the business slowdown hit earlier this decade and corporate orders fell dramatically. Since then, they have rebuilt their business and appear to be on a strong growth path once again (see Figure 2-1). As of this writing, Herman Miller's stock price has doubled since its recent low in 2003, and the company has been growing and profitable, delivering $1.74 billion in revenue and $99 million in earnings in 2006.

One of the unusual ways that Herman Miller "markets" is by regularly providing benchmarks for clients on productivity and environmental impact issues. They even share their environmental findings with competitors in the industry because, as category leaders, they want the industry to get better at building the right kind of living spaces.

It's not uncommon for members of a client company's board, HR department, or C-level team to tour Herman Miller facilities—not to check on their work, but to learn what they might apply to their own businesses. They create best-in-class interior products with extraordinary consistency, decade after de-

Figure 2-1. Herman Miller business performance 2002 to 2006.

Year	Revenue ($ mil.)	Net Income ($ mil.)	Net Profit Margin
2006	1,737.2	99.2	5.7%
2005	1,515.6	68.0	4.5%
2004	1,338.3	42.3	3.2%
2003	1,336.5	23.3	1.7%
2002	1,468.7	(56.0)	--

SOURCE: Hoover's, Inc. (www.hoovers.com). Used with permission.

cade, while also balancing their interest in leading-edge innovation with the daily needs of the customers' staffs and families who will live and work in their spaces.

Even though the company is often the pioneer in developing new designs and materials, they are not the first to spotlight their success. "At one point," according to Kris Manos, executive vice president, North American Office and Learning Environments, "we were the innovator in many environmental areas but we had a corporate modesty that made us reluctant to talk about it. Some competitors scooped us at touting their innovations, even though we had been the real pioneers."[3]

One such case was the time that Herman Miller created a new fabric called "Kira." The fabric employs a panel system made entirely from renewable, bio-based fiber derived from corn plant sugars, and is virtually unique in that it is completely compostable at the end of its life. More furniture companies followed suit and promoted their products more heavily than did Herman Miller. Yet the company's extraordinary reputation for both quality and reluctance to blow its own horn may be contributing to its mystique as the preeminent industry manufacturer.

Much More Than Furniture

Herman Miller's marketing programs are purposely understated, but effective nonetheless. The company does not advertise for the most part, but relies heavily on public relations efforts via trade publications as well as media placements that result in favorable (and accurate) news stories about the company and its achievements. They also host conferences on design and environmentalism and often invite their competitors to take part.

The Herman Miller values are always present when they design brochures or sale sheets or PR releases. If there is even a hint of something being untrue or exaggerated, it never makes it out the door. When Director of Corporate Communications Mark Schurman joined the company in 1993, he was told to remember what former CEO George Nelson had said years earlier: "The truth is good enough."[4]

That principle frequently comes in handy at Herman Miller. Like the time that global account manager Bryan Dozeman and his colleague, designer Gus Pascual, were working with a client. The challenge was to fit as many people into the client's office space as possible. Pascual came back with a design that not only fit the required people, but some additional ones as well. The client was amazed and the conversation that followed went like this:

> **Client:** "Are you sure this is correct? Did you draw this to scale?"
> **Gus:** "Absolutely, I did the building in quarter-inch scale and the furniture in eighth-inch scale."

Client: "But, Gus, that won't work."
Gus: "And neither will your building."

The client got the message and found a larger space. Gus and Herman Miller were awarded the job for the entire new project.[5]

The company's sales efforts are really more like long-term partnering with their customers to learn as much as possible and to establish an association that is nurtured over many years. On many occasions, they have passed on an opportunity to make a quick sale in order to slowly and steadily create a rapport that may lead to more business years later. Of the company's top 300 customers, half have done business with the firm for ten years or more.

Internally, because of the company's reverence for its history and heritage, new employees are given a healthy dose of what Herman Miller is all about, how it began, and how the values of the company are lived every day. The culture is strong and pervasive, and kept alive by "water carriers"—specially designated long-term employees who communicate and debate with other employees about issues that affect their daily work lives. While they are never referred to as internal marketers, that is what they do very well.

What Herman Miller is all about is perhaps best stated on their website: "What arrives on the truck is furniture. What went into the truck was an amalgam of what we believe in: innovation, design, operational excellence, smart application of technology, and social responsibility."[6] (See Figure 2-2 for their sample website page.)

What We Can Learn from Herman Miller

When Tiger Woods appeared at a public function for the first time after his father's death in 2006, he was asked what advice he would give to young people. He replied that the greatest advice he got was from his dad, who told him to always "care and share."[7]

That is a philosophy that Herman Miller has made into a way of life. They deeply care about what their customers need and about making sure that what customers get is the best it can be for them and the world they live in. At the same time, when Herman Miller learns something that will help the industry as a whole, they're equally anxious to share it because it will help all furniture makers. Their sharing is an important part of their marketing program. In the meantime, their competitive edge is secure because they are the best at what they do and even sharing with the competition will not change that.

Herman Miller also approaches design and the manufacture of interior systems in the most holistic manner possible, always thinking about what a new

Figure 2-2. Sample page from Herman Miller website, September 2006.

fabric or chair design or furniture system might mean to the individuals using them, the company employing them, and the environment now and in the future that may be affected by them. The environmental impact of their products—in every sense of the term "environmental"—is critical to their thinking, from conception to design to manufacture to sale. That larger view is simply not present in many other more siloed companies.

Finally, Herman Miller employs practical integrity in their marketing communications as they create a flow of information and word-of-mouth, then let their work and reputation make a sale rather than straining to invade the lives of their prospects. They lead and make sure that they enjoy all the benefits of leadership, but they also use restraint and good sense in deploying their marketing resources.

Herman Miller makes furniture and interior systems of superior quality, which is a critical reason for their success. They market their goods with such practical integrity that the value of their work is magnified many-fold.

Infosys: "The Softest Pillow Is a Clear Conscience"

If you're not in the market for corporate information services, you may never have heard of Infosys Technologies. It is one of India's corporate shining stars, a powerful, up-and-coming IT consulting company that provides software development and engineering, data management, systems integration, and numerous must-have services for the world's corporations.

Thanks to a successful business plan and strong demand for quality work at reasonable costs from outsourcers, Infosys is now making serious inroads into the sales territories of IBM Consulting, Accenture, and other technology heavyweights.

This is another "It all started in the garage" technology story, except this one started in Bangalore, India instead of Silicon Valley. Founded with six friends and $250 borrowed from their wives, N.R. Narayana Murthy and his partners birthed their company in 1981. It was not an easy delivery because India's economy and private commerce were under tight government control at the time. As Murthy explained many years later: "It took about 24 months and about 25 visits to Delhi to obtain a license to import a computer costing U.S. $50,000. It took us one year to get a telephone line. In fact, a retired government officer would have a higher priority for phones than we did."[8]

Ten years later the Indian government finally liberalized the economy, and Infosys revenue grew steadily from $2 million in 1991 to $2.14 billion in 2006.

More than financial reward and global recognition, the young Infosys founders were driven by a compulsion to prove that honest people can finish first, even in a country that had widespread bureaucratic corruption. Murthy and his cofounders were determined from the outset to demonstrate to their peers, customers, and especially to Indian young people that success need not be the product of deception.

In a speech to business students at the Wharton School of Business, Murthy described their values this way: "The Infosys value system can be captured in one line—the softest pillow is a clear conscience. . . . At Infosys, we have stood firm whenever our value system was tested."[9]

Apparently the message got through to future business execs: Murthy has been named the most admired business leader by management students in India five consecutive times. And, despite owning 7 percent of a $2 billion company, he keeps his feet firmly on the ground by living modestly. (Not that many years ago his wife reportedly drove him to the bus stop where he rode to work with some slightly-less-affluent fellow citizens of Bangalore.)[10]

Values Over Profits

The Infosys corporate ethos puts a premium on transparency by operating with the code "When in doubt, disclose." As one executive explained, "If it came to a question of giving up our profits or our values, we would gladly give away our profits."[11] The growing crowd of Infosys shareholders might have something to say about that, but it is one indication of how the entire organization is committed to winning the right way, or not playing the game. Infosys wants always to be seen as a company that simultaneously does what is right, legal, and growth-oriented.

The management of Infosys also believes the company has a strong responsibility to help India as a whole to become economically stronger. Despite its exceptional economic growth in recent years, India continues to struggle with enormous poverty among hundreds of millions of its population. Several founders of Infosys have reportedly subsized meal programs for primary school students throughout India.[12]

For Infosys, this issue of poverty is also an opportunity to help many Indians find prosperity for the first time by joining the company's growing ranks. Both Infosys and another leading Indian technology company, Wipro, received more than one million job applications in 2005 for 10,000 vacancies.[13]

"We would first like to be known as decent, honest, and trustworthy people, and then as smart people." That, the Infosys people believe, gives them permission to claim "predictability," which is critically important in IT work, not to mention in all marketing work. Predictability means delivering what you promise, which is one key difference between great marketers and ordinary ones.

Infosys was the first Indian company to be listed on the NASDAQ. With more than 55,000 employees in twenty countries, Infosys revenue is now well over U.S. $2 billion, and has nearly quintupled in the last five years (see Figure 2-3). As of this writing, the company carries a market value of more than $21 billion, and its stock price is more than twice that of 2002 when the company began its comeback from the tech meltdown.

One of the keys to the company's 25 percent + net margins, and thus to its

Figure 2-3. Infosys business performance 2002 to 2006.

Year	Revenue ($ mil.)	Net Income ($ mil.)	Net Profit Margin	Employees
Mar 2006	2,152.0	555.0	25.8%	36,750
Mar 2005	1,592.0	419.0	26.3%	36,800
Mar 2004	1,062.6	270.3	25.4%	25,700
Mar 2003	753.8	194.9	25.9%	15,940
Mar 2002	545.1	164.5	30.2%	10,740

SOURCE: Hoover's, Inc. (www.hoovers.com). Used with permission.

marketing strategy, is that an estimated 90 percent of its revenues come from its existing clients.[14] It is also telling that, although Infosys only moved into the North American market at the end of the 1990s, that region already represents 65 percent of its total top line. As of this writing, almost all of its revenue, 80 percent of its customers, and 30 percent of its investors are from developed nations.[15]

Where the Earth First Got Flat

For some years now, Infosys has been using a global collaborative system for designing and delivering software to customers, called the "Global Delivery Model." This is an example of how a company that is out-gunned in marketing spending and sales force size can create some competitive advantage using its nimbleness. The Global Delivery Model enables the company to determine system requirements at a customer site in one city, develop the software in another, and deploy it in a third, all at different corners of the globe.

The system enables Infosys to reduce the cost of ownership for its customers, which in turn can trigger some positive word-of-mouth that leads to another project with a new or existing customer. That is the sort of 24/7 service that has led companies like Aetna, Nordstrom, and Aon to repeatedly use Infosys for their mission-critical IT projects.[16]

In the past, Infosys has kept its formal marketing efforts to a minimum, relying instead on the company's fine reputation among current customers. The company's positioning line for many years has been, "Powered by intellect. Driven by values," reflecting its formidable think-based rationality in tandem with its desire to be the best possible corporate citizen.

On its website, the company markets its role as a leader in Indian business by emphasizing thought leadership by its people, including leading-edge books written by employees on global sourcing and knowledge management. They also market their close association with Thomas Friedman and his best-selling book *The World Is Flat: A Brief History of the Twenty-first Century.* In fact, Friedman wrote that he came to the conclusion depicted by his title while sitting in an Infosys conference room in Bangalore with Infosys CEO Nandan Nilekani. "Tom," Nilekani said, "the playing field is being leveled," using a common business phrase that Friedman then expanded into the larger flat-Earth principle he wrote about.[17]

While the fundamental essence of the Infosys brand will undoubtedly remain focused on values, the company has shown some interest in more aggressively marketing its quality to separate itself from the view that India is simply the beneficiary of the trend toward outsourcing in the United States and Europe.

What We Can Learn from Infosys

Infosys is not an Indian company that seeks to undercut the pricing of competition, but a global one that seeks to lead competition and to price according to the quality delivered.

At least part of the successful formula for Infosys has been the combination of strong talent, reasonable costs, and predictable results in a less-than predictable industry. Infosys is a straight-arrow corporate culture that ensures that some of the ethical elasticity that India's bureaucracies are famous for will not be a factor when dealing with the company.

Infosys is also a good company to study about customer retention. They go deep and wide into their customer base, providing support in a burgeoning list of services, always with the same commitment to excellence and honesty in their dealings. Their penchant for accountability is an important reason why they keep getting more business from their current customer base.

The company's dedication to fighting poverty in India certainly serves the organization well, but just as important, it underlines that humanity of the company, and that pays dividends in employee spirit. There is no more critical asset than employee morale in a service business. That is a lesson some other service companies could learn from Infosys, particularly if they are trying to sell customers what they have failed to embed in their own organizations.

The Infosys brand is lagging behind such giant competitors as IBM and Accenture in brand recall and salience, as are a good many other Indian companies. But Infosys has launched a global "Think Flat" marketing effort that positions the company as a transformational service provider in a flattening world. Yet no matter how aggressively Infosys bolsters its marketing, they are likely to continue to do so with the same honesty that they demonstrated in more modest times.

Infosys has gone head-to-head with the world's best in their field and done well. Their determination to continue battling the best should work out well because they offer outstanding value based on trust, which is a benefit base that is infinitely expandable. Yet, if Infosys stays true to form, they will not let elevated marketing spending change the essence of their appeal, namely, their practical integrity.

Delivering services so good that they market themselves, and marketing with accountability over and over again to existing customers, offering superior value, operating with unquestioned integrity—all of these are in the bull's eye of practical integrity.

Infosys may just have the prescription for how Indian companies can expand their influence from this point forward. In any case, they certainly have the prescription for a good night's sleep.

Trader Joe's: "Purchasing Agents for the Consumer"

It's one of the most unlikely success stories to crop up in the retail food industry in recent memory. Trader Joe's is a mushrooming U.S. food retailer that has maintained its initial cachet as a branded retail outlet while growing very fast in size and stature.

Trader Joe's was founded in 1958 as Pronto Markets by grocer Joe Coulombe, who was trying to battle the spread of 7-11 stores in Southern California. The chain was renamed Trader Joe's (and now is often referred to as "TJ's") when Coulombe got the idea for a tropical adventure theme while daydreaming on a beach in the Caribbean. Coulombe eventually sold out to the Albrecht family of Germany in 1988, but Trader Joe's operates largely independently from the corporate parent.

TJ's is nothing if not quirky, and that is an important part of what attracts the passionate loyalty of its shoppers. But there's nothing quirky about their uniquely differentiating mission, which is to bring the best values in food and beverages from around the world, along with the information needed for their customers to make the best decisions.[18]

Eight out of ten products sold off Trader Joe's shelves—some 2,000 labels—are store brands, compared to about 16 percent of total U.S. supermarket purchases.[19] At Trader Joe's, private labels are not just moneymakers, they are trust builders. As former *Progressive Grocer* Editor-in-Chief Len Lewis pointed out, "private labels have created a label of trust between Trader Joe's and its customers. . . . It has become a tacit seal of approval, something that, in the past, was limited to only a few of the most revered national brands."[20]

That's not all their private labels do; the strategy also builds an unbeatable value proposition that is all about quality at a reasonable price, underscored by customers' absolute trust in the Trader Joe's brand.

This is an ingenious strategy that accomplished several things simultaneously. First, the TJ private labels are, by their very nature, both differentiated and differentiating. They provide a uniqueness that requires a shopping trip to Trader Joe's, compared to the store labels in ordinary supermarkets that are usually the same product you can find anywhere else, just with that chain's name on it.

Second, thanks to the careful shopping of Trader Joe's buyers, each of the store-labeled items is superior in quality, yet reasonably priced because they are bought in bulk. This strategy creates a value in the mind of shoppers because they are buying unique, high-quality items at very reasonable prices.

Finally, the TJ-labeled products add to the fun atmosphere of the Trader Joe's brand experience. They carry exotic or tongue-in-cheek names like Two-buck Chuck (aka Charles Shaw) wines, Trader Joe's Chimichurri Rice (from

Argentina), Monopolowa vodka (from Eastern Europe), and Nature's Path Gorilla Munch (an organic cereal from EnviroKidz).

It's a value proposition that most retailers would kill for, and there's no indication it will grow stale anytime soon.

Supermarkets are interested in the masses and often treat them in a mass-like way. Trader Joe's attracts what founder Coulombe used to call "the educated customer." These are people who know quality and nutritional wholesomeness when they see it. Many of them actually search far and wide for products that ordinary supermarkets might not carry, or that they stock on dusty shelves in the back of the store.[21]

Trader Joe's attracts so-called limited-assortment-store shoppers with lower *and* higher incomes, who are drawn to the high-value private-labeled goods. They may run the demographic gamut, but they share in common a willingness to make an extra trip to find great bargains on extraordinary foodstuffs within a unique brand experience.

A conventional U.S. supermarket has about 50,000 square feet, wide aisles, uniformly stocked boxes and cans, and only periodic glimpses of stock clerks who have time to help. Trader Joe's stores are about one-fifth that size and inventory, stocked with odd assortments of distinctive products, and serviced by happy, friendly staffers decked out in wild Hawaiian shirts who seem thrilled that you want them to help you in your search for the strange and wonderful.

The meat, produce, and dry goods buyers in the larger chains are interested in adequate, consistent quality that they can get in bulk without delay. But at Trader Joe's, nothing is sold unless it makes it through the company's tough-minded tasting panel, made up of buyers, management, and staff, who are knowledgeable food people.

In most supermarket chains, managers are running roughly the same kind of operation that their counterparts run on the other side of town, with minor variations in size and clientele. In contrast, Trader Joe's "captains" have a great deal of autonomy in how their stores are operated, giving them much better responsiveness to local customer needs.

Invited In, Not Forced On

The supermarket industry continues to consolidate and struggle to increase sales year-to-year. TJ's, on the other hand, now has 255 stores in twenty states in the United States, and is opening more on a regular basis. Sales of the privately-owned company are believed to have increased more than 20 percent every year since 1990, and now are estimated to stand at well above $5 billion (see Figure 2-4).

When Trader Joe's does announce that they are going to open a store, they

Figure 2-4. Trader Joe's revenue 2001 to 2004.

	Revenue ($ mil.)
Jun 2004	4,000.0
Jun 2003	2,500.0
Jun 2002	2,200.0
Jun 2001	1,900.0
Jun 2000	1,670.0

SOURCE: Hoover's, Inc. (www.hoovers.com). Used with permission.

are welcomed by the community, which is certainly not the case with all retail chains. On more than one occasion, the company has been specifically invited to open a store by local shoppers who have had the TJ experience elsewhere and want to have one in their own neighborhood.

Positioned as the "purchasing agents for the consumer," Trader Joe's advertises on a limited basis and relies on its "Fearless Flyer" to inform customers what's in the store and what's coming up. They don't promote nearly as actively as their competition, mainly because their customers are doing it for them. Blogs and websites like *trader joefan.com* and *tracking traderjoes.com* are helping to spread the word virally, which is far more persuasive than any company-sponsored effort. Single Seattle residents have even started a site that reportedly includes this rally cry: "This is for singles who shop at Trader Joe's and are sick of accidentally checking out attached people while shopping for groceries. Trader Joe's singles, unite and flirt!"[22]

Figure 2-5. Trader Joe's website home page, September 2006.

SOURCE: © Trader Joe's, Inc. Used with permission of Trader Joe's, Inc.

On the other hand, they do promote themselves via their funky Trader Joe's website traderjoes.com, where you feel as if you've fallen into some kind of mind safari. The graphics look like they were crafted by a refugee from *Survivor*. The South Seas imagery and cheeky humor lure you in, not demanding your attention but getting it nonetheless (see Figure 2-5 for Trader Joe's website home page).

Listening and Learning

As a company, they are proficient listeners who take action when there is a customer in need. If a customer asks for an item that is not stocked, the item suddenly appears by the time the customer returns. If shoppers show up before the store opens, the staff may very well open early just because they don't want people waiting outside when they could be inside enjoying their shopping before everyone else arrives.

When Trader Joe's occasionally runs into opposition—such as when animal-rights activists were concerned about how ducks were slaughtered to stock the shelves—the people at TJ's pull the controversial products from their markets or change their sourcing systems. As Audrey Dumper, vice president of marketing for Trader Joe's East, told *Fast Company*, "We like to think of Trader Joe's as an economic food democracy."[23]

Democracies should run so well.

What We Can Learn from Trader Joe's

Trader Joe's regularly provides their customers with something that mega-chains simply cannot deliver: unique values in a unique setting, serviced by committed teams of superior service providers. You may spend ten minutes or an hour in one of their stores, but you invariably find yourself smiling as you discover the unexpected down every aisle.

Trader Joe's listens to customers and responds to their requests quickly and sensitively, engaging people instead of overwhelming them, providing real value at surprisingly reasonable prices, and promoting with a flair that makes them likeable, yet practical as a shopping choice.

Integrity runs throughout the organization as a guide and a gyroscope. They buy organic when they can and steer clear of genetically modified ingredients, products that have unnecessary chemicals, and trans-fatty foods. They treat their people as valuable associates, and their customers as partners.

At first glance Trader Joe's may appear to be almost counter-culture. In truth, it is leading culture, and its rapidly expanding corps of converts couldn't be happier to be ahead of the pack. And why not? As *BusinessWeek* pointed out a few years ago, "For most people, shopping is a chore. Trader Joe's makes it recreation."[24]

All of this is accomplished within a culture of innovation, an entertaining brand experience, and one overriding leadership approach to their business, as expressed by former Trader Joe's CEO John Shields: "You have to have absolute integrity. If you don't have this, just forget about everything else."[25]

This is practical integrity gone retail, a tough business with low margins and high anxiety. But, like great athletes and peerless artists, Trader Joe's makes it look easy. It is anything but.

Patagonia: "We Would Rather Earn Credibility Than Buy It"

Yvon Chouinard is the son of a French-Canadian father who immigrated to Lisbon, Maine, then later moved his family to Burbank, California. It was in sprawling Griffith Park—right in the middle of what was then one of the world's most polluted megalopolises—that young Yvon began his lifelong effort to save the planet.

Yvon wanted to be a fur trapper when he grew up but eventually fell in with what he later described as "misfits," a group of teens who founded the Southern California Falconry Club. The club called for lots of outdoors work, the kind that Yvon found deeply satisfying. One of the adults in the club taught him how to climb rocks and rappel down to falcon aeries high up on precipitous cliffs. Sixty years later he is still an avid and expert climber.

Early on, Yvon taught himself blacksmithing so that he could make climbing pitons (those metal spikes hammered into rock to provide foot and hand support). After taking part in the first ascent of the North American Wall on El Capitan in Yosemite Park, Yvon eventually refined his climbing equipment skills, leading ultimately to the founding (with partner Tom Frost) of Chouinard Equipment, a company that by 1970 had become the largest U.S.-based supplier of climbing hardware.

Paradoxically, Chouinard Equipment had also become a company that created an environmental problem: The hard steel pitons were disfiguring rocks wherever they were used. So Yvon phased out the profitable piton business and replaced it with aluminum chocks. It was the kind of decision that he would make many times in future years, sacrificing short-term profit in order to reduce environmental impact.

The company changed its name to Great Pacific Iron Works in 1973 and added climbing apparel to its wares. Three years later the clothing line was renamed Patagonia, after the rugged area of Argentina. After starts and stops and sporadic growth, the company overextended and ended up with bloated inventories, ultimately causing it to go into Chapter 11 and Yvon to leave to pursue other interests. He eventually returned and, with a lot of help from his friends, finally created some momentum that propelled the company into the Patagonia of today.

Patagonia is a midsize (about $250 million in estimated 2005 retail sales) player in the competitive outdoor apparel business with about twenty stores in fifteen states and another twenty stores overseas. The company has an extraordinary reputation for integrity and a commitment to more than profitability. In fact, Patagonia makes sure that it doesn't get too profitable by donating 10 percent of its pretax profits or 1 percent of its gross sales to environmental causes, whichever is larger.

This is how the company describes its reason for being:

> For us at Patagonia, a love of wild and beautiful places demands participation in the fight to save them, and to help reverse the steep decline in the overall environmental health of our planet. . . .We know that our business activity— from lighting stores to dyeing shirts—creates pollution as a by-product. So we work steadily to reduce those harms. We use recycled polyester in many of our clothes and only organic, rather than pesticide-intensive, cotton.[26]

Patagonia has been honored numerous times for their commitment to the environment, to their own people, and to a powerful sense of integrity. The company repeatedly has been listed among *The 100 Best Companies to Work for in America*, and cited in *Forbes* as among the top 25 companies in the United States in their category. They have been singled out for excellence by *Business Ethics* magazine, and honored at the White House for their environmental zeal. On that occasion, then-President Clinton, who was a regular at Patagonia, commented, "Every time I go into one (of their stores) I feel like I'm on an evangelical mission."[27]

Here is a sampling of what Yvon Chouinard and the fiercely dedicated staff of Patagonia believe in and reflect in their daily marketing-related work:

- ❏ *About customers*: "They are intelligent, they don't shop for entertainment or to 'buy a life,' (and they) want to deepen and simplify, not junk up, their lives."

- ❏ *About marketing*: "Our charter is to inspire and educate rather than promote."

- ❏ *About communications*: "We advertise only as a last resort. The best resources for us are the word-of-mouth recommendations from a friend or favorable comments in the press. "

- ❏ *About image*: "We would rather earn credibility than buy it."[28]

The company does not use billboards because of the impact on the environment. Their catalogs are printed on recycled paper and each product is clearly identified as being made with an environmentally friendly process or material.

On the other hand, Patagonia is more than willing to use "buzz" marketing to promote the environmental cause. Prior to the 2004 U.S. presidential election, the company fielded a $500,000 multimedia "Vote the Environment" campaign among their customers and the general public. The effort did not support specific candidates or parties, but urged the unregistered to sign up, and the voters to support politicians who promised environmental reforms.[29]

Accountable to Nature

"Patagonia," says senior executive Rick Ridgeway, "is not here to enrich our shareholders. Our shareholders are the wild lands and wild animals."[30] Ridgeway, one of the world's foremost mountain climbers (he was the first American to summit K2 . . . without bottled oxygen), used to be an executive vice president until the staff decided that such titles had no place in their egalitarian workplace. Ridgeway makes it very clear that the company's commitments are anything but corporate hype. The people at Patagonia believe passionately in Yvon Chouinard's view that the changes in society tend to come from the national government, local and regional government, and the citizenry itself. Of these, the actions of the citizenry create the most positive and lasting change.

Patagonia's dedication to environmental activism started with Yvon Chouinard, but its epicenter is now found in the company mission that he and others agreed on a few years ago. The product of deep internal examination starting in the 1980s and continuing for years after, Patagonia's values statement is lived on a daily basis by the company's people. As Rick Ridgeway tells it, "Not a week goes by that it's not repeated in the company. Everyone uses it daily." How many companies can say that? The statement speaks in part to being:

❏ *Committed to the Soul of the Sport.* The "sport" is alpine mountaineering and rock climbing, but Patagonia also is committed to supplying paddlers, fly fishermen, and endurance athletes. This is what they call the "silent sports" (no motors), where "the reward for each involves no audience and no prize other than hard-won grace, those moments of connection that break down the imaginary divide between ourselves and the rest of nature."

❏ *Committed to Grassroots Environmental Activism.* Patagonia condemns eco-violence, but actively encourages and helps fund what they call "small-scale citizens' groups who have been working to reverse the historical tide, river by river, ecosystem by ecosystem."

❏ *Committed to Uncommon Culture.* Patagonia was among the first to insist on a casual work environment (shoes optional). Their cultural point of view: "We prefer the human scale to the corporate, vagabonding to tourism, the quirky and lively to the toned down and flattened out."

❏ *Committed to Innovative Design.* Patagonia's designs and the company itself have a "bias for simplicity and utility," which feeds their first design principle that form follows function. The "resulting product is stronger, more versatile, lighter, and often more environmentally sound."[31]

Marketing at Patagonia is as unconventional as the rest of the company's activities. They believe that good products tell their own story, with some help here and there from a website, a quarterly catalog, occasional e-mails to their customers, some channel merchandising, and only minimal advertising. But that advertising they have done—as well as the photos in their catalogs—are dramatic illustrations of the extreme conditions in which their apparel is tested and worn (see Figure 2-6 for sample print advertising).

Patagonia staffers develop their own catalog and creative materials. Decentralized teams work on their own website and catalog areas, but nothing is released without careful scrutiny about whether it meets the company's stringent environmental and quality guidelines. When outside help is needed, Patagonia teams work with suppliers who share the company's passion for environmental causes.

Patagonia also tends to avoid what they refer to as "simplistic marketing statements." The messages they have about product and the environment are too complex to be reduced to a single selling line.

Figure 2-6. Patagonia print advertising.

SOURCE: Photo by Paul Dix. © Patagonia, Inc.

They consider their stores to be a "canvas" on which they portray their product lines and positions via point-of-purchase displays and brochures.

When it comes to marketing research, the company's people believe that they must rely on information from their customers and their own instincts, with the heaviest emphasis on the latter. Their view is that they try to lead their customers, particularly in terms of environmental activism and in apparel designs and fabrics that customers don't necessarily know are possible, such as their successful experiment with all-organic cotton that is now integral to their product line.

One of the most critical components of their corporate cause is the belief that a company must be based on traditional and honest transparency, the kind that can only come from a healthy respect for what buyers and sellers need to know about one another.

What We Can Learn from Patagonia

It would be easy to dismiss Patagonia as a boutique clothing company that has carved out a unique niche and whose idiosyncrasies are not particularly applicable to other businesses. But the company is ahead of the curve on two important fronts that will have major significance for companies everywhere in upcoming years.

First, Yvon Chouinard and his team were concerned about the environment long before most of us had even heard about global warming. Because he and his compatriots saw a link between their business and its impact on the environment—a cause-and-effect that many business leaders are only now acknowledging—they integrated their passion into how they conducted their business. That passion was not about making money, it was about making a viable business that gave back to the Earth instead of taking from it. Companies like Patagonia set the stage for larger companies that are just now following suit, including megacorporations like General Electric ("ecomagination") and BP ("Beyond Petroleum").

From a marketing standpoint, Patagonia has also proved that great products and a strong corporate culture can attract and hold customers with like-minded passions without relying heavily on traditional marketing tools. They have demonstrated that more is not necessarily better and loud is not necessarily persuasive. They have shown others that followed their example that marketing can be successful on many levels, if a company's passion propels whatever marketing initiatives it employs.

Like the other companies profiled here, Patagonia presents their views and their products and welcomes all those who join their parade. Yet, they successfully avoided pushing their perspective into places where it is not welcome. Their marketing efforts are admittedly self-selecting and never likely to create a company of enormous size and scope. But the work they do—just like the products they design—is of pristine quality that doesn't require aggressive marketing to be seen and appreciated.

Patagonia is definitely unique, but its lessons for companies of all sizes are likely to be relevant in many venues and many industries. If conventional marketers look long and hard enough at the Patagonia model, they might find some practical integrity approaches that would greatly improve their own ways of generating profitable revenue, at whatever scale.

Kiehl's Since 1851: "We Don't Do Trends. We Do What We Believe In."

You can tell by the company name that the people of Kiehl's Since 1851 are proud of their roots. It was "an old world apothecary" that John Kiehl opened in Manhattan on the corner of Thirteenth and Third, the same year that a fledgling newspaper that would come to be called *The New York Times* published its first edition. The Kiehl's company liked the East Village location so much that its flagship store is still located there, along with the original floorboards and wood fixtures. (See Figure 2-7 for picture of original Kiehl's location.)

The apothecary evolved into a contemporary pharmacy carrying homeopathic and herbal remedies, oils, OTC drugs, and a few Kiehl's branded products. Gradually the Kiehl's staff began experimenting with new ideas that blossomed into a line of superior hair and beauty products. Apparently they did

Figure 2-7. The original Kiehl's store in Manhattan.

SOURCE: © Kiehl's Since 1851. Used with permission.

good work. The Smithsonian Institution's permanent archive in Washington, D.C., contains 103 Kiehl's products.

Their line covers all life stages, from Kiehl's Baby products to anti-aging creams and lotions. In 2005, they partnered with stylist Kevin Mancuso to produce a Stylist Series of hair products. The packaging is plain and utilitarian-looking which, oddly enough, underscores the specialness of the product inside.

As part of the Kiehl's family legacy, the company also gives liberally to important social and health causes. All of the proceeds of their anti-aging and some other products are donated to charitable organizations. In addition, Kiehl's and its employees have become ardent supporters of various environmental causes including their efforts to slow the loss of Greenland's irreplaceable ice reservoirs due to global warming (*www.clickforgreenland.com*).[32]

The No-Sell Sale

From the beginning, the Kiehl's family sold only natural cosmetics and operated on the principle that natural word-of-mouth was the best advertising. To this day—despite being acquired in 2000 by L'Oreal, one of the world's largest beauty products companies—Kiehl's still sells their products largely with the help of word-of-mouth-generating events and generous in-store sampling.

The Kiehl's products are purposely kept in relatively limited distribution through a small number of high-end outlets like Barney's, Nieman Marcus, Bergdorf Goodman, and about 150 department store counters in the United States. The company has only twenty owned and operated stores, and expects to move very slowly in expanding their retail business, despite the likelihood that demand would far exceed any expansion.

Like Trader Joe's, it's all about the Kiehl's retail brand experience. The moment that customers walk into a Kiehl's store they see the Kiehl's difference in action. You won't find mirrors in Kiehl's that make your blemishes look like moon craters. Those behind the counter are not overly made-up beauty-queen contest dropouts. In fact, Kiehl's normally does not hire make-up experts; they prefer to hire an eclectic array of people, including artists and athletes and even stand-up comedians, all of whom are naturally engaging but have an aptitude to learn and teach about cosmetics.

The company's heritage as apothecary "chemists" is carried through in the training of their salespeople, called "retail partners." They become white-coated professionals after undergoing intensive four-week residency schooling that drills them in the chemistry, use, and application of Kiehl's products. They are taught to perform with the same professionalism of a pharmacist, to never send away a customer without a sample, and to never utter gratuitous words like "fabulous."[33]

The Kiehl's way of "selling" is not to sell at all. In fact, they only recently established a marketing department. They believe that the products will do what they do and no hype will change that. They go out of their way not to bad-mouth other companies and products. They are interested in their customer representatives establishing an ongoing relationship with a customer, and that may or may not mean that a sale is made the first time, or even the second or third time that an individual comes into a store.

Their attitude is, in essence: "Don't take our word for it. Try it and if it works, you'll be back." That's one reason why Kiehl's gives away more than 12 million samples a year, which represents 80 percent of their total marketing budget. The products eloquently speak for themselves. Eventually, their regular visitors tend to become regular customers.

Kiehl's extensive sampling program can also extend beyond the store. One Kiehl's customer representative met the assistant to the president of a major television network, who commented on how much she loved the Kiehl's product line. When Christmas season rolled around, the Kiehl's staffer hand-delivered a gift assortment to the network assistant. News spread through the network headquarters and more orders rolled in from throughout that building.

The company sometimes employs cutting-edge marketing techniques, but in ways that support communities and are more likely to endear them to marketing audiences rather than alienate them. Kiehl's develops customized approaches for each new store opening that are geared toward the interests and needs of the local community. When they opened a store on Manhattan's Upper West Side, for instance, they supported a community effort to build playgrounds in Central Park, a hot topic in that neighborhood at the time. The company has also rented mobile marketing vans to visit local unsung community heroes and promote their important work as firefighters or youth leaders or teachers.[34]

The remainder of their low-key marketing programs includes noninvasive e-mailings, an informative, friendly, but decidedly laid-back website *(www .kiehls.com),* a catalog, and handshake tours throughout communities when new stores are opened.

Not Hip, Honored

Above all, Kiehl's is tangibly real in an industry that is festooned with the illusory. As Cammie Cannella, Kiehl's vice president of Global Education Development, puts it, "It's about integrity and authenticity. They are everything to us. We don't do trends, we do what we believe in. It is not about manufactured cachet, or being hip or cool, but about being honored to serve customers in whatever way we can."[35] That would sound just a bit clichéd if it weren't true.

As in the case of Patagonia and Trader Joe's, part of being real sometimes means being eccentric. Historically, the Kiehl's family members have enjoyed alpine ski racing, aviation, equestrian competitions, and motorcycling. You may find bits and pieces of those experiences in any given Kiehl's store, especially vintage Harley-Davidson and Indian motorcycles. It has nothing to do with what they sell but it says something about who they are. The bikes are out of place, but oddly effective in pulling in male customers—which is why then-CEO Aaron Morse came up with the idea in 1978. Today, men represent 30 to 40 percent of the Kiehl's customer base.[36]

When Kiehl's was acquired by L'Oreal, the new parent accelerated expansion but kept the expensive investments in sampling and training of customer representatives. Those turned out to be very sound investments indeed, since Kiehl's racked up double-digit earnings growth and swelled to more than $70 million in gross sales in 2005.

What We Can Learn from Kiehl's

The Kiehl's story is about maintaining simplicity in everything it does. The products are efficacious, yet the packaging is unadorned. The sales associates are professional beauty consultants. They know they are representing superior quality products, so there's no need to sell them in the conventional sense. The product is allowed to speak for itself, and the customers almost always like what it says about them. And this, in the hyper-competitive health and beauty aids market.

For obvious reasons, customers tend to speak highly of Kiehl's to their friends, which is why *Fast Company* made Kiehl's a category finalist for their 2005 "Annual Customers First Award." Based partly on positive customers' comments and mostly on their willingness to recommend the company to others, the research about Kiehl's by *Fast Company* affirmed the benefits of building products and a business with unrelenting integrity.[37]

The management of Kiehl's and their L'Oreal corporate bosses seem to understand how easily they could upset the practical integrity that has become ingrained in the brand and its products. They are moving slowly to expand the exposure of the brand, and have no intention of letting its growth potential— which is considerable—undermine the power of its simple honesty.

Most companies do not have the benefit of the Kiehl's heritage. But there are always opportunities to strip away some of the nonsense that may be encrusting a product so good that, if left unencumbered, could almost sell itself. Does the packaging on a packaged goods brand always have to scream at passersby, or could it be made more appealing by taking something *off* the label rather than adding unnecessary adornment? If your brand is a service brand, are your people trained as well as they should be? Are they over-selling or just being helpful?

Would limited sampling, as expensive as it might be, be a better solution to fuel slow-but-steady growth, in lieu of more ordinary attempts to shout your way into customers' lives? If not, is it because the product might not be strong enough to create momentum on its own?

Kiehl's definitely has some advantages that other brands will never have. But they also have some lessons to teach us all, including that understated integrity may be a smart way to go for a wide spectrum of brands.

Summary

The companies profiled here market with practical integrity because integrity is part of who they are. It comes naturally to them, but the forces of competition and market changes could easily have pulled them off that course. It did not happen because their sense of who they are is far stronger than the distractions of the marketplace.

They make mistakes like any company, but they are guided in their recoveries by what they believe in, and that includes their customers. They celebrate victories but always remember that their integrity is one of the key reasons for their success. They market in ways that are compatible with what they stand for, which in turn dictate how they should market. They learn from their customers while teaching them, and invariably create vocal advocates in the process.

Name any company in any business, and it probably can learn a thing or two from these companies. If nothing else, they teach us that scale is not as important as commitment, differentiation can be created by integrity, and marketing is most persuasive when the marketer lets the customers do the marketing.

To help make all of this happen, marketers may want to consider adopting some new kinds of operating strategies like those we will explore in Part Two.

PART TWO

TRUE STRATEGIES

CHAPTER 3

Be the One They Can Count On

Build Equitable Partnerships, Fused with Integrity

I n the early 1980s, a major hotel chain commissioned some consultants to create sophisticated research and algorithmic modeling to determine the optimum features for a new brand of properties they had in mind.

But even more sophisticated than the research was the way the company began to talk and listen with intensity to what business road warriors wanted in a hotel experience, some little things that they could count on to make their long days seem a little shorter. When they had finished listening and started building, the company was able to honestly position its new hotels for what they were: a place *for* businesspeople, designed *by* businesspeople.

Today, Courtyard by Marriott is one of the top fifteen lodging brands in the world, and the fastest growing brand in the Marriott family.[1] It is a place that assiduously adheres to business-quality standards that give it a service integrity that thousands of businesspeople depend upon every day.

Marketers and their buyers don't have to play tug-of-war to each get what they want. They are far more likely to achieve their mutual goals if they form a working partnership. And, any partnership is more productive and lasts longer when the partners can count on one another's integrity.

Partners, Not Servants

In marketing we used to assume that sellers made the products and created the services, and they owned them. A more recent theory is that the customer "owns" it all, lock, stock, and brand. The idea is that marketers are simply here to service and provide for every need of buyers, including handing over the keys to the company. Still another view is that brands are not owned by the seller, or even by the buyer, but by the entire collective of stakeholders, who include employees, suppliers, and investors.[2]

Which means . . . what? Marketers are just licensing the rights of the real owners to sell the product using someone else's brand? That's intriguing, but not always feasible.

An even more practical way to operate is to realize that the marketer's role is not to be a servant that provides anything the customer wants, but to be a partner who delivers what the customer needs. In most cases, the buyer and the seller are best served by such a peer-to-peer kind of relationship, based on mutually beneficial rewards, and validated with the integrity of the brand.

For decades, full-commission stockbrokers had ordinary investors believing that they couldn't invest well without the brokerage's extensive research, investing experience, and whatever Wall Street heft bought you. It was marketed as customized investment advice but, in reality, it was closer to a one-size-fits-all service.

Charles Schwab & Co. first rose to prominence because it offered a better proposition: Investors would not pay unnecessarily high commissions for routine work. Instead, Schwab helped investors understand that full service was not always necessary, and that investing could be more of a peer partnership, with the investor playing a more active role.

At first, Schwab was seen as just a low-cost transactional brand. Eventually, though, it began to offer more services, and more investors began to think of the company as a peer-partner in their financial planning as well. For many, Schwab was more respected because it was seen as being more transparent in what it offered and what the investor really received, and this despite the fact that it was low-priced. For millions of customers, Schwab had become a peer-partner, more so even than some brokerages that claimed to offer more comprehensive and personalized service.

Make It Easy on Your Partner

Marketing professor Dipak Jain of Northwestern's Kellogg School of Management has suggested that a transparent partnership with customers can be a distinct competitive advantage. According to Jain, customer value involves the customer's cost of switching divided by the customer cost of thinking (about staying or switching). That means that if a company can reduce the cost of thinking and increase the costs of switching, they are more likely to maintain strong customer loyalty."[3]

Peer-partnering with customers can create this kind of a transparent, low-maintenance relationship that can yield a higher quality of loyalty, particularly when the relationship is based on a mutual expectation of integrity.

The entire Patagonia business is based on mutual expectations of integrity that are reinforced by the apparel that Patagonia sells and the affinity customers have for the brand and company. Patagonia makes high-performance products that deliver the goods in the most extreme outdoor conditions, and they do it with Earth-friendly quality. They count on their customers appreciating that and staying loyal, even if the company doesn't sink a fortune into marketing communications, and even if those customers regularly pay a hefty premium.

More Partnering Yields More Brand Involvement

One consumer company that is particularly adept at inviting the customer into a partnership is Trader Joe's. They have created what they call "360-degree marketing," which seeks to understand not only what people buy in their stores, but why.

Merchants at Trader Joe's consider the customer to be part of their research and development team, so that they can modify their stores to fit the lives of their customers rather than the other way around. The store captains spend most of their days walking the floors and chatting with customers, taking in all they want to say and paying them for their time by responding to their requests.[4] That kind of Trader Joe's experience of mutual respect is too often missing from typical supermarket chains.

IKEA sells furniture and accessories, some of which require assembling at home. IKEA in the UK has formally adopted a partnering positioning:

> Your partner in better living. We do our part, you do yours. Together we save money.[5]

This is partnering that clearly lays out certain tasks the customers must perform (assembling furniture, for example) and what they will receive in return (attractive contemporary furniture of superior value). It is, at one and the same time, an honest value statement and a transparent selling proposition.

Back on the B2B side, Herman Miller designers believe that a business can spend $5 million for a great space or a lousy one. A lot depends on how well the company that works for you listens and diagnoses your needs. They'll walk you through the process of defining a space, determining what is to be communicated by that space. That is, should the space communicate to your staff how much they are valued, or where the company has been, or where it hopes to go, or what? It's done with architectural and furniture design, but it's really about sending messages to those you are partnering with.[6]

Customers of companies like IKEA, Herman Miller, and Trader Joe's are given multiple opportunities to get closer to the company in ways that enable them to receive a superior value or superior quality or a superior buying experience. They become more involved in the brands. They know these companies are doing everything possible to operate as a thoughtful and candid partner to their customers, working together as peers, with a partnership that is fused with integrity.

Integrity Partnerships Create Respectful Partners

In the past, the concept of customers-as-partners has been restricted to business-to-business marketing, where a direct sales force is in regular contact with buyers, and where customers are frequently asked for their input on products and customer service.[7] Salespeople for Oracle, SAP, and BEA Systems, for example, all build as strong a personal relationship as possible with individual engineers, product managers, and others who are responsible for purchase decisions.

Yet customer partnerships for all brands and companies are possible, and even if they cannot be as personal as in the B2B sector, peer partnerships can be approximated in B2C companies. A General Mills brand manager or a Starbuck's marketing manager, for example, can reshape their marketing planning, and their consumer marketing, to be based on an integrity-based peer partnership. That starts with dropping such words as "targeting" and substituting "partnering."

Marketing managers can also stop assuming that they are supposed to provide service to the customer, but not vice versa. If it's a partnership, built on mutual respect for one another's integrity, the marketer should expect to get things from buyers, not just their money.

In the best partnerships, both the buyer and seller expect the partner to contribute something of value. The buyer is typically looking for emotional and/or functional benefits, sound value, periodic innovation, good customer service, and a strong sense that the seller is acting with integrity. The seller is looking to the buyer for a purchase and longer-term loyalty. Sellers should also be looking for information that will help create even more for the partner, which may come in the form of positive information, or even as important learning as a result of a rejection (see Figure 3-1).

If this exchange is successful, it works out to everyone's benefit. And, from the marketer's standpoint, the best partners may be the ones that can't get enough of integrity, because they also make the best customers.

Focus on the Fanatics

The undecideds, the easily swayed, the habitually open-minded—these types of buyers can drive a marketing team crazy. Such buyers have difficulty committing

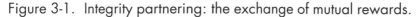

Figure 3-1. Integrity partnering: the exchange of mutual rewards.

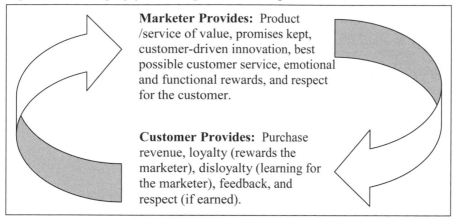

Marketer Provides: Product /service of value, promises kept, customer-driven innovation, best possible customer service, emotional and functional rewards, and respect for the customer.

Customer Provides: Purchase revenue, loyalty (rewards the marketer), disloyalty (learning for the marketer), feedback, and respect (if earned).

to a brand, or have no interest in it, and they never want to get too comfortable with a particular brand of anything because there are so many other opportunities out there that they might miss.

In any market, however, there is usually a segment of customers—sometimes they are in the majority—who are in search of particular product or service qualities that carry value for both the buyer and the seller.

These people know and respect integrity when they see it, and they are always in search of it. They may believe that they have integrity, and they purchase brands that they think reflect who they are. Or, they may buy high-integrity brands because they like to be seen as someone who has an affinity for such brands. Since integrity is not as common as the choices that face most buyers, they tend to selectively search for, find, and stay with integrity when they see it.

Kiehl's spends a lot of time and money training their counter people because they are the ones who have to believe, and convince customers that they believe, in Kiehl's integrity of purpose. That sense of integrity of purpose and product integrity is part of what makes Kiehl's different from and superior to less sincere competitors. It also attracts customers who are willing to pay more for Kiehl's products.

Herman Miller customers know when they walk in the door that they can find less expensive products elsewhere, but the integrity of the company is not as plentiful. Many of Trader Joe's shoppers specifically make an extra trip to TJ's because they do not see the selection, value, or product integrity in more ordinary grocery chains.

These integrity heavy-users may be valuable enough to aggressively pursue for several reasons. First, they tend to value branded products and services that

◆ What If? ◆

What if your customers owned your company? What if they decided how they wanted to be marketed to . . . or with? What if they had to give a "thumbs up/thumbs down" on any of your marketing ideas before you could launch them? What if you had to submit marketing plans to them for them to critique before you launched it? How would that go?

What if your team made up a marketing plan outline that reflected everything you know about the way your customers would do it? If they came up blank, that might mean that you don't know enough about the way your customer thinks. If they come up with a detailed outline that didn't match what you did last year—it might be time to rethink your approach to marketing planning. Either way, thinking about your customer as an active partner in the marketing might change the way you market, and for the better.

are selling all things value-added (which usually carry higher margins). They have learned the hard way that lower quality costs more in the end.

Second, they come to the partnership with a positive outlook about what their experience is going to be. They can certainly be disappointed if they are let down—and that disappointment can be more severe than with other customers. But if they are pleased, they show their appreciation in their fierce loyalty.

Third, they show their appreciation by becoming influential endorsers to their friends and families. They are vocal about their belief in a brand because they are more passionate about it. And why wouldn't they be? They have worked hard to find brands with integrity and are happy to share their enthusiasm with others. And their known devotion to quality at all price levels tends to make them more credible when they pass along a recommendation.

Are there integrity heavy-users in more mundane categories like household cleaners or the rental car business? Certainly. They are the ones studying labels and contracts for value-added benefits. They love a bargain as much as the next person, but they won't get burned more than once trying to save money at the expense of performance.

In short, integrity heavy-users often are most companies' best shot at achieving profitable growth *if* that company delivers on its promises.

*   *   *

A Customer Strategy:
Create Integrity Partnerships

1. Find the Fanatics

Where can integrity heavy-users be found? Some may be tucked inside your current customer base and just haven't been asked the right questions or offered the right incentive to stick their heads up and be identified. Others are patronizing the competition, and aren't necessarily happy with that experience. Still others may not have experienced your products or services, but they are always willing and eager to meet a new friend to form a limited, integrity-based partnership.

Integrity heavy-users are, in fact, everywhere. You just have to know where to look or, more accurately, how to look. The behavior and attitudes of integrity buyers are eminently researchable, using habits and attitudes studies that can track buyer brand or product affinities.

As just one example, a marketer of premium sportswear might also discover that their best prospects tend to buy premium sports equipment with common value propositions, namely, offering products that will outlive the customer. That could offer some co-branding opportunities, and it could also provide important insight into what the integrity heavy-user's entire lifestyle looks like.

Here are a few things to look for when you are designing research to search out integrity heavy-users:

❏ They may be willing to pay a bit more for what they see as a lot more in quality. They seek longevity and durability over flash and empty style.

❏ They scan the marketplace for options like everyone else, but they don't jump for the sake of trying something new. They are thoughtful more often than they are impetuous.

❏ They love the genuine article. They are attracted to all things authentic that don't necessarily rely on enormous marketing budgets to prop up the brand. Some of them are specifically drawn to brands that are understated in their marketing communications.

❏ They tend to stay with a brand they like longer than their more fickle fellow buyers, especially if that brand has found ways to specifically reward them for their loyalty by providing them with even greater value for superior quality. They may be willing to try new products and services, but they are considerably more likely to stick with new products from companies and brands that have proven they can be trusted. Because of that, they are more likely to try brand extensions from trusted "partners" than to seek the same products elsewhere.

❏ They are attracted to brands that more frequently market with a focus on performance rather than price, although they are more than willing to purchase lower-priced items if they believe they are a good value.

❏ They are more aware of the context of the product or brand, such as its history, the reputation of its parent company, the quality of its people who have contact with buyers, and what kind and level of customer service is offered.

Prospects in search of high-integrity brands may be more demanding than the ordinary buyer in terms of the time and attention a company must pay, but it's generally worth it for a company or brand to take the extra time to work with them.

2. Surprise Them with Respect

Marketers are frequently searching for the drivers of brand choice that are the most important reasons why customers make their brand choice and switching decisions. In the same way, marketers might want to consider the degree to which their customers believe that your company or brand literally empathizes with them. Do you treat them as if you were someone that has been there, has experienced their frustrations, and know what will give them faith once again in what they buy?

Infosys co-founder Nandan M. Nilekani once explained that the key to his company's marketing success was its respectability, a Brahmanic trait that is held in high regard by the co-founders, several of whom are of the Brahman caste. "Our vision," Nilekani said, "is to be a globally respected company, delivering the best-of-breed software solutions, employing best-in-class professionals."[8] Needless to say, maintaining integrity in its marketing and sales programs is a critical aspect of that vision, and of building customer respect.

In a way, you're saying to your customers that their fanaticism about needing a company they can trust is completely understandable. You need to prove that you have heard them and have the utmost respect for their point of view. You need to demonstrate to them that you can *be* the customer and operate entirely from their point of view. Your company or your brand is every bit as fanatical about what buyers want as they are.

The research techniques of Max Blackston, a pioneering researcher in the field of brand personalities, have been used many times in the past to help marketers understand what customers think of brands and what customers think brands think of them. This can be especially valuable in consumer service businesses where customer partnerships must be carefully crafted and maintained.

In one study, Blackston's approach was used in the 1980s by a credit card company to determine how much respect a brand garnered from its customers, based on how they thought the company respected them and their time.[9] In another study a decade later in the health-care field, a major insurer segmented potential members according to how much respect they had for various companies in an industry where respect can sometimes be hard to come by.

The fact is that we go out of our way to avoid companies that do not seem to respect us. We could never feel as if they are offering a peer-partnership. These challenges often arise in deregulated transition industries where there are still some staff members that are not all that customer-driven. Note the poor customer satisfaction ratings for more than a few telecommunications, health-care, and utility companies.

A Conversation

"Good afternoon. . . Lower Upstream Water Company. How can I give you spectacular service?"

"Yeah, we've got a busted water line."

"OK, sir, we'll take care of that."

"Thanks. We live on Delmonico Court in Point Roundout."

"OK, let's see . . . Point Roundout . . . around here we like to call that 'Point Way Out.'"

"Very funny."

". . . Okey-dokey, we can have someone out there by . . . noon Thursday."

"Noon Thursday? The whole block could float away by then!"

"Did I say 'noon'? I meant between noon and five."

"You can't be serious."

"Well, sir, we have to take these in the order they come up . . . that's only fair, wouldn't you agree?"

"Fair, yes. Smart, not so much."

"This is Lower Upstream, sir. We take care of everything."

"Uh-huh. Well, just have your guy leave his bill on the curb."

"Sorry?"

"Curbs don't float."

"I like that, that's very funny. Now, for our survey, may I put down that we gave you spectacular service? . . . Sir?"

Fortunately, thanks to the efforts of past and present researchers, it isn't all that difficult to establish segmenting based on how respected a brand is, which is one indicator of the potential for peer-partnering.

General Electric found a promising way to track the respect it receives from its customers. Based on the loyalty work done by Fred Reichheld, director emeritus of Bain & Co., and some pioneering customer satisfaction research by Enterprise Rent-A-Car, GE's "net-promoter score" concentrates on one question: "How likely are you to recommend us to a friend?" The company uses the data to create respect-based segments that Bain & Co. calls "proponents," "detractors," and "passives." The customers rate the company on a 1-to-10 scale, and those rating GE at 9 or 10 are being categorized as "promoters." The net-promoter score is obtained by subtracting the detractors from the promoters.

The system is a quick-response customer satisfaction device, but it also tracks how respected a company is, and whether customers believe they are respected by the company.[10]

Microsoft has succeeded because of its dominance on the PC software market, but it also has not lost that dominance despite plenty of opportunities for superior systems and software to be introduced. Microsoft has earned the begrudging respect of customers and other companies, whose leaders wish they had had the vision and aggressiveness to do what Microsoft has accomplished. However, that respect for Microsoft may be tinged with a dislike for the company's way of doing business or its apparent arrogance, which makes it difficult to garner the full respect of even its most ardent supporters.

If proprietary research is feasible, a company could create a solid statistical research base of brand associations, refined with regression or similar analyses that zero in on respect-related factors and how they apply to various brands in the industry. Matching that data with demographic or other benchmarks could provide some quantification of the size of various respect-based segments. An example of the end product of such work might look like the table in Figure 3-2, which lays out a hypothetical brand life span with distribution of respecting prospects.

However the data is obtained, respect segmentation can provide marketers with some valuable guidance on how strong the partnership is between the company or brand and their users. In many cases, it is integrity that is at the root of the respect customers have for brands and companies, and it is often integrity that prompts those companies to respect their customers.

Figure 3-2. Hypothetical distribution of prospective user respect segments by brand life stage.

Brand Life Stage	Unquestioning Respecters	Watchful Respecters	Fair Weather Respecters	Cynics & Skeptics	Neutrals
New/ Early Growth	3%	10%	15%	20%	52%
Maturing	15	15	20	10	40
Mature	25	25	25	5	20
Waning	10	15	20	40	15

3. Build Loyalty with Involvement

Depending who you listen to, brand loyalty is dead, dying, or never better. In a 2001 Accenture survey, U.S. and UK marketing executives said they believed their customers to be significantly less loyal than in the past. Four years later, a study among 1,000 Americans confirmed that a majority felt the Internet made it easier for them to switch brands because they could find out so much so quickly about other options.[11]

Then again, a 2002 Grocery Manufacturers of America survey reported that 76 percent of U.S. consumers considered the brand first before making a final product selection, and 67 percent claimed that they would "chase" their favorite brand to another store if it were not available.[12]

Whether it is on the rise or on the decline, one thing is certain: Loyalty is increasingly brittle. Loyalty is created when customers believe they can rely on what is being promised. If that trust is shaken they will often reconsider. If it is abused they will often walk away. If something is wrong and it is covered up, they may also rally their friends for the brand equivalent of a political impeachment. (That Accenture study mentioned above also discovered that nearly seven in ten consumers would tell family and friends whenever they had a negative experience with a brand or company.)

Some companies believe that they have created loyalty when they have not, mainly because it is based on forced choice. For example, in corporate banking customers may stick with their bank because of the cost of switching, which is loyalty-by-inertia. But the quality of that loyalty may be relatively poor in terms of customer satisfaction, yet not enough to offset the cost of switching. In the airline industry, frequent user programs create a false loyalty that discourages switching, not because an airline is offering superior value, but because of the investment in user points by ostensibly "loyal" frequent fliers.

Is hollow loyalty better than none? In some respects it is, because it still may enable a dialogue and offer the possibility of an occasional sale. But hollow loyalty can also be a time-released headache because users are itching to switch. While they wait to spring, they may become masters of the un-sell who start conversations like, "Believe me, if it weren't for the miles, I wouldn't have anything to do with that useless airline . . ."

The purpose of creating loyalty beyond the immediate revenue gain is to ensure *future* revenue and the higher profitability that results from repeat purchases. There's not much future revenue in store for a brand that's being slammed hard in the present. Future revenue can be ensured, however, if there's an expectation that a brand or company will respect its customer-partners and operate with integrity.

Maker's Mark is a high-end bourbon first distilled in 1958 in Loretto, Kentucky by William Samuels, Sr. His son, Bill Samuels, Jr., is now the president of Maker's Mark, now part of the Jim Beam family marketed by Fortune Brands, and he oversees the production of about 600,000 cases a year. Every bottle is still hand-sealed with its own unique red wax seal. The brand is supported by low-key advertising as limited as its product supply. Bill Samuels likes it that way because he always runs the risk of running out of bourbon.

Despite—or perhaps because of—this low-key approach to marketing, the Fortune Brands people say the "ethos" of the Maker's Mark brand has attracted thousands of converts who meet with Bill Samuels in his travels to taverns all over the United States. Bill Samuels's chats not only pick up valuable pieces of information from customers, they also enable him to personally demonstrate the respect the distiller has for the interests of their customers.[13]

In 1966, Paul Van Doren drove down to a surfing competition in Costa Mesa, California, walked up to original king of the sport, Duke Kahanamoka, and offered to make him shoes to match his shirt. Since that day, his company, Vans, has earned and demonstrated a high respect for the alternative sports performers, many of whom are now on the Vans payroll as designers, advisers, and spokestars. But of even greater importance is the respect ordinary users have for the Vans company and the respect the company has consistently demonstrated toward them.

Vans is another well-respected brand in the relatively young extreme sports field that includes skateboarding, snowboarding, surfing, and motocross biking. What has made Vans stay special for several decades is how it stays in touch with its customers and uses it brand to forge a mutually beneficial partnership with them.

Furniture leader IKEA has created a new division, called the Small Biz Network, which hosts networking events for small business entrepreneurs at IKEA stores, where they can meet others of their ilk and learn new techniques from experts. Nokia established a communications center in their flagship Moscow store, where customers can use Nokia products to communicate with anyone anywhere at no cost, and more such stores are coming soon to other metropolitan areas.

These companies recognize that strong partnerships require regular involvement with their customers, involvement that offers plenty of opportunities for customers to see the integrity of the company firsthand.

In all of these cases, the involvement with customers and the customers' involvement with the companies have been the hallmark for a mutual admiration between brand and customer, and the foundation for an honest partnership.

4. Do What Good Partners Do

Marketers provide customers with what they want and need, but buyers and sellers must partner because they need each other and could not function separately in the marketplace. And as with all partnerships, the deal comes with mutual benefits and responsibilities.

Building a strong customer partnership—one that creates mutual loyalties between buyer and seller despite differences in the partners—is hard work. Here is a brief checklist of what good seller-buyer partners do to keep their partnerships alive:

❏ *Good partners listen with intensity to one another.* At W.L. Gore, product development teams get into the field regularly and listen to the unvarnished opinions of fans and critics alike to make their products as good as they can be. They have worked closely with thoracic specialists to develop a graft that could save the lives of many, such as athletes with hidden heart diseases that kill unexpectedly. And they developed an improved ionic exchange membrane that didn't seem to have a use until Gore researchers sent the prototypes to fuel-cell scientists who provided the feedback that could give the product enormous potential in the energy industry.[14]

Harley-Davidson, Jeep, and Range Rover regularly attract thousands of users to customer rallies around the United States and elsewhere that celebrate the partnership between brand and buyer. They eat, they drink, they enjoy each other's company, and they share their mutual involvement in their brand of choice. It's an opportunity to hear why customers admire and respect the brands and for the companies to demonstrate how they appreciate and respect input from their users. These are bonding sessions between the drivers, their vehicles, and the brands that they believe in, because they believe the companies believe in them.

❏ *Good partners look out for one another.* Marketers that demonstrate a real interest in their customers as people, not just revenue, have increased their chances of achieving customer respect.

eBay has built the world's largest online community, and its existence depends on maintaining continuous contact and support for its sellers. Ten times a year eBay brings groups of buyers and sellers to its San Jose, California headquarters to listen to their praise and complaints about the way the auction giant does business. After two days and nights of this program, called "Voices," eBay staff stay in touch with the Voices members to track their views over time.[15]

Similarly, Patagonia executives keep a close watch on environmental issues, and every eighteen months or so they hold environmental conferences to listen to what's going on in the field. This serves a dual purpose of supporting causes they passionately believe in and provides regular input on what issues they should be addressing as they design their outdoor apparel and equipment.[16]

❏ *Good partners are honest with one another.* John Deere was a blacksmith who created a superior plow and founded a company that ultimately grew to be a $20+ billion global leader in farming and other equipment with about 50,000 employees in 150 countries. Deere & Company has succeeded over the years for a lot of reasons but the company believes that there is one reason that is more important than all the rest.

In 1964, the company had close to 40,000 employees, and CEO Bill Hewitt felt that a company that size had to be clear on what it wanted to stand for. In the summer of that year, Hewitt issued the first of what was referred to as the *Green Bulletins,* rare but critical internal messages from the leader of the company to its employees. The very first *Green Bulletin* dealt with the most important factors in the company's success. It read in part:

> *Integrity and merit are the bases of our continued success as an organization*
> *and as individuals within it. . . . Of what do integrity and merit consist?*
> *COURTESY in every word*
> *HONESTY in every transaction*
> *PROGRESSIVENESS in every thought*
> *CONSTRUCTIVENESS in every criticism*
> *QUALITY in every piece of work produced*

They may sound quaint, but Deere & Co. has uncompromisingly adhered to these principles, which have driven their success and have occasionally caused them to lose money when they refused to compromise them.[17]

❏ *Good partners respect one another.* It isn't just about good customer service or meeting customer needs. Companies with strong customer relationships genuinely like to be with their customers, and their customers are often willing to reciprocate.

In contrast to Microsoft, Apple likely enjoys much greater respect among its customers than does Microsoft, yet has only a fraction of Microsoft's share of operating systems. Despite that miniscule OS share, it is partly the respect that Apple attracts inside and outside of the computer industry that enabled it to launch new ventures in previously untried categories with a great deal of positive momentum before there was positive cash flow.

A company that started with respect for nutrition in the frequently criticized fast food industry has gained significant respect, and the rewards for buyer and seller have been many and mutual. Fred De-Luca and Dr. Peter Buck had an idea they acted upon in 1965. They created a fast-food joint called "Pete's Super Submarines" in Bridgeport, Connecticut. After a slow start, the company began franchising its operation. Today, Subway is the second largest fast-food chain in the world, in terms of locations, behind only McDonald's. As of 2006, the chain had been named franchiser of the year fourteen times in the last sixteen years by *Entrepreneur* magazine.

One of the real propellants for growth has been the successful advertising campaign featuring likeable Jared Fogle, who is said to have lost 245 pounds on a diet of Subway sandwiches. This is a brand that failed to gain the respect of either the public or the industry until its alternative fare began to make more and more sense in comparison to the carbs and calories of the competition. Now Subway is one of the most successful franchise companies in the United States.

5. Avoid the Turn-Offs

Potential customers in search of brands with integrity are just as likely to move away from the wrong peer-partner as move toward one they have affinity for. Watch out for turn-offs that send all the wrong signals:

❏ *Treating New Customers Much Better Than Existing Ones.* It's tempting to lure new users into the fold by providing them with incentives that you don't feel obligated to offer to existing customers because they're already in the bag. Customers who believe that they are dealing with a high-integrity company or brand may begin to wonder if they made the right decision when the see inequitable treatment. Just because it's done a lot doesn't mean it's liked. Telecom and cable companies that deep discount for new customers are building customer bases at the expense of customer loyalty.

Partnering Implication to Consider: If trial incentives are necessary, simultaneously offer some token of your esteem to your current users, perhaps on an opt-in basis. For a lot of them, it probably won't be necessary to do anything more than make the offer, but the thought definitely counts.

❏ *Assuming You Know Your Partners Better Than They Know Themselves.* Customers evolve faster than companies' ability to track their changes. The Cadillac users got too old to drive and GM figured that the next generation would venerate the old brand the same way their parents did. Kodak was so loved that it assumed that its customers wouldn't abandon the brand when better cameras and better value film invaded from Japan. Nokia thought it had a good grip on what styling cell phone users liked, but missed the boat on the clam-shell phone.

Partnering Implication to Consider: If your company is not conducting annual tracking studies with periodic fill-in gap research, start now. If you're running the research and it's not being reviewed regularly at the highest levels, start now. If you assumed something—no matter how minor—about your customers that turned out to be wrong, reevaluate all of your recent results and the methodologies used to obtain them. Try to "be the customer," but be sure to fully understand what that entails by doing the homework.

❏ *Giving Your Partners What You Think They Need (Without Asking Them).* Even when customers and marketers are operating as partners, the customers are the ultimate arbiters of what's working because they can always walk away. If they had really understood what their customers wanted, Quaker would have left Snapple's quirky brand personality intact when they purchased the brand for $1.7 billion. Less than three years later they sold it for a fraction of that amount because they felt they knew better than their customers how to integrate it into the Quaker beverages system. (It's supposed to be a partnership, not a dictatorship.)

Borders and other mainline bookstore chains failed to see that their customers and their potential customers were browsing in their stores and buying online. By time they caught on, Amazon had already cornered the lion's share of the online market. Many book buyers were not interested in paying more for books so a store could serve cappuccino.

Partnering Implication to Consider: Are your customers trying to help out their "partners" and no one is listening? Are your corporate priorities taking precedence over what the market seems to need? Build an analysis that compares, point by point, all you know about what your customers have indicated they want with what the company's corresponding actions have been. If there's a gap, it's a problem, whether it's been identified as one or not.

*   *   *

A Summary and a Few Questions

Every successful marketing program begins with an accurate and thorough understanding of current and potential buyers and what makes them buy what they buy. Those potential customers are going to yield the best possible result for marketers who treat them as partners, not targets. In particular, those partners who are inclined to search and buy high-integrity products may be the most valuable segment for a brand or company to focus on. They are not hard to find if the right research is employed to identify and learn from them.

Some additional questions to consider:

1. Do you treat your customers as partners, or as nameless sources of revenue? Have you tried to envision them as a single partner? Do you consider your major marketing decision within the context of "what would our partners think?"

2. Do you know your customers well enough to establish what *they* would describe as a real partnership? Have you delved into what motivates them to buy, and what would motivate them to accept a lasting partnership with your brand and company? Are you assuming certain things about your customers that you have no right to assume?

3. Do your customers respect your brand and your company as much as you claim to respect them? Have you really asked your customers how

much they respect you, and if so, have you actually made any marketing decisions based on that feedback?

4. What could you do that you are *not* doing now to become a better
partner to your customers? What has stopped you from doing it?
Would it be possible to draw up a formal "partnership agreement"
that would accurately describe what your customers would want included in the contract? Would just the exercise of creating such an
agreement help your marketing team to better understand the mutual
obligations you and your customers share?

5. If you could identify your integrity heavy-user customers, what
changes would you make in how you market to them? Could you use
an ongoing tracking study or some proprietary attitude research to
focus on this group? Would the findings be actionable, or just treated
as nice to know? Are you prepared to reshape your marketing programs to emphasize such groups if you can confirm that they would
create higher lifetime value than more conventional segmenting?

Sellers and buyers need each other just as in any strong partnerships. And, as
we will discuss in Chapter 4, strong partnerships can create superior products
and services, forged with integrity.

CHAPTER 4

My Product, My Self

That's Not a Product You're Marketing, That's Your Word

The 1979 Academy Award–winning movie *Kramer vs. Kramer* starred Dustin Hoffman as a successful New York advertising executive. According to one behind-the-scenes story, Hoffman—who was famous for his method acting—shadowed a real-life Manhattan creative director through his daily routine.

At one point, Hoffman asked if he could borrow the man's clothes just to get an even better feel for the part. Absolutely, said the flattered exec, except for his Levi's. Nobody borrows his Levi's.

In their heyday, Levi's were more than just a pair of jeans; they were like a friend you could count on. They were both what you wore and who you were. They might have been unwashed for months, or looked hopelessly overwashed. They might have worn spots on the butt or on the knees, or they might not have had any knee fabric left at all. They might have carried the stains of a misspent youth, or the proud remnants of the greatest Stones concert ever. They were far more valuable than the cash it took to buy them, and in some countries they were actually bartered like currency.

They had integrity, an integrity that traces more than 150 years to when Levi Strauss made durable pants for California gold prospectors.

You can't count on creating classics like Levi's, but you can invest whatever you make with integrity, as if it is your own integrity in product form. Because it is.

Marketing Honor

No product will last forever. (Even Levi's die.) Today, in fact, few versions in most categories of products will be current for very long after they are introduced. Not many customers will be satisfied with the same service year after year.

71

Innovation is a price of entry and a prerequisite for sticking around in virtually every industry.

What should never change, however, is the explicit or implied product or service guarantee that is grounded in the integrity of the brand. Any product or service benefits are manifestations of that integrity.

Max DePree, the former CEO of Herman Miller, once explained how he came upon a simple definition of "honor." It was: "A fine sense of one's obligations." That, he concluded, was also a pretty good description of "quality." Marketers, just like furniture makers, must have a firm grip on their obligations if they hope to market products of quality.[1]

In January 2006, *BusinessWeek* named its fifty best-performing large U.S. companies. Topping the list was Paccar, Inc., the Bellevue, Washington manufacturer of Kenworth and Peterbilt long-haul trucks. Later that winter Paccar received the National Medal of Technology from the U.S. Commerce Department for their heritage of outstanding innovation. Stockholders also rewarded Paccar for delivering strong earnings for sixty-seven consecutive years; its stock price has multiplied nearly six-fold in the last five of those years.[2]

Ask anybody who knows anything about long-haulers and they'll tell you that Paccar makes great trucks, custom built to every new owner's specifications. But those Peterbilts and Kenworths you see rolling down the interstate aren't just superior vehicles, they're 18-wheelers hauling the latest shipment of Paccar integrity. And that's one load that never leaves the truck.

A 2004 Ponemon Institute study of more than 6,300 U.S. consumers reported that a company's overall reputation for product and service quality is the single most important factor in finding companies trustworthy.[3] That same year, however, Yankelovich Partners found that 63 percent of its respondents agreed with the statement that "even well-known, long-established companies cannot be trusted to make safe, durable products without the government setting industry standards."[4] Those findings say as much about integrity as product performance.

To understand the full leverage of products built with integrity, we have to first look at what can stand in the way of that leverage.

Saturn's Product Integrity: How Many Times Can It Go to the Well?

General Motors announced in December 2005 that a product line that once had great promise was being cut to the bone. Facing a shaky financial future, GM decided that it would be shuttering the Spring Hill, Tennessee Saturn plant that had been feted in so many memorable commercials over the years.

Saturn was the home-grown GM success story that couldn't keep pace with its own aspirations. In the first few years of the brand's life, thousands of U.S. Toyota and Honda owners switched to Saturn, hoping that, at last, America had found a way to compete with the vaunted Japanese manufacturing expertise. A Saturn cult grew up in showrooms and summer rallies, not unlike that for another American icon, Harley-Davidson.

But when the hoopla and elegant advertising were pulled back, realists discovered that Saturn never matched its rivals in the J.D. Powers quality ratings. The broken dream to build superior products had overwhelmed brand hope. By 2005, Saturn's annual sales were 25 percent below their 1994 peak of nearly 300,000 units.[5]

For ten years the entire Saturn line consisted of basically one model. To make matters worse, the initial "L" and later Ion models were, in the view of most critics, stunningly dull, even compared to some of their more pedestrian rivals in the lower-end of the Toyota and Honda lines. Then, the Ion sedan was listed as the "least safe American car of 2006" by *Forbes* editors.[6]

Yet the biggest reason why Saturn stumbled may have been because the line was touted everywhere as the "different kind of car"—with an obvious comparison to more conventional cars like those made by its parent, GM. That did not sit well in the tradition-bound offices of GM's senior management.

As of this writing, Saturn is hoping to regain customers with a new hybrid model, a crossover SUV, and an Aura sedan that has critics interested, if not over the top. But hopes were so high in the beginning of its brand life and thrown to the ground so hard, the question still remains whether the Saturn brand can be trusted.

Saturn hopes to negate the naysayers but, to make that happen, they will have to recapture a sense of product integrity, which makes the brand's new, enigmatic slogan a question as much as a positioning statement: "Like Always, Like Never Before."[7]

Doubt Comes in Multiple Flavors

Doubt is fed by information extremes, either a great deal of information that prompts questions, or too little information that raises questions about what might be going on behind that curtain. From a buyer's standpoint, doubt can be a very good thing. With doubt we can move closer to the truth, and without doubt we are the rightful prey of those with something to hide. From a marketer's view of things, however, doubt can be a trust corrosive.

Doubting buyers come in different flavors, depending on how often and how severely they've been burned. For example, the *disillusioned* ones are those whose good faith is shaken by a bad experience. These people are a little stunned—and maybe more than a little annoyed—by whatever may have disappointed them, and it can taint the way they look at things from that point forward. The consumers at the wrong end of a 2006 Toyota Prius hybrid recall might be counted in this group; they thought they had bought the perfect car for the twenty-first century from the world's best car company, only to discover that the twenty-first century has recalls that look a lot like the ones in the twentieth century.

Then there are the *born skeptics* who are more comfortable with questions than answers. These people are difficult to satisfy because they are more comfortable being unsatisfied. That's their problem—unless they generously share their skepticism with others, as many of them do, then it's the marketer's problem. In the B2B world, IT managers, directors of shipping, and heads of purchasing are likely to be among this group.

Next would be *hard core cynics* who know that life will never meet their standards and are not shy about making that sad reality known to others. They are not likely to change their minds but they are very capable of changing the minds of those they know, usually through a depressing repetition of what's wrong with the world. Cynics rarely make valuable long-term customers.

Finally, the *fatalists* believe that nothing good lasts forever and if it did, we couldn't do much about it anyway. This is a milder form of cynicism that is less harmful to companies and brands. Fatalists are willing to be convinced, but it doesn't take a lot to dissuade them if someone presents new evidence, because life is bound to change, usually for the worse. The notoriously fickle customers in the fashion industry include some fatalists, who are rarely surprised to hear that what they just bought is already out of style.

Doubters and skeptics and cynics and fatalists can stop a trial in its tracks, poison a prospect pool, and slow or even halt the growth of a new brand or new approach to selling. Doubt can cast a shadow over product claims or imply that a brand is not good enough to deliver on its promises. It only takes a sprinkling of these doubt dispensers to make many more question their own sound judgment. Doubt has caused major damage to the GM, Vioxx, and K-mart brands, among many others. And so doubt zigzags across a fine line between converting would-be buyers and letting them slip away (see Figure 4-1).

Figure 4-1. The fine line between buy-in and push-back.

Conversion Stage	Likely Adopter	Likely Rejecter
Initial contacts with brand	Gain in positive familiarity	Awareness of (search for?) something disquieting or a superior feature from competition
Investigation	Expectant information search	Probe into area(s) of concern
Interest	Gradual increase in affinity	Gradual increase in doubt
Information sensitivity	Greater sensitivity to new information about product	Greater resistance to new information
Buying consideration	Seriously consider trial	Resist trial
Trial	Try product or service	Reject trial, or test-try with expectation of disappointment, and to confirm suspicions
Usage	Use product or service regularly	Reject product or service
Commitment	Usage loyalty and advocacy	Express disappointment or vocal counter-selling

When Integrity Stumbles, Doubt Doesn't

Customers are often taking as a matter of faith that a product will deliver what is promised. (The fact that the promise has been packaged or branded well is no guarantee, of course, that it will perform well.) For companies known for their integrity, the product is the expression of their reputation—a tangible representation of their promises kept. Companies that play a bit fast and loose with the facts are asking for push-back from their customers and their own people.

It's been said that the U.S. electorate will forgive just about anything of their leaders except being lied to. Such integrity lapses have crippled countless politicians—including more than one U.S. president—and a good many brands whose managers figured that covering up was better than 'fessing up.

One now infamous example involved two historically close companies that appeared to temporarily forget that they were supposed to be marketing their integrity, not just their products.

Over a series of years, several Firestone tire models that were original equipment on Ford Explorers had been linked to 125 deaths and 250 injuries worldwide. The brand debacle that ensued was made worse by very public feuding and accusations between Ford, the maker of the Explorer that carried most of the original equipment tires involved in the scandal, and Firestone, owned by Bridgestone in Japan. Ford-Firestone was a partnership that had lasted for more than ninety years, and to this day, the two families remain very close. (Ford Chairman Bill Ford's mother is the granddaughter of Firestone founder, Harvey Firestone.)

The impact of the subsequent worldwide tire recalls was devastating. Following an embarrassing series of revelations in the press, Ford and Firestone sales plummeted and trust levels in the two brands fell between 14 to 48 percent in major countries around the world. It has been estimated that the recall cost Ford 15 to 20 percent of its Explorer sales that year, and it cost Firestone a onetime charge of $750 million. Within a year of the full recall, the CEOs of Ford (Jacques Nasser), Bridgestone-U.S. (Masatoshi Ono), and Bridgestone Corp. (Yoichiro Kaizaki) had all resigned or been ousted.[8]

In addition, largely because of the scandal, Ford lost one-third of its estimated brand value between 2001 and 2002. At least part of that loss was because consumers were concerned about the safety of the Ford and Firestone products. The other part was no doubt their concern that the integrity of the companies had seen better days. The lingering impact of the scandal, followed by subsequent poor business and design decisions, has resulted in continuous Ford brand devaluation ever since (see Figure 4-2).

Eventually the Explorer brand itself made a comeback, but not without very expensive recuperative marketing and sales efforts. The Firestone brand is still struggling and wasn't helped by still another recall in the summer of 2006.

The integrity of a car or tire company is tested with every vehicle that leaves the assembly line, and there will always be flaws in those products. Yet if a

Figure 4-2. Decline in Ford brand valuation.

	2002	2003	2004	2005	2006	**DIFF 2006 vs. 2002**
Est. Ford Brand Value ($ Billion)	$20.4	$17.1	$14.4	$13.2	$11.06	-$ 9.2
% Chg vs. Prev. Year	-32%	-16%	-29%	-8%	-16%	-45%
Ford Global Brand Rank	11th	14th	12th	19th	30th	19-place decline

SOURCE: Interbrand estimates with data provided by Citigroup, J.P. Morgan Chase, Morgan Stanley, and *BusinessWeek*.

company is operating with practical integrity, the crisis becomes far more manageable, and sometimes avoidable.

Back when Saturn was a car of promise and promises kept, its 1993 voluntary recall of 350,000 vehicles was cleverly transformed by marketers and retailers into a positive marketing event that proved that the company was serious about its commitments. More recently, Toyota decided to implement a massive production slowdown in order to fix quality control problems, despite unprecedented demand for its products at the time. These kinds of preemptive, voluntary moves can actually reinforce a company's integrity reputation before breakdowns can cause major brand equity losses.[9]

And therein may lie the most important lesson of all about defusing doubt: Assume the worst is coming and preempt it before your integrity is thrown into doubt even more than your product's performance. By maintaining a practical integrity approach to all aspects of marketing, including product and quality control upgrades, such decisions become easier to make and the consequences easier to live with.

A Conversation

"So what do you think of our product news?"

"I'm in favor of product news. News is good."

"You don't know what I'm talking about, do you?"

"Let's just assume I don't."

"We're losing some of our customers, my friend. It seems that one of our worthy competitors has put a big red burst on their label that says, 'CONTAINS NO CHOLESTEROL!'"

"They've got a lot nerve, those people."

"Now, some of our loyal users are heading out, so . . ."

". . .We need product news. But we don't have product news . . . do we?"

"That's why we're going to make some. We're going to need a burst of our own."

"OK. And what do we put on our burst: 'We REALLY don't contain cholesterol?'"

"Cute. How fast can we get a 'No Cholesterol' burst out there?"

"About three weeks before the first labels hit the shelves, then another ten weeks to make it to 80 percent distribution."

"All right. Not great, but OK."

"So, just one thing . . . Call me a stickler but doesn't the human body create cholesterol when our product is consumed?"

"Your point being?"

"That a 'No Cholesterol' burst is just a bit . . . oh, I don't know . . . misleading?"

"Absolutely not. The burst is pure fact. We don't contain any cholesterol."

"So . . . it's up to consumers to train their bodies so they don't create cholesterol in the blood after eating our product?"

"Just fix the label, clown-boy."

"I'm all over it . . . right after my cancer-free cigarette break."

Products That Embody Integrity

Is it possible to create doubt-proof products? No more than it is possible to create earthquake-proof houses or flood-proof cities. But marketers can build doubt-*resistant* products by incorporating practical integrity into what they sell.

In-N-Out Burger is a legendary fast-food chain founded by Harry and Esther Snyder in 1948 in Baldwin Park, California, about twenty miles east of Los Angeles. For those in the know, In-N-Out has transcended fast food and become a cultural icon that refuses to make the mistake that so many iconic brands have made in the past, namely, to compromise on quality in order to increase capacity.

After returning home from World War II, Harry Snyder decided to make the building of a better burger into his life's work. He used fresh ingredients, hand-cut fries, hand-picked meat and vegetables, and shakes made with real ice cream. As the family business took off, so did another hamburger outfit down the road run by the McDonald brothers that was eventually sold to an entrepreneur named Ray Kroc. But the Snyders soon made it clear that they were not going to go the franchise-and-sell-out route taken by the McDonald brothers. To this day, the In-N-Out Burger outlets are all family owned and company run.

The chain's menu of burgers, fries, and drinks is basically the same as it was in 1948, compared to McDonald's, which has added an estimated thirty-seven items to its core menu since its inception, and tested untold more. Carl Karcher, the founder of Carl's Jr's, once told the *Los Angeles Times*, "Everyone in the fast-food industry envies In-N-Out. We're working on new products every year and In-N-Out keeps the same menu and knocks them dead."[10]

All the ingredients are still fresh off the truck, including the hand-diced whole potatoes, produce shipped in every other day, and hand-selected beef. No microwaves or freezers are allowed on the premises. The employees are all "associates" and are treated as if their last names were Snyder. Many of them have been at the same location or within the company for a generation or more, compared to an industry-average annual turnover rate in excess of 100 percent at the lower levels.[11]

Today, the 200 + -store chain stretches over California, Nevada, and Arizona, and could expand still farther, depending on plans management is now pondering.

The company's mission is a challenging promise that's very tough to deliver in today's very tough fast food industry:

> Give customers the freshest, highest quality foods you can buy and provide them with friendly service in a sparkling clean environment.[12]

In-N-Out Burger is much less inclined to market aggressively than its competitors, and has proven that its quality markets itself, which is helpful because their marketing budgets aren't even in the same ballpark with the industry giants. In-N-Out runs an estimated $1 to $2 million in advertising each year to keep the awareness fires stoked. That's compared to an estimated $765 million spent annually in measured media by McDonald's, and projected half a billion dollars more in unmeasured channels like buzz marketing. (See Figure 4-3.)

Fast-food chains in general don't attract very high customer commitment, according to research conducted by TNS in March 2003. Yet, despite low marketing support, In-N-Out and a few smaller chains enjoy far more loyalty from their customers than do their higher-profile competition.[13]

In another study by Quick Track research, In-N-Out was rated highest among all fast-food chains in taste, friendliness, order accuracy, and ingredients served. That is especially impressive considering that the wait times at In-N-Out can be much longer than for other chains. The food, people seem to be saying, is well worth the wait.

The mushrooming In-N-Out legend is reflected in slavishly loyal customers, like the man who claimed he programmed his PDA to lead him to a new In-N-Out Burger every day, or a Boston convert who happened to be visiting Southern California, and provided a typical In-N-Out testimonial when he shared his revelation online: "I can honestly say, with no exaggeration at all this is hands

Figure 4-3. Fast-food advertising spending comparisons.

Advertiser	2005 Estimated Annual U.S. Ad Spending
In-N-Out	$1 – 2 million
McDonald's	$765 million
Wendy's	$375 million
Burger King	$269 million

SOURCE: *Advertising Age,* excepting In-N-Out estimate by Upshaw Marketing.
*Measured media only.
**Estimate based on various press reports.

◆ What If? ◆

What if you ran your marketing programs the way In-N-Out Burger runs its operations? What if your product claims had to be as simple and straightforward as In-N-Out's? What if your customers were told that they'd have to wait longer than they do for the competition's product, but that it would be worth it? What if you had to reduce your marketing spending down to 1/765th of the level that your largest competitor spent? (OK, how about one-fifth of what they spent?) What if you didn't expand your business until you were actually ready to take on all the extra burdens?

Would you go out of business in three weeks, or would customers begin to realize that your quirky way of working might mean that you were more authentic or genuine than the competition? Would it completely disrupt your marketing operations, or give it more focus? Would it be worth it to study companies like In-N-Out Burger and others like them to see what might actually apply to your business?

down the best fast food I've ever had. There isn't even a close second."[14] (See Figure 4-4 for rendering of In-N-Out store on their website.)

In-N-Out employees—from the newest fries fryer to company management—believe that the other guys sell food, but that they are selling food with a promise that never gets broken. The difference—at least for them—is a difference made possible by the company's values that are grounded in practical integrity, and guaranteed by a personal commitment to that integrity.

Integrity Begets Authenticity

It is commonly believed that marketable authenticity is rare and can only be built around a venerable product, or through a legendary founder, or from a history that's rich with storytelling and myth. In fact, while authenticity is tough to come by, it is not necessarily serendipitous. Authenticity can be born, reborn, and rehabilitated (Converse shoes), accidentally created, then capitalized upon (Sony), acquired—although not necessarily managed well (Sears/Land's End), and even methodically engineered (Virgin brands and pre-GM-managed Saturn).

Yet, it can also be the product of rigorous discovery and nurturing, especially in those companies with a competence in practical integrity. Real authenticity can be an invaluable tool in building or turning around a brand or a company because its power comes from the power of integrity that often originates in a single person's word.

A question that often comes up about authenticity is whether it requires the company or brand to have enjoyed a long and storied history. The definitive answer is: yes and no. Venerable companies like Coca-Cola, John Deere, and Pendleton have certainly been around for many decades, but their longevity simply gave them a longer time in which to prove themselves.

Figure 4-4. An In-N-Out store on company website, September 2006.

SOURCE: © In-N-Out Burgers, Inc. Used with permission.

But age is not necessarily a precondition for authenticity, nor is it a guarantee that authenticity will always stick around. Trader Joe's was established in 1958, and Patagonia in 1973. It didn't take decades for them to develop a sense of authenticity, because authenticity was in their DNA when those companies were formed. In some cases, legitimate authenticity can be uncovered, dusted off, and presented as the genuine article.

In the world of popcorn there was—and will always be—only one king. Orville Redenbacher really did spend forty years of his life creating 30,000 strains of popcorn, working alongside his friend Charlie Bowman in the fields and labs of Valparaiso, Indiana,

When they cross-bred the optimum kernal, they formed their own company and sold their product in mason jars, first to Marshall Field's in Chicago, then to other gourmet food shops. Orville liked to tell the story about how he asked a Chicago marketing firm to name his product. They came up with all kinds of wild ideas, he said, but in the end he decided his own name was just a bit better. Thus was born "Orville Redenbacher's Gourmet Popping Corn." The product was ultimately sold to Hunt-Wesson Foods, whose marketing and distribution made it America's favorite brand.

But as Orville aged, Hunt-Wesson and its advertising agency worried how they would maintain the authenticity of Orville the legacy without Orville the man. That's when they recruited Gary Fish, Orville's grandson. They gave him a bow tie, asked him to change his name legally to Gary Redenbacher, and tried to pass the torch.

It didn't work. There was only one Orville. Gary Redenbacher—despite his own brand of charm—just couldn't be an authentic corn expert because he was really something else. You can't fake genuine authenticity. Witness the 2006 reincarnation of a long-deceased Orville as a creepy digitized spokesman (dubbed "Orville Deadenbacher") that attracted the wrong kind of attention, and undoubtedly eroded net brand equity.[15]

Puma: Authentic, Hip, or Authentically Hip?

Like companies such as Nokia and Samsung, Puma A.G. is one of those organizations that just needed the right CEO to reinvent itself and attain profitable growth. But beyond the wisdom of its new leadership, Puma the company and the brand have skyrocketed to new success because they represent a particular brand of authenticity, or an old kind of hip.

Puma AG was founded in Germany in 1948 by Adi Dossler, who was the estranged brother of Rudolph, the founder of the Adidas empire. Although the brothers were credited with literally founding the sports apparel business, by 1993 the Puma brand was an also-ran shoe on a track owned and operated by Nike, Adidas, and Reebok. Puma AG was $100 million in debt, sported a brand that had little or no equity or meaning, and was surrounded by a terminally Teutonic organization content to follow in the leaders' wake, picking up what was left behind until it expired from self-absorption.

Enter thirty-year-old CEO Jochen Zeitz, who promptly discovered that there was a need for a new sense of individualism (a critical part of the "post-modern" world), with shoes and apparel that had the performance cachet of the professional athlete, but which appealed on a parallel level with the everyday athletes and nonathletic lifestylers.

Puma offered specific shoes for runners and soccer players, but also hip, often retro looks for street athletes, segmented by customer need and channel preference. Since they couldn't outspend their competition, they launched a series of innovative marketing efforts that included off-the-wall in-store merchandising (a cooler filled with shoes), clever partnerships (a BMW MINI-inspired driving shoe called the "MINI motion"), and cool promotions (more than 500 pairs of $250 shoes made from second-hand clothes offered online . . . after they had been displayed at a London art gallery).

Revenue nearly quintupled in five years to $2.1 billion by 2005. Earnings, which had been nonexistent at the turn of the decade, leapt to $351 million several years later. Athletic apparel chains of all sizes continue to clamor for more stock and have seen Puma sales increases by as much as 300 percent in one year.[16]

Constantly catering to a wide swath of segments and providing them with the right style is not an easy task and it will eventually cause the slowdown of Puma's amazing growth of late. Nevertheless, this is a company that has found a brand and selling methodology that can be endlessly replenished, if they stay tuned to what some see as authentically hip. Their main challenge will be to stay hip when too many people are wearing their shoes.

* * *

A Product Strategy: Not Just a Product, Your Word

It is impossible to separate a product's performance from the reputation of the brand that it is marketed under, or the company that made it—unless that company operates as a "stealth" parent whose identity is separated from the brand (e.g., Procter & Gamble in the United States). The integrity of both the brand and the company are either expressed by the brand, or belied by it. Consider some initiatives that might address the issues associated with both product and integrity.

1. Make It Personal

Product integrity has to have a genesis in someone's personal integrity. Somewhere in the value chain, one individual or team or group took charge and incorporated their personal sense of what's right into what was made right. It's a good story when it happens, and an even better heritage when it happens regularly.

General Motors has seen better days, and there is well-founded doubt about the company's ability to fully restore confidence in its products. But, despite its massive business challenges, GM also has some good stories to tell about personal pride. One of them gives a glimpse into what built that massive company when it was founded by Billy Durant in 1908, and managed into leadership by Alfred Sloan in the 1920s.

The managers of a General Motors plant in Wilmington, Delaware used to show a film to their people that began with a GM executive announcing that the plant was going to be closed in three years, and the decision was final. The general manager in the film talks to his people and tells them that, if they can't change the decision, at least they could make the company realize how dumb the decision was.

With no other incentive, the workers set out to build cars so well that dealers began asking for cars specifically made by that plant. Three years later when the time came for the plant to be closed, management reversed their decision. The personal pride of those employees of a struggling company had changed the unchangeable, and in the process, the best possible GM cars were produced and sold.[17]

Some Encouraging Moments of Integrity

There are many little moments in marketing that don't get talked about a lot but that represent the best of marketing integrity. Here are a few recounted to this author by a marketing executive of a major U.S. consumer packaged goods company:

I once managed a brand where we went to a new type of plastic for the packaging. It passed all of our routine testing. After hitting the market, some real torture tests were done and it was found that the bottle could crack under very unusual circumstances. There was no legal or regulatory requirement to change this, but the general manager said it is never worth losing sleep over it if we had done something wrong. Despite huge costs and hassle, he ordered removal of all this product and got R&D to develop a new bottle in record time.

We also had some products that contained chemistry where there were some preliminary findings that in absolutely huge quantities this material could build up in the environment. These were not really even official findings, and the amount we use is nowhere near problematic levels. We immediately reformulated (to correct the problem).

In each of these cases there was no legal or other need to take action. The company seriously believes that we should never overthink these issues, but instead just do the right thing. The benefits of this are: 1) We take action very fast. The principle is clear, there is little debate. 2) You are empowered to take actions because you know how strongly the company feels. 3) Your loyalty to the company goes up because you feel good about it, and I feel I can look anyone in the eye and say we are not some corporate evil doer.

This company's integrity is obviously ingrained into the operating system of the organization. Where that is not the case, an individual or team or unit can take the initiative by preemptively preventing any questionable products or promotions from getting out the door.

2. Let's Have Some Applause for the Flaws

While it's always important for a marketing team to be enthusiastic about the product or service they market, it is even more important that they be relentlessly candid with one another about its flaws. Customer doubt is best dispelled by coolly analyzing what can cause buyer doubt and by quickly reversing the cause. One helpful first step may be a thorough flaw audit.

A *product flaw audit* can involve a meticulous examination of 1) how well the product or service performs according to empirical measurements, 2) how the product is perceived by the customers and prospects you care about and how those views may veer from the empirical findings, 3) what product or service actions must be taken to rectify perceptions, and 4) how the resulting changes can best be marketed to customers. Special emphasis can be placed on those components or other elements that are contributing most to existing doubt and purchase resistance.

But be aware that when a team concentrates on its product's flaws, some of their peers may begin to believe that the team is not fully committed to the product, which discourages candid analysis. However, the "W" in any SWOT (Strengths, Weakness, Opportunities, Threats) analysis should be the longest and most thorough section. If, after laying out the product's imperfections and vulnerabilities in detail, the team is ready to move forward with enthusiasm, then it has improved its chances of dispelling buyer doubts in the marketplace. In some cases, doubt actually has to be cultivated to help destroy it.

Microsoft tries to provide its users with bug-less software but historically has had many problems trying to pull that off. In July 2001, a PC worm called Code Red slowed down massive amounts of Internet traffic and cost companies all over the world billions of dollars in repairs and lost productivity. Among the corporate victims was Microsoft's own Hotmail servers. It happened again in the fall of 2002 when another harmful worm named Slammer attacked the Microsoft database software.[18] Microsoft's credibility as a protector of its users' data was slipping away as the company watched.

Bill Gates created a new ten-year initiative called "Trustworthy Computing," and e-mailed his concerns and plans to 50,000 Microsoft employees. According to one analyst: "The joke inside Microsoft has been that quality is job 1.1—the real bugs don't get fixed until after the release, when the service patches come out. It's not yet clear that quality really is a top priority across all of Microsoft's lines of business."[19]

Was the problem with Microsoft's quality control, or was it virtually impossible to protect software as ubiquitous as Microsoft's from insidious attacks? The last thing Microsoft needed was to send a message that it, of all companies, has been overrun by its own bugs.

Beginning in 2004, the company's Center for Software Excellence began staging a series of "prediction markets" in which programmers bid on release dates. By watching where the programmers placed their "bets" the company discovered where the people doing the work were less optimistic than their bosses about when projects would be ready for release.

Microsoft learned the value of dealing candidly with doubts internally before they could be raised by customers. It is only by becoming the ultimate skeptics of their own technologies that they will eliminate a strain of skepticism that could more virulently attack their integrity than any software bug.

3. Build a Perpetual Integrity Machine

The term "product integrity" is usually interpreted narrowly, referring to performance against specified standards. But within the larger context of practical integrity marketing, those standards expand to include greater commitments than just to product specs. When your ultimate product is your commitment to the customer to market with integrity, consider another set of objectives:

❏ *Product development projects and refinement programs achieve and maintain quality integrity regardless of market or company circumstances.* Reducing product or service quality to make short-term numbers is a formula for inevitable product, brand, and company decline. It has happened in beverages (the demise of Schlitz beer due to cost-cutting formula changes), technology (the slide of Apple hardware's quality in the early 1990s), and retailing (the service quality falloff at Sears and Montgomery Ward). Worse, the decline in product quality calls into question the integrity of the entire organization.

Conversely, superior quality can turn around a company that is heading in the wrong direction and imbue it with both product integrity and greater belief in the integrity of the company as a whole.

For years, Samsung Electronics had virtually guaranteed its bottom-rung profitability by creating generations of mediocre products. Then in 1997, CEO Yun Jong Yong changed course abruptly by declaring, "Our future will depend on our brand equity."[20]

Hundreds of millions were invested in R&D, manufacturing, design, marketing, and sales development until Samsung created a superior global brand with the products and infrastructure to support it. Samsung's product line was gradually upgraded until it was every bit as innovative and reliable as Sony's, the industry standard for mass audience electronics.

Samsung is now the fastest growing brand of its kind, buoyed by a new product integrity that has cut a swath through the industry.

❏ *Product improvement programs never shut down, just as integrity can never be permitted to slide.* W. L. Gore, the maker of GORE-TEX® and Glide® Dental Floss, considers innovation to be at least as important as making money, and their structure, or lack of it, is designed to cultivate new ways to do everything possible. Their teams of associates, who own 25 percent of the privately held company, are set up to encourage hands-on innovation and product improvement. It is innovation that cuts across hierarchies (which are frowned upon at Gore), the usual turf wars (neither turf nor wars reportedly exist), or what the bosses think (there aren't any of them, either).[21]

The product integrity of Gore products and the integrity of the W.L. Gore people are fused into one offering to its customers.

❏ *Products are built with such integrity that they virtually market themselves.* Some great products don't require major promotional efforts because the word spreads so quickly and persuasively that formal marketing is largely unnecessary.

Google and Amazon built brands of enormous value and breadth without any significant marketing support by creating and continuously refining their products until the world noticed that they were becoming indispensable tools for the lives of millions of users. But they would not have sustained that status if their services, response time, or data retrieval systems had failed as often as a typical American automobile or desktop computer program. Their reliability extends beyond being a product attribute; it is a reflection of integrity.

Patagonia is another company that spends very little on formal marketing but has built a high-integrity brand by always stretching their innovativeness, usually with the objective of making their products more Earth-friendly. Back in 1993 Patagonia became the first outdoor clothing manufacturer to adapt fleece to enable it to be made with post-consumer-recycled (PCR) plastic soda bottles. Today they make thirty-one products with PCR fleece and have saved approximately 86 million bottles from landing in the trash, which is enough fuel to fill the gas tanks of 20,000 Chevy Suburbans.[22] Even underwear is sometimes recycled, including by customers who have a hard time parting with it (see "Ode to Underwear").

Ode to Underwear

One of Patagonia's commitments to the environment is to encourage recycling of every conceivable product, even someone's underwear. Their "Common Threads Recycling Program" has accepted many pairs of Patagonia underwear, returned by customers for recycling. Here's an excerpt from one customer who gave up one pair only after a lot of soul-searching:

Dear Patagonia:
Inside this envelope you'll find the remains of the first pair of Patagonia underwear I ever owned. I send them to you not knowing where else to turn. I only hope you can reincarnate them into a pop-bottle-fleece . . . We've been through so much together, it's hard to imagine saying goodbye. But I must find closure. To heal. To move forward. To seek out the next adventure. Before I do, if I could have a few words . . .

Oh sad, sad day. Oh somber mood of winter. Oh, for the end of an era. Oh underwear, how can I ever express the love I feel for you? I know I've dragged you through the mud, snagged you on slivers and raked you over the coals. I know I've sat on you your entire life. I'm sure you've often felt smothered. . . .

Wherever you're going, don't forget the good times. Like beach cruising in the early Pacific chill on the Baja in December. Or mountain biking the misty woods of Scotland in search of sacred stone circles. Or what about Fairbanks at 40 below? And don't forget all those nights in the sleeping bag when it was just you, me, a few yards of Primaloft and the endless Alaskan wild. . . . Well, I guess, it's time to say goodbye. Please take good care of this rag. Please find a suitable end. And please, if you think there's any way you can help ease the pain of my loss, don't hesitate to send me another pair. I couldn't bear the thought of wearing any other brand so close to my behind.

Sincerely,
Tracy Ross[23]

How do you intentionally create such self-marketing products? Consider rewarding the most marketable product innovations and elevating "marketability" as a highly visible goal for product development, or publicly rewarding development teams that come up with products whose features and quality virtually "market themselves." Or try linking the incentive pay of the product development leaders to that of marketing leaders, thus encouraging more cooperation between the two historically separate groups, and creating more marketable innovation in the process.

4. Sell Integrity Where It Has Leverage

Integrity, like honesty, is not usually a subject you can boast about practicing because buyers tend to doubt most those who claim they need never be doubted. However, there are ways to determine the most effective integrity-related benefits that might be offered.

The oft-quoted caution from the late Harvard Professor Theodore Leavitt is as applicable today as it was when he first told his students, "People don't want to buy a quarter-inch drill. They need a quarter-inch hole."[24] We don't buy TiVo because it's fun to have still another remote in the family room, we buy TiVo because it's fun to have more control over television programming. Corporate buyers don't acquire just IT systems, they purchase productivity. The benefit guarantees that are offered from brands and companies are at the core of their value proposition.

A benefit tier analysis could be helpful in determining where the most leverageable benefit promises reside, and that could help marketers and their product development colleagues to zero in on benefits that might best underscore the brand's or company's integrity. Most marketers have opportunities to mold and direct their benefits at multiple need levels, but only one of those levels will be optimum for creating the greatest impact on the customer's purchase decision.[25] Here are the key steps in this type of an analysis:

❑ *Establish the industry's parameters of need.* Using a model based on your industry parameters, determine the full spectrum of needs, wants, desires, and aspirations that your product or service might address without endangering its integrity in the eyes of customers. This needs to include "drivers of choice," the reasons why consumers or business customers choose a particular product, brand, or company over alternatives.

❑ *Determine the benefit type.* Each type of benefit can have a different form of impact on the perceived integrity of the product or service.

❑ *Identify the possible integrity implications of the benefits in question.* Based on the analysis of benefits and opportunities, apply the findings to the brand and determine likely implications.

❑ *Agree on specific marketing actions that will capitalize on the leveragability of those benefits.* Determine how the marketing programs will make the best use of the observations and analysis to reinforce product, brand, and company integrity.

See Figure 4-5 for an example analysis summary, which uses hypothetical observations and Starbucks as an example brand.

5. Drive the Marketing Machine Right into the Product Group's Garage

With some notable exceptions, marketers and product development teams run on parallel paths that only occasionally intersect. That's partly because the two disciplines require two sets of skills, and because the organizations often report to different senior executives. Even when both departments report to a single chief marketing/product officer, they can be at odds, requiring executive management to arbitrate disagreements.

The result of this separation of work and responsibilities is that marketing is often not in the room when many critical product decisions are made. That can be very unfortunate for the planning process because, in these circumstances, marketing ends up being positioned internally as the team that is only supposed to sell whatever product development creates.

Instead, the marketing and product development teams should be fully integrated as early as possible in the development process (see Figure 4-6).

Figure 4-5. Product/service integrity benefit analysis example: Starbucks.

Customer Needs/ Wants Parameters	Benefit Type	Possible Product Integrity Implications	Possible Marketing Leverage
Need for "wake-up" drink in the morning.	Generic category benefit	Too generic for brand or product integrity to be relevant.	Poor. Little or no proprietary opportunity for Starbucks brand.
Need for a comfortable, people-friendly place to enjoy food and drink.	Experiential "belonging" benefit	Requires that retail stores are equipped to be inviting third place, while not increasing customer wait time.	Opportunity to base marketing programs on this benefit. However, tends to take emphasis off product quality.
Need for convenient place to buy product.	Functional service benefit	Must guard against losing brand's specialness when distributed in grocery stores, airlines, etc.	Enables broad distribution, but convenience claim could also diminish quality integrity.
Willingness to pay more for prestigious branded product.	Psychological "badge value" benefit	Perfect match for Starbucks "you're worth it" type of positioning, backed up by high-integrity service.	Reinforce alignment between premium product integrity and strategic direction.
Need to begin busy day with comfort food in comfortable place.	Psychological comfort benefit	All non-coffee offerings (e.g., accessories, music CDs) should reinforce core brand integrity with products of same quality as coffee products.	Promising ways to reinforce experiential brand, but could focus on core products.

When marketing is working more closely with product development, especially at the early stages, it creates a series of positive benefits for both teams:

❏ *Marketing can inject customer needs directly into the product development process.* In consumer product or service companies, the marketing teams and their research colleagues are the keepers of more information than any other about customer needs and wants. In B2B situa-

Figure 4-6. Traditional versus enlightened marketing influence.

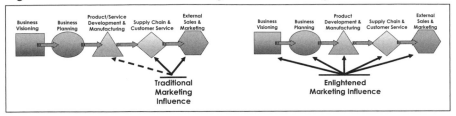

tions, the sales force also stays on top of customer needs, of course, but they often base their conclusions on anecdotal observations. The marketing team, on the other hand, can provide more projectible, quantitative research findings that can help product and service managers to build more reliable integrity into what marketers sell.

❏ *Marketers can help develop more competitive products.* In all types of companies, it is the marketers who are generally the keepers of the competitive intelligence, and they usually are the authors of the most comprehensive competitive profiling and analyses. Their perspective could be critical when developing products. For example, a product that works well according to some internal standards but does not perform well against the competition is not likely going to add to the brand's reputation for integrity.

❏ *Marketers can help transform products into agents of integrity.* No product or service is safe from replication, and it is especially vulnerable if not shielded by a unique brand encasement. Even when there are patents and proprietary trade dress that are protecting specific designs, they are not protecting market spaces or positionings in the minds of potential customers.

In some categories—like credit cards, airlines, or computer peripherals—there are relatively few opportunities to create substantive differences among products, except in how their identities are projected through their brands. If product development groups encourage marketers to participate as early as possible in the process, they will have the best chance of turning products into superior performing brands that can enhance and extend the company's reputation for product integrity, as well as corporate integrity.

Doubt can erode equity, but product and practical integrity can repel doubt. A well-integrated product-marketing process can create products of such quality that their performance is the most compelling evidence of the integrity of a brand and the company that created it.

6. Avoid the Turn-Offs

If your product is the embodiment of your brand, and you recognize the value of each, it should be relatively easy to see the product pitfalls coming. What isn't as easy to see is what damage can be done to your integrity when the product under-performs. If it's a minor problem, it may be overlooked. If it's chronic, it may never be forgotten. Some customer turn-offs to avoid:

❏ *Assessing Quality Primarily Against Competitive Standards.* There's always a temptation to do only what is necessary to be more appealing than competition, but without regard to absolute standards. Companies with strong product integrity compare their performance to the ideal, not to the common denominator. Leaders—such as Hewlett-Packard in printers, Apple in personal electronics, and Google in search engines—are all competing against themselves as much as or more than against their competition.

  Product Implication to Consider: Remove all competitive comparisons from product spec reviews and focus on the ideal profile from the customer's standpoint. Look at competitive products only after performance-against-ideal has been evaluated.

❏ *Mining for New Revenue with Marginal Line Extensions Can Undermine the Brand's Integrity.* One way to pretty much guarantee that your customers will wonder what your brand stands for is to stretch it where it should not go. Mercedes had a hard time in the United States, convincing some prospects that its early C- and E-series cars and early M-series SUVs were of the same quality as their more expensive models, especially after they suffered a series of recalls and service issues that lowered their J.D. Powers reliability ratings.

  BMW, on the other hand, has delivered on its promise to incorporate superior performance all the way from their 7-series to their 3-series. Both companies operate ethically enough, but Mercedes' troubles a few years ago raised doubts about their commitment to product integrity at lower price tiers.

  When a company attempts to extend a brand line because of the allure of broadening the revenue base, it carries certain risks even beyond the costs of the launch: It also risks undermining the brand's perceived integrity.

Product Implication to Consider: Line extensions are less expensive in up-front costs than launching wholly new products. However, their hidden costs can be extreme if, as in the examples above, they are a bust in the marketplace because what appeared to be a logical extension was anything but logical to the buyer. Don't extend a winning brand until it has been verified that no harm will come to the parent brand's integrity if the extension fails (or for that matter, if it doesn't).

❏ *Adding Products Because You Can.* Despite the hard lessons learned in the past, companies continue to build and launch look-what-we-can-do! entries that are products in search of a need. In 2001, Microsoft Tablet PC was hailed by no less than Bill Gates himself as destined to be "the most popular form of PC sold in America."[26] That never happened, largely because Microsoft built a product that only a small percentage of people needed, mostly those who need to write down things on the run.

Product Implication to Consider: Brand and company reputations are generally built on meeting customer needs, and only occasionally on providing products before customer know they need them. Invest heavily in need and dissatisfaction research before committing to product development, and brand and company integrity will be protected.

❏ *Building Perceived Improvements Instead of Actual Ones.* Realities have a way of catching up with perceptions, especially in this time of continuous peer-to-peer sharing of information and opinions. Miller Clear beer and Pepsi Clear were clearly not an improvement because they were aesthetically at odds with consumer perceptions and had no real reason for being. For many, America Online was not a better way to go online than . . . going online. Windows Millennium had so many problems that the most you could say for it was that it made us appreciate XP that much more.

Product Implication to Consider: Don't settle for "nice to have" concepts or "nifty new idea" products. Innovation that falls short of meaningful change can be found at every inventors' convention. Weigh the projected benefit of the "improvement" against its projected impact on the current brand integrity. Then, lean to the conservative side.

*   *   *

A Summary and a Few Questions

Doubt can be an insidious threat to the quality of the current revenue base, and a corrosive threat to future growth. Customer commitment and potential user interest can evaporate quickly when the integrity of the company or brand comes into question. Conversely, integrity can be the most important ingredient in any product, especially when it has been demonstrated over long periods of time. A company's or brand's integrity is the ultimate "product" that is for sale, even though it must be marketed more subtly than standard product features.

Some additional questions to consider:

1. *Does the performance of your products or services match the integrity values you have established for the company? If not, why not?* Does your product enjoy the same respect from your customers as your most enthusiastic stakeholders have for your organization?

2. *Are you selling benefits that legitimately meet or exceed the expectations that your marketing is creating?* Are your marketing efforts supporting a realistic view of your product, or idealizing it and thus putting the credibility of the brand and company in jeopardy?

3. *Are your marketing and product development programs operated on separate tracks in your company, or are they integrated and supportive of one another's efforts?* If they are not in synch, could the problem be rectified by more frequent, in-depth communications and contact between the two groups? If an organizational impasse is involved, can you enlist the support of other managers to help sort through the problem and get product development and marketing on the same track?

4. *What metrics have you established that gauge product integrity, and what impact might they have on the company's integrity, and vice versa?* Is the product designed and produced with such quality that you can assess its impact on marketing over time?

Superior product performance—no matter how the customer may define "superior"—is a fast train to credibility. In Chapter 5, we'll take a close look at how practical integrity can help companies achieve a leadership share of credibility in their markets.

CHAPTER 5

Win the Credibility Race (and It *Is* a Race)

Grab the Leadership Share of What Customers Believe In

1968 was a year of promises made and never kept.

In January, the carnage of the Tet Offensive destroyed President Lyndon Johnson's promise to end the war in Vietnam. Martin Luther King, Jr. was assassinated in April and Robert Kennedy in June, striking down their promises of social change and leaving a country torn by strife. In July, Chicago "police riots" created a sham of the promises wafting from the Democratic National Convention. The promise of freedom in Czechoslovakia was crushed in August by Soviet tanks. Two months later, hundreds of students seeking promises from their government were murdered by troops and police in Mexico City's Tlatelolco Square.

In the final month of that interminable year, Broadway producer David Merrick premiered a new musical titled, aptly enough, *Promises, Promises*. For the following 1,281 performances the cast reminded audiences that promises are as fragile as the human beings who believe in them. By that time, we didn't need to be told.

The marketing arena is filled with promises that are less dramatic but just as brittle as those proffered by politicians and playwrights. And, while marketers routinely spend months conjuring up complex strategies and street-tough tactics, at the end of the day they had better be in the promise-keeping business or it's going to be a short night at the theater.

Baloney on Lie

When the people we count on to help us sort the truth from the baloney become part of the sandwich, we all have a problem. The First Amendment ensures that the free press will remain free. Unfortunately, the Founding Fathers forgot to put something in there about the importance of the free press pursuing unbiased truth as hard as they defend their own freedoms. That may be because newspapers in Revolutionary times were not known for their objectivity, as noted by Thomas Jefferson who once commented, "Advertisements . . . contain the only truths to be relied on in a newspaper."[1]

And if it weren't enough that the press has once again veered toward bias—in all directions of the political compass—now there are an alarming number of fabrications masquerading as fact emerging from newspeople and even the scientists that we all thought were the last of the truth-tellers. Some sad examples:

❏ Stephen Glass, an associate editor of the venerable *New Republic,* wrote an article about a teenage hacker in the Spring of 1998 that reportedly was chock full of fiction, as apparently were many other pieces written by Glass for the magazine.[2]

❏ Jan Hendrik Schon, a celebrated researcher for the highly regarded Bell Laboratories, was fired in September 2002 after it was learned that he had altered key data in dozens of scientific papers that were touted to be breakthroughs in their field.[3]

❏ In January 2004, veteran and award-winning *USA Today* foreign correspondent Jack Kelley resigned after admitting that he had concocted parts or all of at least eight stories over the course of many years.[4]

❏ The following year *New York Times* reporter Jayson Blair filed fabricated stories and lied to editors about his own credibility, a scandal that ultimately cost Blair, his executive editor, and his managing editor their jobs, and the *Times* a large slice of credibility.[5]

❏ In July 2004, the Tribune Company admitted that two of its newspapers, *Newsday* and the Spanish-language *Hoy*, had reported overstated daily and Sunday circulation, which prompted the Audit Bureau of Circulations to place sanctions on those papers, as well as the Chicago *Sun-Times*, which had done the same.[6]

❏ South Korean scientist Hwang Woo Suk, a world-renowned cloning expert, resigned in December 2005 from his prestigious Seoul National University post after admitting that his most famous published research had been faked, calling into question the entire global cloning scientific process.[7]

In an inevitable sign of the times, an academic journal surfaced in early 2006, called *Plagiary: Cross-Disciplinary Studies in Plagiarism, Fabrication and Falsification*. Commenting on the familiar link between selling-at-all-cost and dubious behavior, the executive director of the Center for Academic Integrity at Duke University said, "We are creating this kind of winning culture that is causing a lot of people to take shortcuts, to over-invest in the chase for stardom. It's a corruption of the kind of marketing culture of, 'If I can get it to sell, then I have done well.'"[8]

Credibility as Gatekeeper

Credibility is, to coin a phrase, a terrible thing to waste. Yet businesses and brands may be doing just that if they assume that buyers will believe anything simply because it is repeated again and again.

A study by Yankelovich Partners, called "The State of Consumer Trust," found that as many as two-thirds of Americans believe that businesses would take advantage of the public if they had the opportunity, and if they did not believe they would be discovered. As many as one-fourth of Americans believe that there is literally nothing that business can do to recapture their trust once it is lost.[9]

Credibility in marketing usually involves current and potential customers recognizing a brand's expertise and trusting that brand to deliver whatever it promises.[10] That is one of many reasons why companies must win the race they may not even know they are in, a race to gain the lead share of credibility which, like the lead share of market, can create important competitive advantages.

Credibility is the "yin" to the "yang" of relevance. If a brand is credible but not relevant, the prospect has no interest. If the brand is relevant but not credible, the prospect cannot trust the claims and thus is not likely to be interested, either.

The Responsibilities of Being Credible

Strong brand or company credibility is a powerful defense against competitive encroachments, a motivating point of pride for company staff, and a strong platform from which to launch new products and initiatives. Marketing that generates credibility usually is based on a certain set of actions by a marketer, such as:

❏ *Delivering What Customers Interpret as Relevant and Substantive in Their Lives.* What is credible is genuinely important to the lives of customers, or at least in the lives they would like to lead. It strikes home as above debate, often at a gut level that may be hard to articulate, but which can become a significant competitive advantage.

We tend to believe in products like John Deere tractors and Oshkosh kids clothes because they seem to deal with authentic basics that we find comforting. The longer such brands deliver on that promise, the greater the burden to continue delivering. They have reached that sought-after, yet narrow ledge that champions climb onto, enjoying the view but ever-mindful that a strong gust or a misstep could lead to a nasty fall from grace.

And customers often mourn such falls by great brands that stumbled into becoming lesser forces in the marketplace. We are saddened by the state of brands like Levi's, Sears, and Kodak because, before they faltered, they were the commercial gold standards of what was real in our lives. (And many of us are rooting for them to climb back up to that champion's ledge once again.)

In contrast, brands like Apple's iPod, Motorola's Razr, or the Red Bull energy drink are powered by relevance of a completely different kind. Anything but reassuring or comforting, they are nevertheless an integral part of many lives. But at the base of their popularity—in addition to their cool factor—is a product that delivers what it promises, if not more.

❏ *Adhering to a Mutually Understood Definition of What's Honest.* Corporate governance scandals aside, customers would like to believe that the company they deal with is delivering a product or service honestly and ethically. People may hold a skeptical view of business as a whole, yet believe that the particular companies they are loyal to are adhering to a higher standard. At the same time, the companies would like to believe that the customers will respond in kind, leading to the healthiest possible partnership.

Which companies are leading in honesty? Most of us would probably put Procter & Gamble, Whole Foods, and Timberland on that list, because they are rarely, if ever, accused of lying to their customers, or to anyone else for that matter. This does not automatically make them successful, of course, but it helps to eliminate unnecessary obstacles when they market.

❏ *DWYSYWD: Aligning Promises and Delivery.* Credibility is established by keeping promises that are relevant and meaningful to the customer. The same dynamic works between buyers and sellers. A prerequisite of any partnership they may form is that each will, in the words of credibility experts James M. Kouzes and Barry Posner, "do what you say you will do, or DWYSYWD."[11]

Sellers must deliver what is promised if they hope to have credibility in the marketplace. Buyers, of course, are under no obligation to do what sellers ask them to do But if they want to get the most they can from the seller, they need to be honest about what interests them most, and "reward" the seller with valuable information, input, and their patronage. As we discussed in Chapter 3, this candid exchange of information and opinions between buyer and seller are how productive customer-marketer partnerships may be formed and strengthened.

❑ *Being Candid . . . **Especially** When It Hurts.* Companies with robust credibility maintain that advantage by dropping the marketing spin when necessary in order to be clear and candid. It is a risky decision, but there are times when it must be done to be sure that credibility is not lost along with other collateral damage that might take place.

The most dramatic need for candor occurs when a company fouls up and has to admit it, such as the famous 1982 Tylenol poisonings crisis, which was well handled by the parent company, Johnson & Johnson, or the 1999 Coca-Cola product contamination problems in Europe, which were not handled as adroitly.

But companies that are candid when they don't have to be are relatively rare animals. Patagonia is one such company. Despite their strides in making eco-friendly garments, they are very aware of the balancing act they must maintain in order to compete realistically in the marketplace, as they frankly point out in one of their catalog essays in 1997:

> The fact remains: the clothing industry is dirty, and the production of our clothing takes a significant toll on the earth. No Patagonia products are genuinely sustainable. . . . There remains a direct connection between the manufacture of our clothing and the cascade of woes affecting the natural world. . . . We're not blind to that connection. We're aware of an immediate environmental crisis. But we also have a commitment to making the best quality products we possibly can. So we've deliberately chosen a dual focus: We will reduce our impact on the earth—but we will also continue making the best outdoor gear available. Sounds simple. But that challenge involves countless trade-offs that our customers should understand.[12]

You have to give Patagonia a great deal of credit for 1) recognizing that trade-off, 2) admitting it to their customers, and 3) explaining how they are doing their best to reconcile the rock and the hard place. That's pure credibility speaking.

A Conversation

"Afternoon, everyone. It's been some time since our executive council met, and I'm sorry about that. We're so busy executing that we never seem to take enough time to plan our next moves. I'll try to get better at making that happen.

"In the meantime, a couple of things need to be discussed today. The big one is how we're going to make those stretch numbers for the remainder of the fiscal. But before we get to that, Ben here—some of you may have met Ben from market research—Ben is going to briefly summarize some research he just completed about our competitive standing in the marketplace. We decided to add some questions to our quarterly tracking study and they've come back—what would you say, Ben?—they've come back a bit sour for the last three periods.

"Basically, it seems that some people think we, ah, exaggerate a bit. I guess we're not considered the most credible company in the world. So big deal, you might say. You know and I know that we're credible, but for some reason there are a quite a few people out there who don't get that. Bill, you and your marketing magicians had better think about driving our message harder because they're just not getting it. We'll have to round up some more dollars to do that . . . maybe from your reserve fund.

"Anyhow, I ran into Ben in the elevator the other day and he said something like, 'When they stop believing you, they stop buying you.' Personally, I think he may be overstating the case, but I figured we'd all let him say his peace, then we can jump into those revenue numbers.

"OK, Ben, why don't you go ahead. See if you can lay the whole thing out in about five minutes or so . . ."

When It's a Zero Sum Game

Competitors in every industry are in a race to convince prospects that their brand should be preferred because theirs can be believed. In essence, it can become a zero sum game, a race for a finite amount of credibility in any given industry.

Many industries certainly include more than one credible competitor. Aquafina and Evian, Met Life and New York Life, Intel and AMD all compete head-to-head and are all considered as credible options for buyers in their markets. But simply being known as credible is the table stakes that gets you on the buyer's short list. The ultimate decision is often based on which competitor is *more* credible when each competitor is claiming to offer the best water, insurance, or chip.

Conjoint research is one helpful tool that forces respondents to do what all prospective customers do in their heads before making a purchase, that is, winnow the choices down to two or three, then settle on a final choice based on benefits and trade-offs. Credibility may be the ultimate driver of choice because it sheds a positive light on all stages of possible purchases. In other words, if I am choosing between two insurance companies, the degree to which I believe one over the other (i.e., its credibility) affects my purchase decision for my initial purchase. And assuming that the company performs as promised, it also may influence my insurance purchase habits indefinitely into the future.

When assessing credibility, we consciously or unconsciously rank our options by believability. If you can track these views across a buying population, you can create a "share of credibility" graphic, such as the hypothetical example in Figure 5-1, which tracks the percentage of a buying population that finds one company more credible than its rivals. Of course, the shares can be influenced over time by events in the marketplace, or product innovation, or any other factor that might affect credibility in buyers' eyes.

The zero sum game can be made easier when buyers decide that one brand better fits their needs than another, in which case those buyers may assign more credibility to the chosen brand.

Figure 5-1. Example shares of market credibility.

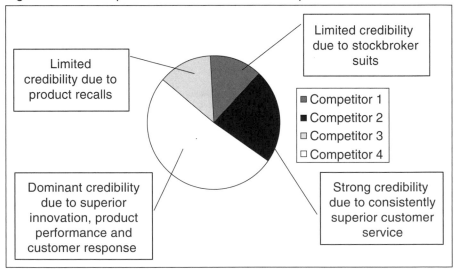

For instance, if members of a buying committee select Sun Microsystems servers over those from IBM because they believe that Sun's servers better fit their company's needs, they may continue to respect IBM, but they have thrown in their lot with the Sun brand. Assuming the company has a good experience with Sun, they are more likely to find future Sun claims to be more credible, if for no other reason than they are looking for post-purchase reinforcement.

So, even though the committee's members may respect IBM, and even though that brand has done nothing to lower its credibility in their view, their previous purchase choice and experience have given both the relevance and credibility edge to Sun in this particular case.

In other words, a positive experience with a product gives the brand a definite edge in the share-of-credibility race. The companies that have made promise-keeping habitual have the greatest probability of maintaining that edge.

Disruptive Integrity: The Competitive Advantage for Promise-Keepers

The companies that have mastered the artful science of relentless promise-keeping are always at an advantage, whether in good times or bad.

You could hear the snickering far beyond Silicon Valley in the 1990s when the respective founders of the online Big Four—eBay, Google, Yahoo!, Amazon—

◆ What If? ◆

What if you added "share-of-credibility" analyses to your regular management reports? What if you asked marketing research to design a portion of your tracking study to provide in-depth data on the credibility of your brand or company, with over-samples of your most important user segments? What if you were to create "credibility segments" that identified different credibility attitudes about the company by demographic, geo-demographic, and psychographic profiles? What if you issued a quarterly "credibility index" that reported to the entire company how credible the brand and company are in the minds of its customers and other constituencies?

If these analyses yielded surprising results, would they make any difference in how you marketed? Would your management suggest that you not share them with everyone in the company, but only with them? Would the results make a difference in how your marketing team approached their jobs? Or, would the idea be abandoned after the first negative report?

first promised that their modestly intriguing ideas would become major new forces in their respective businesses. The snickering escalated to catcalls when the tech boom melted away paper fortunes, and so-called pure plays looked less pure and not all that fun.

But these nascent giants did what all great football linebackers instinctively do: They "stayed at home," refining their technologies and inventing new ways to viral-market without extending into too many directions at once. As of this writing, the Big Four now represent a combined annual revenue of $25 billion and a total market capitalization of more than $100 billion. But this time around there's considerably more heft than hype in those numbers.

In the mid-1980s, Harley-Davidson was on the brink of being sold for scrap. Most of their old "choppers" seized up, and virtually all left an oil stain wherever they were parked.[13] It wasn't hard to find Harley dealers whose idea of great customer service was staying open past noon on Saturday. Harley's competitors, mostly from Japan, were cheaper, more reliable, and just as fast around a curve.

What pulled the company and brand out of the identity pit, among other things, was a commitment to regain its credibility by renewing its commitment to product reliability. Harleys were ultimately transformed from eccentric mechanical liabilities into beautifully crafted, all-American treasures whose customers sometimes waited half a year for delivery. Now, Harley is a $5 + billion global empire and sports more than 1,000 HOGs (Harley Owner Groups) clubs worldwide with 350,000 members. Improved products attracted new customers to the brand, but it was the brand's credibility that rebuilt the company.

On the other side of the planet, India's Infosys was being born just about the time that Harley-Davidson was being reborn. One of the principal tenets upon which Infosys was founded was the concept of keeping promises—promises to stakeholders, promises to the industry, and promises to India as a nation.

The Infosys integrity contributes directly to its credibility, both of which are closely guarded and once in a while leads to some financial loss. A few years ago, the company was offered a project worth $10 million U.S. at a time when their total revenue was $500 million. After Infosys was selected, the customer suggested they take an approach that Infosys didn't agree with. Infosys stood firm that its approach was the best route, but lost the customer because of their refusal to create work that they did not believe in. The project was awarded to another company, launched in a different way, and ultimately failed.[14]

Companies that market and sell and operate with high integrity are often put in the position of standing up for what they believe in and risking enormous amounts of revenue in the process. But Infosys and others have proven that practical integrity will eventually pay off, creating rock-solid credibility that leads to more business from buyers in search of a company they can trust.

But more than helping to achieve standard business goals, integrity that is adhered to can become positively disruptive to the competition, especially if in the past one or more competitors did not always take the high road. Saturn accomplished that during its early years of promise in the automobile industry, Charles Schwab did so in the securities industry, and Trader Joe's has done so in the grocery business. These companies did not make inroads simply because they had better ideas, but because they built those ideas on foundations of integrity. (See Figure 5-2.)

The Gentrification of Street Cred

"Street cred"—originally meaning the credibility (and respect) earned on the mean streets of urban centers—is about what's real and trustworthy in places where reality comes down hard and where trust is often thought to be for children and fools. Legitimized by stoop buzz and pushed by rappers, some of the mainstream brands that have gained street cred in the past few years include Cristal Champagne and Remy Martin Cognac, Mercedes and Cadillac, and Nike and Adidas.[15] (See Figure 5-3 for ESPN's tracking of street cred.)

Can you engineer street cred? A lot of companies are trying. Nissan, for example, tried to build some urban buzz around their latest Altima that included planned graffiti attacks on mass transit advertising, calling for readers to go to "ElectricMoyo.com."

Nike has learned some lessons the hard way about street cred. That company's usual approach of using big-time athletes and major marketing investments has built much of its $14 billion business. But that strategy was more of an obstacle than a boost to company's efforts to crack the burgeoning skateboard shoe field in 1997. "They did almost everything wrong," according to Fran Richards, sports consultant and former publisher of *TransWorld Skateboarding*.

Figure 5-2. Example of disruptive integrity.

Brand	Industry	Disruptive Integrity	Impact
Charles Schwab	Investment Services	Demonstrated that there is not always a need for full commission services.	Established beachhead with discount brokerage, and expanded to a major financial services player.
Trader Joe's & Whole Foods	Retail Grocery	Provided superior service and policies that reflected social consciousness.	Both companies have carved out robust shares at the expense of conventional grocery chains.
Patagonia & Timberland	Outdoor Apparel	Tied apparel design, manufacturing, and sales directly to environmental issues.	Both companies have attracted significant followings, based on combination of product performance and social consciousness. Their actions have influenced numerous other companies and industries.

Figure 5-3. The ESPN Guide to "Street Cred."

STREET CRED: A COMPARATIVE CHART			
Category	High Street Cred	Some Street Cred	No Street Cred
Tattoo	"Thug Life:	A cross	Harry Potter
Cell phone ring tone	2Pac "Until the End of Time"	"Mission Impossible" theme	Celine Dion Chrysler ads
Cologne	Fahrenheit	Eternity	Old Spice
Slang term	"Fo shizzle my nizzle"	"Straight trippin,' Boo"	"I'm not gonna pay a lot for this muffler"
Postgame props to …	Jesus	Mom	Teletubbies
Retro clothes	Wes Unseld jersey	Mesh trucker hat	Aquaman underoos
Offseason hobby	Gangsta rapper	Jazz musician	Collecting "Hello Kitty!" memorabilia
Car feature	xbox	Geo-navigational device	"Baby On Board" sign
Cadillac Escalade Upholstery	Imported Italian leather	Suede	Something with cow prints
On-flight game of choice	Dominoes	Poker	Electronic Battleship
Parole violation	Driving under the influence	Skipping town without notifying proper authorities	Removing tags from mattress
Favorite periodic element	Cobalt	Lithium	Boron

SOURCE: "ESPN-Page 2," ESPN.com, January 30, 2006. Used with permission of ESPN.com.

Nike distributed "ads that many skaters found cheesy, product that wasn't focused on the market."[16]

When the company regrouped in 2004, it had figured out new ways to create street cred, and how to be patient enough to build this high-margin business more slowly. Avoiding the high-gloss ad campaigns of seven years earlier that had turned off the street skaters, Nike created its own skateboarding sub-brand, then purposely under-distributed some models, like the hard-to-get Dunk Low Pro SBs that became collectibles. Most of their shoes are never sold in malls, but only in skateboard equipment stores.

What Nike did borrow from its past successes was to enlist well-known riders like pro Richard Mulder, to help design the latest Nike entries into the market and to help with crucial sell-ins to key distributors and retailers. Rather than place ads in a way that would make the famed masterbrand stand out, Nike purposely blended in with the other competitors' advertising to avoid looking like an outsider.

Still, Nike will be Nike, and it is expected that they will continue to expand their distribution and sign up many more athletes in the near future. They have now successfully created "sub-businesses" in skateboarding, golf, and other sports. But their approach to more grassroots sports has changed because of the need to build a more genuine form of street cred.[17]

Arte des Logos: Credibly Fresh

In 2006, Rob Walker of *The New York Times Magazine* discovered on the streets of lower Manhattan what he labeled "The Brand Underground," a subculture of downtowners who make their living by living their own brands. In a cosmopolis at the epicenter of a polymorphous world, it works.

They are under-30s who create their own economies by designing and selling elaborately designed T-shirts and hats and other identity gear under brands called "aNYthing" and "Barking Irons." They have co-opted the street cred that Nike and Adidas built and turned it into something more home-grown, a version of street-real that is refined until it is raw. It's a form of in-your-face *arte des logos* and, because this is New York, it's naturally bubbling uptown so the very rich can look like the very poor. Ultra-chic Barney's bought into the idea in a New York minute, as did other retailers looking for the latest "whassup?" The Barking Irons line alone grew from a few hundred to as many as 12,000 shirts a season.

The key, Rob Walker writes, is that these street artists are not just printing shirts with brands, they are creating brands with ideas. Each of the designs has a story behind it. One Chicago store owner found it to be irresistible when he said: "There's something meaningful behind it. There's something to talk about."

It's a different kind of credible that's young and fresh, not old and legendary.[18]

Credibility Killers

Credibility lapses can kill perceptions of integrity much faster than it takes to build the integrity in the first place. Credibility killers can be viewed along two planes: one dealing with how intentional the malfeasance was, the other with how great an impact it had on net brand equity. As Figure 5-4 suggests, they can

Figure 5-4. Varieties of credibility killers.

	Intentional Integrity Breaches	Inadvertent Integrity Breaches
More Impact on Net Brand Equity	Conspiracies to defraud Mismanagement for financial gain Cover-ups of illegal actions	Regulatory abuse due to ignorance Poor products due to inadequate QC Unintended environmental damage
Less Impact on Net Brand Equity	Advertising to the vulnerable Selling while warning against overuse Implying superiority without verification	Accidental use of unfounded claims Using misleading labeling Promoting products that under-perform

include several combinations of short-sighted behavior that never seems to end well.

Many of the best known and most valuable brands in the world (Coke and Pepsi, British Air and United Airlines, Apple Computer and IBM) have assiduously kept promises for decades at a time, then failed to deliver on their promises for a variety of reasons. When that happens, a precipitous loss in credibility can torpedo an otherwise solid marketing program and, far worse, do major damage to net brand equity.

When a North Carolina lab found minute traces of benzene in Perrier bottles in 1990, the PR aftermath was mishandled. The company lost significant share and category leadership, ultimately becoming the victim of strong growth from Evian and others. In stark contrast, Intel dodged disaster four years later when its Pentium chip was found to be faulty at high computation levels. Only a full recall and a commitment to equity building saved the brand and sub-brand from major hits.

Boeing, the global aircraft manufacturer locked in a contentious competitive battle with Airbus, fired its second CEO in thirteen months in March 2005. Harry Stonecipher, the man most responsible for creating a critically acclaimed ethics program at scandal-plagued Boeing, was fired by its board when it was discovered that he had maintained an ongoing affair with a Washington D.C.-based Boeing employee.

The company's reputation, already damaged from alleged sweetheart deals with the Pentagon and illegal industrial spying, suffered more embarrassment because of a very visible unforced error. Ironically, the Pentagon had already decided to reinstate Boeing in contract bidding (thanks to the ethics program put in place by Stonecipher!).

The good news for Boeing was that this was a case of contained integrity leakage. The bad news came later when it was learned in June 2006 that the company had to take quarterly charges of $1.15 billion for those separate ethics violations plus some late delivery fees, more than wiping out their profit for that quarter.[19]

Integrity can take a lot of effort to maintain but even more effort when it lapses, partly because it is very difficult to field a strong offense when you are spending all the time on the defense.

After a lot of internal soul-searching Boeing has become one of the leading corporate bloggers as part of an effort to be more transparent to the public. The blogs include "Randy's Journal" (Randy Baseler is a Boeing marketing vice president), for example, which discusses product and marketing strategies, and "Flight Test Journal," which covers the testing of the 777 aircraft. The previously secretive company has also built blogs for employees, to hear what they have to say about everything from corporate strategy to ethics.[20]

The Prices We Pay

Companies often pay a wide range of penalties for behavior that lacks integrity. First, a company's overall reputation can be seriously damaged. As is true for individuals, the reputation of a company is its foremost asset and the one it can least afford to damage. That is one reason, no doubt, why three-fourths of investors polled by Harris Interactive in 2003 said they were less confident than in the past about the trustworthiness of corporate managements.[21]

Employee performance can also suffer greatly in terms of morale or productivity. It is likely that a company whose people know it has demonstrated questionable integrity will experience a significant drop-off in work levels and attendance, not to mention the less measurable drops in morale. In some broad-scale research of 1.2 million employees among fifty-two mostly Fortune 1000 companies between 2001 to 2004, workers in 85 percent of the companies studied experienced major declines in positive employee attitudes and behavior after the first six months of employment. And, that was without any major credibility crisis.[22]

Another form of equity breakage may occur when employees are not operating with integrity themselves. The Mitsubishi Corporation—Japan's fourth-largest automaker—endured a series of debilitating blows to its reputation beginning in 2000 when it was revealed that company employees had engaged in a massive cover-up to hide defects in its truck and bus vehicles, which had caused numerous deaths of and injuries to Japanese citizens. A police raid in 2004 produced incriminating proof that the company had maintained a "culture of cover-up," partly blamed on the Japanese ethos of following orders without question.

Making matters worse, Japanese government officials began random stops of Mitsubishi trucks and buses for inspections, and demanded weekly updates from all automakers about internal safety reviews. It was a bad experience for the company, and a potentially more damaging blow against its net brand equity in Japan.[23]

Brand equity killers are maddeningly agnostic; they can crop up indiscriminately within or outside any company or any brand at any time, no matter how robust they might have been up to that moment. Predicting, or at least forestalling, integrity breeches requires a systematized approach.

Is It Smart to Fiddle with a Legend?

Do you torpedo authentic when you try to improve it? Kraft Foods had a real dilemma: consumers were clamoring for food companies to eliminate trans-fats, those nasty little secrets in so many of our favorite foods that boost the wrong kind of cholesterol. But one of their legendary products was change-resistant. Peter Wilson, the senior director of technology at Kraft, and his team spent more than 30,000 hours, 200 recipes, and 16 different product lines, trying to de-trans-fat Oreo, easily the world's favorite cookie.

Unfortunately, trans-fats were a critical component of the creamy-crunchy Oreos. Says Wilson, "The ultimate food product is low in calories, carbohydrates and sodium and has no trans fats. That leaves you with only a handful of things—like a carrot."[24]

Ironically, a study by the Hartman Group found that a majority of U.S. consumers had heard about trans-fats, but only about 14 percent expected to go out of their way to avoid them. Of course, some of these same issues arose when Coke created Diet Coke and Miller created Miller Lite. Having a better version of a good thing is often a good thing.

It was a long, tough road, but Kraft food scientists (a job title not to be pondered too long) finally discovered the solution in a combination of canola oil and, of all things, previously defamed palm oil. The new Reduced Fat Oreos were introduced in late 2005 and look faintly oxymoronic sitting on the shelf. It seems likely that the authenticity of this family favorite may have taken one for the team in order to survive in a world concerned about obesity.[25]

*   *   *

A Competitive Strategy: Win the Credibility Race

Here are some specific suggestions on how brands and companies can build a leadership share of credibility:

1. Build an Integritometer

Ultimately, all metrics must link to increased revenue and/or profitability, or they are going to be considered no more than "nice to know." Regrettably, credibility is one of the most amorphous of all attributes and thus resists quantification. But there are some simple ways to find at least some tangential evidence about how much credibility a brand may have in the customers' view, and to what degree that might affect sales.

Create a scorecard of credibility that compares what your brand or company has promised in any and all marketing programs with what the actual product/service realities were. For example, if a software company promised its customers and the industry specific upgrades on particular dates, how often did it deliver on those dates? How many times have those kinds of promises been broken, and how far off were they? An example of a credibility scorecard (an "integritometer") can be found in Appendix A.

Establish how credible your brand or company is believed to be by each of its constituents, using the criteria provided earlier in this chapter. In customer research, ask respondents to rate the accuracy of claims made ("honesty"), the relevance of benefits to customer lives ("realness"), and how well the brand is known for delivering on its promises ("promise-keeping").

Then track responses over time and identify any linkage between ratings of credibility measures and purchase intent. If possible, cross-reference findings against actual sales in the marketplace by time period. With whatever information can be reliably gathered, establish credibility norms, above and beyond customer or employee satisfaction norms.

2. Make the Most of Intrinsic Credibility

Everything says something about your brand's credibility and nothing says it more dramatically than the fact that you have stayed true to its original vision, even if changing market conditions may have required regular updating of that vision. For mature brands and companies, heritage can also be celebrated as a basis for credibility, especially if your past was founded on integrity.

When Nathan Swartz made his first pair of shoes in 1918 he invested in it the quality that would later become the famed Timberland line. When John Deere made a breakthrough plow design in 1837, he knew he was onto something that would stand the test of time if he marketed it with the same integrity that he built into the plow. When N.R. Narayana Murthy and his colleagues founded Infosys in 1981, and Yvon Chouinard founded what would become Patagonia in the early 1970s, and D.J. DePree founded Herman Miller in 1923—they all were determined to build businesses with integrity as their bricks and mortar because they knew that their credibility depended on it. Unlike many other companies that talk a good game, they and their successors have never stopped relying on their integrity to sustain and protect them.

Another source of credibility may come from stellar product or service performance. The Titleist golf equipment company, part of the Fortune Brands stable, has marketed products that are consistently ranked highest among its peers, year after year. Golfers look at Titleist golf balls as the gold standard because of that performance, a view that is nicely reinforced by paid endorsements from leading pros. But the net impact from endorsements is that much more powerful because the golf ball itself, unlike other golf equipment, is largely identical for pros and amateurs.

If a brand seeks emotional connections with its customers, the right use of a credible celebrity can still be an effective tool for reinforcing the credibility of a brand. Tiger Woods might make Buicks look good to some who have never seen a golf course they didn't like. Martha Stewart undoubtedly owes some of her fame to the fact that she makes uneasy homemakers feel more confident and credible because they can now make anything into a good thing.

American Express, a distant third in credit card usage but very aggressive in its marketing and distribution efforts, has repeatedly validated its cards' credibility by using celebrities in communications channels that resonate with their marketing targets. Recent campaigns have sponsored Jerry Seinfeld as his favorite hero, Superman, in a series of "web-isodes," famed photographer Annie Leibovitz in art exhibits, and Sheryl Crow in concerts. The company's "This is My Card" campaign is an insider's look at what motivates stars like Robert DiNiro and Ellen DeGeneres.[26]

Getting Real

The latest approach to building credibility is the wild and crazy idea of letting real people tell their own stories. The successful Dove "Campaign for Real Beauty" campaign, featuring people who look like real people, is an example of how advertisers are turning back to reality for inspiration. Unilever's Dove beauty product sales have taken off in recent years, along with the brand's esteem, thanks to some smart line extending and even smarter marketing communications.

Using the equity of skin care wrapped up in the Dove brand, the "Real Beauty" campaign, introduced in 2004, is based on global research that found that a majority of women strongly agree that society expects women to be as physically attractive as possible, that such attractiveness is highly valued by men, and that the media and advertising have set standards for what's beautiful that are unhealthy and unrealistic.[27]

The "Real Beauty" campaign tries to define and portray what is true and authentic, and it gives prospective buyers more reasons to genuinely like the Dove product line because the brand seems to understand what concerns women about the out-of-reach standards that society sets.

Dove claims to have increased traffic at their website by 200 percent and, while the bar soap category declined at about 2 percent a year, the total Dove business has been increasing by as much as 30 percent annually.[28] In addition to its performance gains, the Dove brand is getting credit for tapping into something genuinely credible that real people can resonate with.[29]

3. Establish a Credibility Protocol

Credibility, whether it originates with a genuine heritage or must rely on other sources, can be built methodically. Here are some ways to do that:

❏ *Demonstrate to the buyer your own faith in what you sell.* Don't overlook the value of such promotional old-standbys as guarantees, warranties, money-back offers, or whatever will clearly communicate that the buyer has nothing to worry about because you know you will deliver on what you promise.

❏ *Establish an inviolable system for authenticating all factual material before it is released.* Beyond whatever legal reviews are standard procedure in your company, the marketing department itself should have a proven system for verifying the veracity of claims that are going to be made in marketing communications. Such a system is an important double-check on the legal review because marketing staff may have a better understanding of the context in which the claim is appearing.

❏ *Lead the industry in self-policing.* Make it clear to internal and external stakeholders and customers that you are doing everything possible *proactively* to maintain impeccable integrity in what you sell and how you sell it. That could include proposing self-regulatory guidelines through your industry association. Or, you might consider establishing self-policing programs within your marketing organization, and offering to share lessons learned with other companies.

❏ *React positively to credibility challenges.* If your brand's or company's credibility is challenged, be proactively positive in responding to that challenge. Consider it to be an opportunity to prove the brand's worth. That attitude turned disaster into saving grace for brands like Tylenol, Jack-in-the-Box, and Denny's, which have all have come back from troubled times to reestablish strong momentum in their respective markets.

Better yet, consider some periodic scenario training in which you envision some issues that could be problematic in the future and rehearse responding with actions.

❏ *Overall, rely on transparency to validate your credibility.* Transparency in all things sends several messages: To your customers, it communicates that you have nothing to hide, which means that they have nothing to fear. To your people, transparency is both a reminder of the need for their diligence, and a reinforcement of the integrity you want them to live by. And, for the management of the company, transparency is a continuous symbol of the standards that you should profess and live.

You don't have to look that hard to find credibility guidelines in the best of companies. Johnson & Johnson calls it their "Credo"; Patagonia calls it their "Uncommon Culture"; the people at Herman

Miller believe in and talk about the "Things that Matter." These companies have thought through what they believe and put their values into plans that are the foundations of their credibility. But then, so have a lot of companies. The difference is that some companies make it a part of what they do, not just what they say they will do.

Even if similar values guides have been proposed in your company, assign someone to adapt them specifically to marketing issues and challenges. Broad ethical goals and procedures may be helpful for the entire corporation, but marketing credibility and the practice of practical integrity deserve their own focused set of guidelines.

4. Protect Your Net Brand Equity

A brand's *net equity* is the bottom-line assessment of whether credibility has been maintained or sacrificed. To protect your net brand equity, consider taking these specific steps:

❏ *Conduct a full equity audit.* Determine what your equity assets are, with a particular focus on intangible brand assets (awareness, familiarity, salience, likeability). Wherever possible, find a way to quantify them and track them over time.

❏ *Determine where brand equity is most vulnerable.* Are your products or services vulnerable to breakdown? Are your customers easily swayed by competitive counterclaims? Are your marketing communications claims not entirely verifiable? Where will equity loss strike first?

❏ *Prepare countermeasures, and be prepared to launch them at a moment's notice when marketing credibility is threatened.* This is a primary tenet of crisis management: Assume the worst will happen and prepare for it. Be ready to launch whatever measures are necessary to help minimize or forestall equity losses. These actions should be separate from, but closely coordinated with, any actions by your corporate communications team. Remember: You don't just need a crisis plan, you need a crisis capitalization plan.

❏ *Learn from your mistakes.* As actions are taken that result in equity loss—and they *will* happen—meticulously track, measure, and codify what occurs and what are and are not successful as countermeasures. There's no point in repeating history, especially when it comes to credibility threats.

❏ *Stay away from marketing tools that do more harm than good.* We've all seen them, been bombarded by them, and been occasionally offended by them. Some examples are:

- Direct mail pieces from some of the biggest companies in the country, designed to look like government checks to prompt the addressee to open them quickly.
- Come-ons that promise low, low prices on printer ink cartridges only to discover that they are remanufactured by the supplier.
- Retailers that must be terrible businesspeople because they regularly are "going out of business," are "way overstocked," or "have no choice but to lose money."
- Online marketing from otherwise smart marketers whose invasive messages annoy more than sell.
- Telecommunications plans that offer such deep discounting to new customers that they eventually alienate their core customers who overcome inertia and move on.
- Nonprofits that exploit their exemption from the "Do Not Call" registry to hound would-be donors until they are driven into a "Do Not Give" mode.

5. Avoid the Turn-Offs

Lose your credibility and you might as well close up shop. Introduce a new product and fail to establish its credibility and you will wish you had saved your money. In marketing, credibility is like air: you can't see it, taste it, or touch it, but you'll find out very fast if you're running short. A few suggestions on how to avoid losing your credibility:

❏ *We just have to educate them.* "Educating" the consumer or business customer is a viable strategy if you are an industry leader and have the funds to invest, but it's an uphill struggle at best. Educating the customer about credibility is even more of a challenge because credibility is so often a subjective issue, and pounding away with your "defense" may only further undermine your credibility.

When the credibility of such companies as Wal-Mart (because of labor practices), Gap and Starbucks (sourcing), and Merck (Vioxx) were called into question, the best first step was to correct the problem that was the focus of the controversy, and to let the world know the problem was being corrected. Sending out messages that try to offset negative publicity with positive spin may produce an effect that is polar opposite to what was intended.

Credibility Implication to Consider: Most types of credibility crises are like natural disasters in disaster-prone areas: They are always shocking and rarely surprising. Plan, evolve, and rehearse the most credible counter-crisis moves to restore credibility. An easy guideline to remember is to simply tell the truth or, if your legal eagles advice against it, tell as much as you can without altering the truth (and consider getting other legal eagles).

❏ *If the majority of our buyers believe we're credible, we're credible.* This part of marketing is not about democracy. The majority of those you survey may believe your messages, but it only takes a small minority of unbelievers to cause real problems for your brand or company. In most of the credibility cases that turn ugly, it is that minority that begins to push back. Today, that's all it takes for the press to pick up on the story and run with it ("According to the people we talked to today on Main Street . . ."). Neither the press nor the public tend to know or care about the statistical projectability of small samples; they only care that some number of people are claiming that yet another company has allegedly lied to them.

Credibility Implication to Consider: Some believability problems can be foreseen and handled efficiently if the company has maintained meticulous and frequent credibility tracking. Other, more unexpected crises cannot be predicted, but they can be anticipated and trained for (see the "A Summary and a Few Questions" section below).

❏ *Can't we get some traction from our heritage?* Using heritage as a proof point may not be relevant to all of today's consumers, but it's often one of the more feasible options. However, if your heritage has little or nothing to do with what you are now, it may waste some credibility points.

The Saab automobile brand name is an acronym for the original corporate name, "Svenska Aeroplan Aktiebolaget," which translates to "Swedish Aircraft Company." Beginning in 2006, the company advertised that its roots and design philosophy as an aircraft maker enable the company to build cars like it used to build jets. That is probably a bit of a stretch for some people, but it is based in fact and thus is less likely to hurt the carmaker's credibility, and it may help to differentiate it.

Sometimes a brand can project a faux authenticity by creating a heritage that is even more of a stretch than Saab's. Bombay Sapphire gin is a premium-priced entry whose name and packaging imply a heritage to Victorian England. There are no real connections, however, to Bombay the city, to the famous Bombay Sapphire jewel, or to anything else from the Victorian era. (The name actually refers to the origins of generic gin.) The same situation exists for Haagen-Dazs ice cream, whose name implies old world roots, but which was first created in the early 1920s in Brooklyn, New York.

But are the historical roots what is being sold here, or is it simply the innocent imagery of well-crafted brands? The Haagen-Dazs and Bombay products are rich in flavor and quality, so why can't their brands' "authenticity" be product-based, rather than heritage-based? And so it can, but brand managers may want to file this away for future use: Any confusion about their heritage could limit its marketing options if they hope to make more of what they now simply imply.[30]

In a free market economy, we have a right to sell people things that they don't need, and they have the right to buy them. But in the future, the issue will not necessarily be about whether a brand or company has the right to do such things, but whether such things are doing a service to either buyers or sellers.

*   *   *

A Summary and a Few Questions

Marketing credibility is a gatekeeper to the customer's trust. Every marketer should be trying to achieve a leadership position in the race for marketing credibility. There's often only so much to go around, and the victors are the ones that capture the lion's share of believability. That will give those marketers a distinct competitive advantage and limit equity damage when the inevitable mistake is made in the marketplace.

To accomplish this and more, establish a sound tracking system ("integritometer") and protocol to support credible claims and filter out those that can do more harm than good.

You might begin by asking these questions:

1. *Do you have an accurate and timely way to assess your brand's or company's credibility among your customer-partners and prospects? How ex-*

plicitly do you probe credibility issues in your current research? What questionnaire design or other measures have you taken to ensure that you get accurate feedback about your credibility? How clearly have you differentiated your brand credibility from your corporate (reputation) credibility?

2. *How would you rate your company's or brand's ability to keep its promises, compared to your competition?* Breaking promises to your customers is never a good idea, but you may gain some understanding of your relative credibility by objectively gauging your credibility performance against those of your competitors.

3. *Do your marketing programs contain anything intentionally or inadvertently deceptive?* Where is your brand or company most vulnerable to credibility challenges? The first cut at this is easy: Make up a list of past and present claims and have someone determine if any deception has been used. Then confirm or rebut those findings with some in-depth interviewing of representative customers. But don't stop there. Run credibility-crisis scenario drills, envisioning everything from a questioning by a watchdog group about a support claim, all the way to a major product disaster that affects hundreds, if not thousands, of customers.

4. *How has your net brand equity been impacted in recent years by the happenings in your industry?* Are you finding that your brand or company is hit harder than others if and when your industry is questioned about its credibility? Have you attempted to establish your net brand equity after some difficult events in your industry may have had an impact on it?

5. *Are you able to establish a link between credibility and market results in your business?* Is credibility a given in your business, or regularly at issue? Have you seen business declines when your company or a competitor has suffered some credibility setbacks? If these measures have not been considered, a thorough analysis may save time and money when/if credibility issues begin to affect your business.

Credibility is tough to get and easy to lose. As we will discuss in Chapter 6, marketing communications is one of those tools that can lead to either credibility loss or gain, depending on how well it is managed.

CHAPTER 6

Promote Honestly, Not Just Legally

No Weasels Allowed

DILBERT: © Scott Adams/Dist. by United Feature Syndicate, Inc.

*D*ilbert offers the quintessential cynic's view of business life. The luckless title character languishes in a world peopled with incompetence and irrationality. What's just a little disturbing is that the strip's dialogue carries a ring of truth, even familiarity. We laugh at the absurdities that Dilbert and his colleagues endure because we see hints of them in our own lives.

The Way Marketing Will Always Be?

It's likely that few marketers deceive blatantly, but it's also safe to say that a good many stretch the truth, or omit critical but negative information about their products, or find a way to couch facts to make the products sound better than they are.

When marketing honesty is abused in a big way, we shake our heads, wonder what gets into people, and move on. But we think of more subtle deceptions as harmless, or just the way things are, have always been, and always will be. We call it human nature. We call it by benign names, like "puffery" or "weasels." Or, if we admire it, we call it "aggressive marketing." But whatever we call it, it is becoming riskier because more customers are demanding to know what's real and are inclined to reject what isn't.

A few examples of why "marketing integrity" is considered by some to be a contradiction in terms:

❏ A major video rental chain advertised in 2005 that it was eliminating all late fees on games and movies, which can be a significant obstacle to more frequent rental. Test trials had demonstrated that dropping the fees increased business.

The offer carried a caveat, however: Renters had a free one-week grace period, but then were billed for the full purchase price of the rental, less the rental cost. If they returned it after that week, they got a refund for the purchase price, less a stocking fee, but the consumers might be inclined to just keep the video and leave the charge on their credit card.

After forty-seven states claimed something was afoul, the company settled for total fines of $670,000 and agreed to substantially alter the way it advertised the policy.[1]

❏ The court proceedings in wrongful death suits against a leading pharmaceutical firm reportedly revealed a set of embarrassing internal e-mails—including one titled "Dodge"—that referred to marketing and sales techniques used on physicians. Another e-mail allegedly encouraged sales reps to "neutralize" physicians who were opposed to the use of this company's major drug. Claimed safety issues with the drug and the subsequent loss in consumer trust has likely contributed to a 50 percent decline in the price of this particular company's stock over a recent five-year period.[2]

That firm was hardly alone. The pharmaceutical industry in total paid more than $2 billion in fines between 2001 and 2004 for allegedly illegal marketing activities. The activities included salespeople purportedly paying doctors to prescribe off-label uses of a company's drugs—which prosecutors claim the company knew had no effect—and for allegedly hiring ghostwriters to craft articles proclaiming the salvation of off-label uses, then inserting the doctors' names as the authors.[3]

It is little wonder that a 2006 Kaiser Permanente survey found that only 18 percent of U.S. consumers believe drug ads "most of the time," about half the level reported nine years earlier.[4]

To add to the industry's problems, in June 2006 the American

Medical Association called for a temporary moratorium on all direct-to-consumer advertising until the AMA could figure out if the practice was a benefit to consumers.[5] Not a good sign of things to come.

❏ A few years ago three of the major life insurers all admitted to marketing "interest-sensitive" life insurance policies during the 1980s and 1990s. Reportedly their sales agents told subscribers that the policies would yield returns that would pay for any premiums due over the years. But when interest rates fell, subscribers ended up losing far more than they might have retained with standard policies, sometimes including their entire life savings. Multiple class-action suits later, the firms agreed that their sales and marketing people had been—as politicians like to call it—overzealous.[6]

A Conversation

"Morning."

"Morning. Hey, I was just thinking about the Project Fireball launch."

"Me, too. We sure gave that puppy the right code name."

"Yeah, well . . . I'm thinking maybe we're stretching things a bit."

"Oh?"

"Yeah. So, I know it's an exciting product and everything . . ."

"Exciting? It's killer. It's liquid heat. It's gonna light a fire under the brand."

"I know, I know. I was just thinking . . ."

"What?"

"I was just thinking that the product doesn't . . . quite . . ."

"What? Talk to me."

"Well, it's not exactly as good as our ad campaign claims it is."

"You got Legal to sign off, right?"

"Right."

"So we're covered, right?"

"Right."

"OK, then."

"Yeah, but the product. . . ."

"Not our problem, bro. The product people make it. The Legals sign off on it. We market it, and that's that."

"Uh-huh . . ."

"Am I right?"

"Yeah, I guess you're right."

"You guess?"

"No, I see your point. I do."
"Then we're cool?"
"Yeah, we're cool."
"OK, then."

Weasels and Other Self-Inflicted Wounds

Persuading buyers has become more difficult because of what buyers believe about the message and the messenger. In a 2003 study the U.S. public rated advertising practitioners, for example, just above HMO managers, insurance salesmen, and car salesmen in terms of honesty and ethics (see Figure 6-1).

Why would advertising executives be rated so low? At least part of the reason has got to be that—rightly or wrongly—the ad industry is not known for employing the truth so much as whatever it takes to sell whatever they are selling. Their frequent use of "weasels" can't help.

The nonmammalian version of the term "weasel" is believed to have been coined by political commentator Stewart Chaplin in the nineteenth century. Chaplin called weasels "words that suck the life out of the words next to them, just as a weasel sucks out the egg and leaves the shell." Bullmoose Party candidate Theodore Roosevelt frequently accused his 1912 Democratic opponent, Woodrow Wilson, of using "weasel words," which he decried as "one of the defects of our nation."[7]

In marketing-speak, *weasels* suck the meaning from a claim and leave only its shell remaining. One form of weaseled advertising claims that "Nobody is better than our brand." That kind of weasel is often factually accurate but the consumer's takeaway may be that the advertised brand is superior, particularly when the claim is read with conviction by a sonorous announcer.

Figure 6-1. Rating of honesty and ethics of professions, November 2003 (highest and lowest rankings).

Highest Rated Professions	% Rating Ethics as "High" or "Very High"	Lowest Rated Professions	% Rating Ethics as "High" or "Very High"
Nurses	83	Stockbrokers	15
Medical Doctors	68	Advertising Practitioners	12
Veterinarians	68	Insurance Salesmen	12
Druggists/Pharmacists	67	HMO Managers	11
Dentists	61	Car Salesmen	7

SOURCE: "Public Rates Nursing as Most Honest and Ethical Profession," *Gallup Research Report*, Gallup News Service, December 8, 2003.

Another weasel form employs hedged modifiers (no relation to the hedgehog) that serve a similar purpose. If a marketing message proclaims that a new product is "better" in some way, it's common to omit the comparison point, leaving the unanswered question: better than what? Quite possibly better than before but still not as good as alternative brands.

The massification of the Internet has led to a rise in weasel sightings. For instance, virtually all online travel agencies claim to offer the lowest possible airline and hotel rates. In reality, they may be at parity—sometimes by contract—with the lowest online rates of major airlines and hotel chains, or only modestly higher, which is not worth the consumer's effort to worry about.

So you may only get the lowest fare online if you bought it at a certain time, from a certain vendor, with certain Draconian penalties attached. Commented one industry analyst: "They're really just marketing gimmicks. There's nothing wrong with them, but I don't think it's going to move the (travel sales) needle for you."[8] It may not move the sales needle, but it could gradually undermine the credibility still further of the travel industry, an industry that could always use a bit more trust from its customers.

The problem from a buyer standpoint is that weasels, and their promotional pal "puffery," dodge the truth, if not hide it. Sometimes that's not important and sometimes it can make the difference in what buyers think of a brand, or even what they buy. Even when they may appear to have only a minor consequence, weasels and puffery can turn into a way to self-inflict doubt among your customer base. (See Figure 6-2 for examples of equity draining.)

A Sampling of Marketing Malfeasance

In January 2006 this author asked some past and presents colleagues in the marketing industry to provide him with examples of dubious marketing integrity that they were personally familiar with. Below is a sampling of what was received (with names and traceable details omitted):

❑ Retail chains and other companies have purposely launched store branded products and packaging that were virtually identical to that of the national branded competition. When one C-level executive was challenged internally by an employee about using this practice, his response was, "If a customer buys our product thinking that they're buying the other guy, I'm O.K.

Figure 6-2. Weasels and puffery that can drain equity.

Weasel/Puffery	What It May Really Mean	Possible Impact
"Virtually eliminates (fill in the blank)"	"Virtually" is a relative term that many people don't hear. Usually comes with legal caveat that many people don't hear/read, e.g., ". . .when used regularly over a 1-month period."	May provide temporary competitive edge, but likely to leave some users upset when their problem doesn't disappear after a week of product use.
"Preferred by doctors"	Often refers to doctors who receive free samples and may receive financial payments for their "endorsements."	If you ask your doctor and she or he doesn't "prefer it," there's good reason to disbelieve the next claim you hear from that brand.
"Best around"	We believe that our product is the best available (although we don't have statistically projectible research to prove it).	May never be challenged by regulatory agencies but there are plenty of reasonably credible blogmasters and watchdog groups to call the marketer's bluff.
"43% more powerful than another leading brand."	We usually don't hear the "another leading brand" because it's unspecific. The "43% more" claim may be the only takeaway, and "more powerful" can be interpreted many ways.	Perfectly legal, but if the "other leading brand" is "leading" in the sense that it is not dead last, this could set the marketer up for over-promise because the comparison base is so poor.

with that. We need all the customers we can get, even the stupid ones."

❏ An ad agency was told by a client to boldly promote the fact that his product was "sugar free," and to emphasize the health benefits of high fructose syrup versus sugar, despite the fact that there was no evidence that there was any advantage. The agency resisted, and ultimately resigned the account, which presumably was given to another agency to do as ordered.

❏ One national energy association conducted annual surveys that probed how the public felt about their energy fuels. When the numbers started to head toward the negative, the association instructed its research supplier to rephrase the questions so as to make sure that the numbers always looked good. The firm was never specifically asked to "lie" about the results, only to "find the truth." The "truth," in this case, turned out to be as flexible as necessary to make the association's products look good in subsequent press releases.

❏ Even the largest and most prestigious food and household products companies downsize a package while keeping the same price, thus reaping a "hidden" price increase and commensurate profit. Another common practice is introducing "hernia size" packaging and increasing the "flow rate" of toothpaste and detergents by increasing the cap size, all of which research has proven encourages consumers to use more than they need because they seem to have so much on hand. These "improvements" are advertised as making it easier for consumers to consume, and so they are.

Masochistic readers can find more examples in Appendix B.

Buzz, Stealth, and "Human Spam"

The challenge for marketers is how to start a conversation with a generation that includes many who prefer not to be hammered by commercial messaging. One answer that is rapidly becoming mainstream is *buzzing*, and variations on that technique.

"Buzz," the world's original method of marketing, is planned and executed (or the spontaneous creation of) word-of-mouth sharing about a brand, product, service, or company. Word-of-mouth marketing is often cheaper than traditional media, relatively easy to seed and sow, and believed to be 50 percent more influential than radio and television advertising.[9] (See Figure 6-3.)

Although it is called "buzz marketing" or "viral marketing," it may also be close to "stealth marketing," which is marketing that isn't supposed to look like marketing. "Stealth marketing," observed one industry exec, "is buzz without the disclosure."[10]

McKinsey analysts estimated as far back as 2004 that more than two-thirds of the U.S. economy was largely or partly impacted by buzz.[11] Buzz marketing spending is conservatively gauged to be about $200 million in spending as of this writing, but its future may be unlimited. And according to research conducted by

Figure 6-3. Trust in forms of advertising.

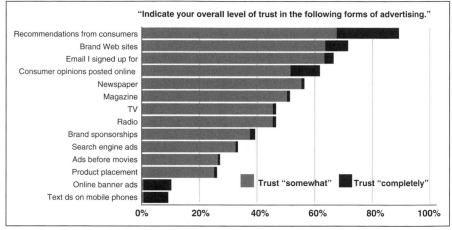

SOURCE: "Consumer-Generated Media and Engagement Study," Intelliseek (now owned by Nielsen BuzzMetrics), 2005.

the now-departed *CMO* magazine, buzz marketing is the second-fastest growing form of marketing channel, behind the omnipresent e-mail marketing.[12]

Here are some examples of successful stealth and/or buzz campaigns, each with some element that could be considered questionable:

❏ *The Fake Tourist.* One electronics company launched a campaign for one of their cameras in 2002 called "fake tourist," in which actors and models pretended to be tourists who were genuinely excited about the product and "spontaneously" demonstrated it for onlookers. A Bloomberg report called the campaign "human spam," while *BRAND-WEEK* named its creator "Guerrilla Marketer of the Year"—a perfect example of how creative marketing can be applauded by some, and considered questionable by others.[13]

❏ *"Best Movie I've Seen Today!"* A motion picture studio distributed fictitious quotes from fictitious film critics to spread positive buzz about one of their pictures. Things went from bad to worse when it turned out that two of the "moviegoers" interviewed in a commercial for the film were studio employees.[14]

❏ *I Was a Teenage Blogger.* In 2004, a soft drink brand reportedly established an in-house blog to push the introduction of a new drink, and flew teen bloggers and their parents to the corporate headquarters for a one-week orientation. The teens were then allegedly sent back home with instructions to spread the word on as many blogging sites as possible, without revealing that they were working on behalf of the company. The teens were not compensated with cash, but did receive promotional items.[15]

❏ *Stop Me Before I Shill Again.* A major word-of-mouth marketing company has built a strong business by recruiting teens for research and viral marketing purposes. Attracting leading firms as clients, the company enables teenagers to become part of major buzz marketing programs, including for a very successful flavored milk that reportedly increased sales by 18 percent in test markets.[16]

At the request of a special interest group, the FTC informally reviewed the firm's marketing methods in January 2006, and reportedly was not concerned that the company does not fully disclose the extent to which the teens are used as word-of-mouth vehicles.[17]

Other critics have not been so sanguine. They have pointed out—and this author agrees—that using teenagers as word-of-mouth sales and marketing agents is not a worthy enterprise for any marketer. Nor does it seem advisable that any word of mouth company should operate without *insisting* that all of its operatives disclose to their friends/contacts that they are working on behalf of a client, regardless of whether that agent is paid for the work.

In 2005, the buzz marketing community created a Code of Ethics through their Word of Mouth Marketing Association (WOMMA). (See Appendix C for the Code.) To its credit, the code calls for marketers to have their operatives disclose that they are paid by sponsors. But like most professional organizations, WOMMA has no way to enforce that policy.

The Rewards of Blogging

One of the hallmarks of the much-heralded "Web 2.0" is a rapid rise in mega-blogs. Frequented by the latest generation of online addicts, usually in their teens and early twenties, these sites feed a seemingly bottomless need to stay in touch with one another. Mega-blogs like MySpace and YouTube have created online meeting tents so enormous and organic that they're among the most visited sites on the Web.

Unlike traditional websites, MySpace is more of a place to hang out than a destination. According to *Fortune* magazine, by August 2006 MySpace had signed up 100 million individuals, and every day was adding the equivalent of the population of Scottsdale, Arizona.[18] Erected in 2003 and purchased by Rupert Murdoch's News Corp. in 2005, MySpace today is the sweet spot for the teens and preteens who live online. One reason for that may be that many young people do not really distinguish the net from the "real" world all that much. In fact, for all intents and purposes, the Internet *is* the real world to them.[19]

Other comprehensive online social networks have sprung up throughout the United States and offshore, including Facebook for college students, concert marketplace Buzz-Oven, and video and photo share site Photobucket. Some are stand-alone and some are tucked inside larger blogs. They are used to share intimacies, buy or swap things and services, but mostly to just stay in touch with friends and strangers, and with friends who last month were strangers.

These meeting places are an advertisers' dream—as long as advertisers don't wear out their welcome. Big hitters such as Coke, Sony Pictures, and Procter & Gamble find MySpace and other mega-blogs to be excellent places to test new ideas for young people. The campaigns are low cost (as little as 10 percent of a major TV campaign), easy to mount, theoretically easy to evaluate in terms of success and return on investment, and carry the highly persuasive messaging via word of mouth. Mega-blogs may be the most effective antidote yet to the continuing erosion of network TV, newspapers, and other conventional media channels.

Mega-blogs also enable marketers to become part of the fabric of an authentic communication among the younger generation, and early indications are that blog users actually appreciate major advertisers legitimizing their efforts. It is believed that MySpace alone may account for as much as 15 percent or more of all online advertising, and rising, despite the fact that the blog does not allow pop-ups or spyware in its advertising.

The Risks of Blogging

There are also risks lurking in every corner of the buzz world, including the prospect of some restrictive regulations. As of this writing, numerous state regulators have been investigating MySpace for allegedly enabling child abusers to contact and meet children under age 14. (MySpace prohibits its use by younger children but may not be able to stop it.)[20]

Another risk is that blogging will be turned against marketers. A large retailer launched a major blogging buzz campaign in 2005 in which citizen-bloggers were enlisted to support the company in a series of public controversies, allegedly using verbiage written by the company itself. The company reportedly contacted bloggers through its PR agency and provided them with blogging material. The company did not encourage the bloggers to say where they got the information, but allegedly did suggest that they should not lift exact language from the company prompt piece lest it be noted by the press. Which, of course, it was.[21]

Influence peddling through blogging is becoming a common part of a communications plan among many public relations agencies and their clients. Being criticized in the press for the way they do it is not part of the plan, and certainly can be a counter-productive way for a company to diffuse negative publicity around other issues.

Although many of these online initiatives are perfectly legitimate, marketers who try anything just because they can may end up on the wrong end of regulation or, worse, buyer anger. Before marketers launch any new program that may involve camouflaged marketing they should carefully analyze whether the possible negative consequences are worth it. Major abuse of buzz marketing will undoubtedly bring critics and government agencies running to the rescue. Marketers should preempt them and use their influence to make sure the vehicles they support are squeaky clean.

At a time when buyers have never been more doubtful of sellers, what seems like a creative or innovative idea may not be all that smart, even if initially it builds awareness or trial. If some of the targeted consumers feel betrayed by the technique, they may tell everyone they know. The word-of-mouth door swings both ways.

The Slippery Slopes of Public Relations

Public relations is becoming one of the most important tools in the marketer's toolbox. As it receives more well-deserved credit for marketing successes, it also is getting more attention than some PR professionals would like. The job of public relations is to manage reputations from behind a curtain, after all, not in front of it. But because a lot of the industry's best work is done behind that curtain, missteps can often appear to be surreptitious.

In early 2005 Armstrong Williams, a popular black political commentator, strongly endorsed the federal government's "No Child Left Behind" initiative and urged other black journalists to follow suit. There was nothing shocking about that, especially since many people supported the program.

But what Mr. Williams didn't tell his listeners was that he had been paid $240,000 by the U.S. Department of Education to promote "No Child Left Behind." The clear impression he left was that his opinions were his own. After a mini-scandal heated up over the incident, Mr. Williams reportedly explained to *USA Today* that he regretted taking the money, but that returning it "would be ludicrous because they bought advertising, and they got it."[22]

Child magazine's technology editor, James Oppenheim, appears regularly on local television shows and reviews toys for interested parents. On one program, Oppenheim touted the benefits of products from Atari Inc., Microsoft Corp., Mattel Inc., Leapfrog Enterprises Inc. and Radio Shack Corp., but allegedly failed to mention that he was paid by those companies to praise their products.

Oppenheim once positioned himself as a "consumer advocate" whose "pledge is to tell the unvarnished truth about the products reviewed." More recently, he reportedly changed his bio to read "technology expert and industry spokesperson."[23]

Syndicated columnist Doug Bandow was suspended from his Copley News Service position in 2005 and forced to resign his post as senior fellow at the respected Cato Institute when it was discovered that he had taken dozens of bribes to write as many as twenty-four stories praising the clients of infamous lobbyist Jack Abramoff. Receiving up to $2,000 per column, the topics of his writing were often allegedly suggested by Abramoff himself, a fact that Bandow omitted from his write-ups.[24]

Sadly, many chief marketing officers don't seem to believe that the questionable practice of paying to place stories in otherwise legitimate news editorial is all that questionable. In a 2006 survey of 266 senior marketing executives, nearly 50 percent said they had paid for an editorial or broadcast story placement, and nearly half of those who had never paid for a placement said that they would be willing to do so. In a survey conducted a year earlier, 65 percent of consumer respondents said they believed that all product placements were paid for.[25]

Marketers will always want to make full use of smart public relations to sell their wares, but whatever they pay in fees and expenses could be investments in brand equity loss if the discipline is not tempered with integrity controls. To its credit, the PR industry is very sensitive to these integrity issues. But, like in the word-of-mouth advertising field, the public relations industry is not capable of enforcing any integrity guidelines, as the ongoing fall of "the wall" demonstrates.

The Fall of "The Wall"

Since the first crude newspaper was cranked out by hand in fifteenth-century Germany, publishers have sprinkled advertising content throughout their editorial pieces. But over the course of many decades, much of the U.S. media at one time had erected a figurative but very real "wall" between editorial decisions and advertiser content and influence. (One possible originator of The Wall may have been *Chicago Tribune* publisher Colonel Robert McCormick, who in the 1920s reportedly insisted that advertising salesmen and editorial staff use separate elevators in the *Tribune* building.[26])

In smaller media outlets that might be subject to more economic pressure from advertisers, a local car dealership, for example, might have a real impact on pending stories that criticize auto row businesses. By and large, though, many editors have kept The Wall as high as possible.[27] But now The Wall is turning out to be about as strong as the original New Orleans levees.

In the spring of 2005, Morgan Stanley threatened to pull advertising from publications in which it received negative publicity. Not long after that, oil colossus BP demanded that they be notified in advance before any print publication in which they were advertising was running a story mentioning their companies. Both companies said they had no intention of interfering with editorial policy, but editors were not buying it.

The Hearst Magazines group recently asked U.S. adults which advertising medium they trusted. The highest level was the 21 percent of respondents who trusted magazines, compared to 12 percent for TV commercials and 7 percent for online advertising.[28] (The magazine industry didn't comment on the fact that nearly 80 percent of adults claim not to trust advertising in any one medium.)

In October 2005, the American Society of Magazine Editors (ASME) held their ground and refused to loosen guidelines that prevent advertisers from embedding commercial messages in editorial content. As Mark Whitaker, the ASME president, put it, "Trends in advertising are going to come and go. The one thing that's going to keep you in business is your relationship with your readers, and if you jeopardize that, then you jeopardize the franchise."[29]

Trusting information requires that we are familiar and comfortable with the source. Nowadays, we're not even sure we know what the source is. That sentiment is applicable to advertisers as well as readers because at least some advertisers do not want to use vehicles that might compromise their own reputations. If the integrity of the carrier of the message is suspect, so may be the message and its sponsor. That's why you don't see many upright advertisers in marginal magazines or broadcast vehicles.

Meanwhile, the relentless march of advertising into editorial space continues. The *Wall Street Journal*, one of the most well-respected newspapers in the world, opened its front page to advertising in the fall of 2006. About the same time, the *New York Times* began selling ads on the front page of its business section and on the front of its Sunday Metro section.[30]

And for one of the first times ever, a mass consumer magazine—Hearst's *Shop Etc.*—began selling its cover to advertisers in July 2006, as did celebrity magazine *OK!* The publisher of *OK!* commented at the time, "We want to have integrity, but we also want to have a point of difference, to say that we will work very hard for [advertisers'] business without confusing or misleading our readers."[31]

Good luck with that.

The Real and Questionable Potential of the Net

When the dot-com boom whimpered away, the value of using the Internet as a relationship marketing tool was discounted in excess, just as its value had been celebrated in excess. But when the economy adjusted, marketers began to discover even more creative ways to engage visitors with a brand via online tools.

Now that marketers of all types are finding their online sea legs, buyers are subjected to spamming, e-mail harvesting (the unauthorized collection of e-mails), e-mailing lists that cannot be opted out of, phishing (tricking someone into providing private information, usually by claiming to be their legitimate product/service provider), and a myriad of criminally fraudulent behavior that has only been multiplied by the Internet's scope and influence.

As online advertising spending spirals upward to a projected level of $25.9 billion by 2011, new kinds of brokers have emerged, called "wranglers," who attract large numbers of key target members to an online happening, then open the door to advertisers.[32] Examples include Action Media's custom-car show called Hot Import Nights, the gaming network Xfire, various mega-blogs, and RSS—real simple syndication that alerts users as content is updated.

What users don't see when they get there is traditional advertising. Instead, messages are woven through the content in a sort of digital version of product placement. Users can drop out of the experience at any time, so those who stay tend to be loyal to the content.[33]

Another potential online gold mine is Internet video, which has been projected to become a $1.5 billion market by the end of this decade.[34] With a stampede heading to online from traditional media, it might not be long before online video competes head-on with some enormous rivals. The cost of production is low, the time to market is short and the attention of the viewer is believed to be far higher than more common forms of advertising.

Advertisers like GM, Unilever, and American Express are moving fast to meet the younger buyers where they now live. In fact, online video advertising is growing faster than what is ironically being called "traditional online advertising," which grew by one-third to $12.9 billion in sales in 2005. And most important of all, these online videos are not subject to the corrosive growth of digital video recorders that threaten to undermine viewership of all but the most entertaining television commercials.[35]

Here again is a new channel that will likely explode in another couple of years. The videos will probably be the victim of a paradox: They will be the best place to promote online, and the best place to find those who prefer not to be marketed at. Because that combination of factors is likely to tempt marketers to do what they shouldn't, now would be the perfect time for participating advertis-

◆ What If? ◆

What if you polled customers about how honest they thought your marketing communications are? What if you compensated marketing team members based on the results of that survey? What if you proposed to your management that examples of questionable marketing or sales or product development actions be reviewed in the executive committee meeting (without attributing blame to any individual, of course)? What if you created an awards program that honored the individual who most contributed to practical integrity in the marketing department each year? What if the prize was worth, say, $5,000, just to make sure everyone was paying attention?

What if you were called before a congressional committee in a nationally televised hearing to discuss your company's marketing communications programs? Would it be a good career moment, or a bad day?

ers to come together and decide what represents legitimate online promotion and what should be avoided.

For instance, should online video product placement be accompanied by guidelines about when advertisers should reveal that they are buying that placement? Or, would it make sense for advertisers to explain via advertorials why online product placement makes valuable suggestions for people to consider purchasing, in order to prevent future backlash by those who feel they are being used?

Various online marketing channels may be destined to be the most powerful vehicles ever conceived. Better to be clear that practical integrity is being planned and practiced now, rather than see the power of the channel be used as an excuse to muzzle marketers in the near future.

The Slow Fade-Out of Tolerance

Outside of the United States, honesty and fair play in marketing communications have often been legislated, and more or less achieved. In Japan and Sweden, in particular, strong laws and relentless pursuit of offenders have made advertising and other channels considerably more straightforward and easy to navigate. Violators are dealt with harshly and some are treated as criminals.

That day may yet dawn on American shores, and those who don't believe it need only remember that executives were rarely prosecuted for financial malfeasance just a decade ago.

What you have read in this chapter may appear to be a litany of isolated examples. It is not. Communications deception—blatant and subtle, egregious and minor—can be found in virtually every consumer and business-to-business industry. Nor is it confined to small, deviant organizations that don't make much of an impact on the marketplace. Large, often market-leading companies are stretching integrity issues everyday, including some that have demonstrated their integrity in many other venues.

The standards are changing, the customers are less tolerant, and the regulators are more aggressive than ever. It's time to reconsider communications integrity as the default position of your marketing programs. If it isn't, it should be.

*　　　*　　　*

The Communications Strategy: Promoting Honestly, Not Just Legally

The 2006 Hewlett-Packard boardroom debacle, in which the private lives of reporters and board members were reportedly violated, was entirely avoidable. The former U.S. federal prosecutor, who was hired by HP CEO Mark Hurd to investigate the matter, struck to the heart of the matter when he told the *New York Times*, "[Investigating the board] is not the test, it is the given. You have to ask what is appropriate and what is ethical."[36]

Marketing communications will always be subject to skepticism, doubt, and occasional outrage, just because it is a company's most visible selling channel and thus carries its most explicit sales messages. Unfortunately, marketing communication instruments are just too strong for some less-than-scrupulous practitioners to resist, and just too easy for them to stretch where they shouldn't go.

But there are some strategies that a company can employ to maintain successful momentum *and* maintain the kind of integrity that will benefit the company in the long-term. In general, you might want to assume that every fact and every implication will be subject to an audit by customers and/or someone who has no vested interest in anything but learning the unvarnished truth. Or, as one corporate policy puts it, assume that everything you produce will be on tomorrow's front page.

Some specific recommendations:

1. *Check in frequently with your internal and external customers to ensure that they are hearing what you are saying.* This should be standard practice for all marketing programs, but it's especially helpful in determining whether your credibility is suffering because your marketing communications claims are in doubt. That could be crippling when

you consider the people who are inheriting the bulk of the buying power in the United States.

The twenty-something segments known variously as Gen Y, the Millennials, and "Generation ®" may be harbingers of the marketplace to come. Now totaling about 100 million buyers in the United States alone and representing at least $175 billion in buying power, these young adults are commercial old souls who are bone-weary of hype and attempts to wedge brands into their lives.

Gen Yers expect marketing messages to be customized, engaging, and simple enough to be understood while multitasking.[37] One advertising campaign that typified this approach was an Arizona Jeans brand commercial that used teens mocking other ads that try to sound like them. The tagline: "Just show me the jeans."[38]

One way to begin is to periodically poll the younger members of your marketing team to see if they themselves believe in the authenticity of the marketing claims they are helping to propagate.

Second, be sure to incorporate message credibility questions in your awareness and attitude research. For example: "Do you believe all you read and hear about this brand? If so, why? If not, why not?" Questions that specifically home in on honesty usually give customers an opportunity to be candid about what they believe about a brand or company. And the respondent base should be large enough to allow cross-tabbing against young adult segments without slicing the pie so thin that the numbers are no longer projectible.

Some industries will attract more negativity in research responses than actually exists, because it's tough to pass up the chance to slam marketers. But good researchers will be able to craft cross-questioning that gets at genuine beliefs.

Of course, if either of these measures uncovers significant levels of distrust, the company should proactively address them. Letting them fester would result in a decline in net brand equity.

2. *Reveal to customers as much as you want them to reveal to you.* Transparency has become the most frequently mentioned antidote to the corporate truth-stretching that we've all been reading about, and that likely applies to marketing. As the unconventional advertising vehicles grow in importance, marketers have an increased obligation to let their audiences know who or what is behind the effort.

If a buzz campaign is launched, be up-front about who is the sponsor. If a spokesperson PR program is in the cards, make sure the spokesperson clearly explains what company is paying them to endorse a brand.

These disclosures may sound like they will damage the persuasiveness of the messaging, but they will more likely enhance its credibility. In a 2005 study by Northeastern University, more than 75 percent of the respondents said that revealing the sponsor of a buzz campaign was a "nonissue," and the rate that the message was passed along was 70 percent *higher* than in the nondisclosed cases.[39]

It is a trademark—not just a guideline—of such companies as Trader Joe's, Kiehl's, Patagonia, Timberland, and Herman Miller to be completely candid with their customers about what they can and cannot do. Those companies and others like them would rather not mount marketing communications of any kind if it meant holding back information that their customers need to make a decision.

And now, there are even more reasons for other companies to do the same.

3. *Use your integrity (with humility) as a competitive advantage.* Marketing communications with practical integrity can be used as a strong competitive advantage, although some companies prefer not to make use of it. Nevertheless, in an age when integrity is at a premium for many consumers, being straightforward about how straightforwardly you market could accomplish several things.

First, consider reassuring customers that their trust is well founded, but without saying "you can trust us." If you dig deep enough into the websites of such companies as Trader Joe's or Whole Foods, you'll find some statements about the integrity of their organizations, but that is not how most of their customers find out about that integrity. They see it in the quality of the food that never falters, in the honesty of the promotions, and in the candid way that they talk about their food on their websites.

It may be helpful to modestly point out the things you do to benefit the customer, possibly as a way of saying that it's your way of showing appreciation for their business. Or, you could invite customers to help you choose one or more of your staff who exemplify the integrity you try to demonstrate in everything the brand or company does.

Second, you might want to separate yourself from your competition by regularly announcing innovative communications that demonstrate your transparency. That could include discussing how the components or ingredients of your products are selected, or some "backroom" stories about how you go about improving a particular service.

One of the marketing communications that further reinforced Patagonia's integrity reputation was an essay in its Spring 2006 catalog. The essay thanked other companies—including some of its direct competitors—for joining Patagonia in an important industry improvement: "We tip our hat to the following companies who now use varying amounts of organically grown cotton in their clothing: Hanna Andersson, Marks & Spencer, Mountain Equipment Co-op, Nike, Nordstrom, Norm Thompson, Prada, Stewart-Brown, and Timberland."[40]

Fielding the right kind of communications may also draw positive awareness from prospects that otherwise might not have been tempted to learn more about your brand. In 2005, GE launched its "Ecomagination" initiative and is funding it to the tune of $1.5 billion a year. The program to commercialize environment-saving programs is projected to create $20 billion in revenue from Ecomagination projects by 2010.

The company has put major marketing communications behind the program and, like BP's Beyond Petroleum positioning, it may very well provide GE with additional competitive advantage against its less future-leaning rivals.[41]

Finally, you might want to establish your company as a resource for accurate and credible information within your industry. This kind of role requires a lot of work to build and maintain, but if customers and others can count on your brand or company for objective information, they will surely be more likely to trust you when you have something to sell.

4. *Try telling the unvarnished truth, then try again.* Marketers are not generally paid to tell everything they know about their product, service, or company, but only the positive things. There's certainly nothing wrong with being an advocate, as long as advocacy doesn't lead you to create inaccurate or misleading information.

   Researchers from two universities in Canada gave subjects marketing material with advertising claims, then later provided them with credible evidence that the claims were, in fact, highly deceptive. The result was that the subjects became not only "defensive" (skeptical) about the first set of claims, they subsequently became defensive about additional claims for another product altogether. In other words, deceptive marketing can create long-term skepticism on top of onetime doubt.[42]

Herman Miller was about to introduce its revolutionary Aeron chair in 2002. The chair was hailed as a breakthrough by, among others, *Los Angeles Times* writer Preston Lerner, who reported that the industry was transformed by the introduction of the Aeron, "which set new standards for ergonomic efficiency while emerging as an I'm-so-cool icon . . . it forever changed the landscape of the modern office."[43]

As part of the launch marketing, someone in the company suggested referring to Herman Miller as the "world's leader in cross-performance work chairs." The marketing communications department pushed back and said that the phrase was basically meaningless (i.e., a weasel) and it didn't add any value to their customers' evaluation of needs. Max DePree, the CEO at the time, commented wryly that "the truth is a real constraint." The truth DePree was talking about included making claims that meant something, not that were just nice sounding. The line was neatly shelved in the round file.[44]

5. *Avoid the turn-offs.* You may think you are working with marketing communications tools, but those "tools" may be nothing short of weapons. In the time it takes to play a sponsored videogame, your marketing communications decisions can make your day or unmake a lot of good work. Because of its visibility and potential impact, marketing communications is one area where it is particularly critical that marketers avoid any outbreaks of "hoof-in-mouth" gaffes, or overzealous spending. Some no-no's to watch out for:

❑ *Killing Your Brand Softly.* The little hedges, weasels, puffery and various forms of exaggeration are probably harmless enough on a onetime basis. But sooner or later, someone will notice if what you promise in marketing communications does not match what they experience as a user.
   Marketing Communications Implications to Consider: As other brands begin to raise their credibility standards, yours could be left in the cold. Get tough on the accuracy of your claims before your most loyal customers question their trust in you.

❏ *Letting Our Expert Out There Tell Them How Great This Thing Is.* It's becoming clear how relative the term "expert" is, and what the new rules are for sending them forth to tell your story. The general public is gradually wising up about how many of the "experts" of the world are working for the companies they are recommending. All other things being equal, a good product or service will succeed in the marketplace. No need to make it tougher, though, by connecting its brand to questionable spokespersons.

> ***Credibility Implication to Consider:*** In light of all the unpleasant revelations in recent years about paid spokespersons, consider adopting four hard and fast rules: 1) pick your spokespeople the way you pick your doctor, with just as much scrutiny about qualifications; 2) when it comes to identifying the relationship between the company and spokesperson: disclose; 3) disclose; and 4) disclose.

❏ *Marketing to Those Who Don't Understand That You're Marketing to Them.* Veterans of PTA and school board meetings know the battle cry: "You can do what you want to me, but don't try it with my kid!" Marketers who are actively soliciting business from younger children and anyone else who is not capable of fully understanding the implications of marketing are rolling enormous dice with their brands and their companies.

You didn't read it here first, but you are reading it again: given the skeptical world that we now live in, such marketing will inevitably be lassoed to the ground by government intervention, customer anger, public outcry, or all of the above.

The Kaiser Family Foundation reported in a 2006 study that 38 percent of food-oriented websites encourage children to purchase products, that 85 percent of leading food brands that employ TV advertising also used branded websites directed at children, but that only 18 percent of such websites clearly explain that they are advertising. Just as predictably, the report's release was followed by a gaggle of politicians who decried the data and the trends.[45]

> ***Marketing Communications Implications to Consider:*** The phrase "playing with fire" does not do

justice to the dangers that lie ahead for marketers who are still free to market to the very young or otherwise gullible, but whose freedoms may soon be curtailed with unreasonable force. Better to market with self-imposed constraints than to be constrained by forces that could wreak more havoc than any competitor.

*　　　*　　　*

A Summary and a Few Questions

Violators of marketing integrity will always be with us, but the bolder they get the more likely they will attract all the wrong kinds of attention to the industry in general. Too many of us in marketing are unnecessarily self-inflicting wounds.

It's now becoming more urgent to reassess the credibility of our marketing as new and very exciting communications vehicles are coming to the fore. The suggestion that we market honestly, not just legally, requires that marketers stay ahead of trouble by policing ourselves before others do it for us.

Here are a few questions to consider in the meantime:

1. Do you know what your customers consider truthful and untruthful in your industry? Have you found out what customers and prospects are most concerned about in terms of honesty and fair play? If not, you may be unnecessarily adding to your future marketing challenges.
2. Has your brand or company ever harmed its net brand equity by intentionally or inadvertently deceiving your customers with your marketing communications? Did you thoroughly analyze the incident(s)? Do you understand what happened, why it happened, and what the full short-term and long-term consequences were?
3. Does your company use buzz or stealth marketing responsibly? The term "responsibly" is certainly not very definitive in this new channel, but if you do your research you will discover how the public in general, and your customers in particular, believe that term should be defined. (See Appendix C for the Word of Mouth Marketing Association Code of Ethics.)
4. What protocol do you have in place to detect and stop deceiving marketing communications before they get out the door? The standard legal checks are a good start, but rarely the final say. You might

consider setting up a rotating panel of customers and prospects to see what they believe are honest communications, and what might be less so.

5. Do your communications programs follow both the letter and the spirit of applicable laws? Now this *is* one for the attorneys, but be certain that they have been given carte blanche to be very candid, and encouraged to take an issue up the command chain if they think it risks problems in the marketplace. The spirit of the law is technically a legal term, but it perhaps should best be interpreted by those who are being asked to buy the product or service. Buyers may not know the letter of the law, but they likely have a good feel for its intent.

CHAPTER 7

Be There When They Want You There

In Their Mind, Not in Their Face

The "Bay to Breakers" is the longest consecutively staged footrace in the world. First organized in 1912 to help cheer up San Franciscans struggling to rebuild after the 1906 quake and fire, the 12K event stretches from the shores of San Francisco Bay to Ocean Beach. As many as 125,000 men, women, and children have been known to run the race, many of them dressed as animals, buildings, and insects. . .or not dressed in anything at all.

A tradition of the day is a pre-race "tortilla toss," where thousands of tortillas are flung like Frisbees and fill the air above the heads of the runners as they wait to start the race.

So it usually happens like this: You warm up your long muscles in the chilly morning air, your heart rate speeds up in anticipation of the starting gun, you psych yourself up to tackle the long Hayes Street Hill . . . and then you're hit in the face with a cold tortilla that's stamped with an ad promising a 15 percent discount from a local massage parlor.

This Bridge Is Sponsored By . . .

It's likely that the vast majority of today's marketing audiences don't care to be an audience as often as marketers would like. That's a nice way of saying that it's time to find a better way to market to buyers than battering them until they can't get out of the way. Integrity among nations and individuals takes many forms, not the least of which involves respecting everyone's right to live without fear of invasion—that is, invasion by force or forceful invasion of privacy.

Estimates vary widely about the extent to which we all are exposed to commercial messaging. In 2005, a reporter for the UK newspaper *Guardian* strapped on a pair of glasses equipped with a tiny camera, and reported that he was "exposed" to 250 commercial messages in his typical London commute over the space of 45 minutes. Assuming a similar return home and many exposures during the day and evening, it's easy to see why the number that is most frequently quoted is 3,000 to 3,500 messages every 24 hours. (By the way, the reporter claimed to be able to remember only one brand out of the 250 he was exposed to.[1])

Whatever the number is, the commercialism that used to seep into our lives is now way above flood stage. A few over-the-top examples that are becoming more commonplace:

- ❏ *Headvertise*, an outfit out of Providence, Rhode Island, pays college students $150 to wear temporary decals on their foreheads for a week. Sometimes called "skinadvertising," you can also commission a grilled cheese sandwich bearing an image of the advertiser's choice."[2]

- ❏ In an attempt to earn much-needed revenue, U.S. airlines are now using tray tables, napkins, ticket jackets, seat-back cards, boarding passes, and even air sickness bags to carry advertising that pops up with meals and pops out with clear air turbulence.[3]

- ❏ In France, Siemens converted the classic Parisian bistro table into an advertising platform for a cell phone introduction in 2000. Oblivious to criticism from all quarters, the media company's representative claimed he saw only potential, saying, "There are 62,000 cafes in France. That gives us a great opportunity."[4]

- ❏ In the summer of 2006, the Walt Disney Company advertised its "Little Einstein" DVDs on the paper liners used in pediatricians' examining rooms.[5]

- ❏ In the summer of 2006, cell phone leaders Verizon and Sprint said they would begin testing commercials on their cell phones that might force users to watch messages for up to ten seconds before their calls would be put through.[6]

- ❏ In July 2006, the board of directors of the Golden Gate Bridge, Highway, and Transportation District voted to explore sponsorships for the world's most famous bridge. Said board member Al Boro, "People use our bridge all the time for advertising. It's about time we find a way to capitalize on our own asset."[7]

Then there's sports. Every major professional sports facility in the United States carries a sponsor's name, as do innumerable sports tournaments, with the notable exception of golf's Masters Tournament. But the other golf tournaments make up for it with mellifluous-sounding events like the Cialis Western Open, the Michelob Ultra Open, and the Crestor Charity Challenge.[8] Moving over to the track, we have The Kentucky Derby presented by Yum, and NASCAR presented by Craftsman. The logos on NASCAR driver uniforms are so dense that barely an inch of naked fabric can be found. Every college bowl game is presented by some brand, and let's not forget the Tim Weber Air Shows brought to you by Geico.

In one of the few times that consumers actually pushed back, purist baseball fans demanded that Major League Baseball pull out of an announced deal in the summer of 2004 with Sony Pictures. The plan had been to paste "Spider-Man 2" ads on the bases to promote the movie's upcoming release.[9] (The promoters didn't seem to be concerned that Spidey's face would be smashed mercilessly by fleeting cleats.)

In Radio, Less May Be More

Some radio stations have begun to run less advertising and have consequently attracted more listeners. The bold move was prompted by a May 2005 Arbitron and Edison Media Research study, which reported that 47 percent of listeners claimed they would listen "a lot more" to a station if there were fewer commercials, and that 44 percent said they would listen more if the commercials were shorter.[10]

Stations in the top ten U.S. markets pulled back their commercial time by nearly 8 percent in December 2005 and began raising advertising rates as audience levels increased. Clear Channel landed a first-quarter profit of $96.8 million in 2006, doubling its first-quarter profit from 2005. Advertisers are happy as well, according to the company.[11]

Nearly one-fourth of research respondents said that they were aware of stations that had fewer commercials and shorter commercial breaks. And the number of those thinking that radio has more commercials than in the past declined significantly. The jury's not in yet on this idea, but stay tuned.

We may be seeing the dawning of an era where a media industry actually begins believing that less is more. On the other hand, Clear Channel's outdoor advertising division announced in September 2006 that they were planning to install table-top ads in up to 200 malls by the end of 2007. So much for reducing clutter.[12]

Product Plots

Media buying company Magna Global estimates that there will be more than 25 million U.S. households with a digital video recorder (DVR) by 2008.[13] A study by media agency MindShare found that 79 percent of consumers purchased DVRs in order to skip commercials, and research by TiVo and Starcom Worldwide confirmed that more than 70 percent of TiVo owners did, in fact, skip commercials.[14]

In 2006, KFC aired a TV commercial that included an embedded message requiring a DVR to slow it down in order for viewers to read about a special promotional offer. The use of "branded tags"— logos that pop up when commercials are fast-forwarded— are also becoming more common.[15]

As advertisers lose large chunks of their audiences to online video games, mobile phone mania, and mega-blogs, they have moved full speed to embed their messages in places formerly reserved for a plot.

Television product placement represented as much as $2.5 billion in revenue in 2005, and it was expected to increase by 15 percent a year for all media through 2009.[16] Perhaps the most dramatic placement to date has been Oprah's 2004 give-away of Pontiacs to each member of her entire theater audience, costing GM 276 cars and obtaining in return what the placement organizer claimed was at least $70 million in publicity.[17]

It's been argued that TV product placement is no more intrusive than the wholesale sponsorship of radio and early television shows by Texaco, Procter & Gamble, and Philip Morris. The difference is that the product placement is generally not all that obvious—which is the whole idea—and has led critics to cry "foul" because viewers don't know they are being "manipulated" into watching a commercial event in the middle of something that is supposed to be commercial-free (a valid point if there were any aspect of our lives that was still commercial-free).

Movies are the ideal venue for product placement. There are on average about 110 minutes of plot and characterizations to plop a product into. Virtually all of the audience will sit through the entire length of the movie—with tickets at nine or ten dollars a pop, who's going to leave?—and they will be every bit as mesmerized as they are with any computer game or TV show. Even better, there are no distractions to prevent them from seeing the commercial exposures. Big-time actors happily provide virtual endorsements. What's not to like, if you don't include the audiences?

We've Been Had

In their efforts to reach consumers whether or not they want to be reached, advertisers are creating new commercial environments that are less blatantly commercial but significantly more immersive. For example, Procter & Gamble produced 90-second sitcom "episodes" on *Nick at Night* supporting their Febreze line of fabric care products, and Ford has created 90-minute theatrical films to promote the Lincoln Zephyr and Mercury Milan. *The Fairway Gourmet*, a series on purportedly commercial-free PBS, is set in the resorts of Hawaii and paid for entirely by the Hawaii Visitors & Convention Bureau.[18]

But the big money may yet turn out to be in the video gaming business. Forrester Research estimates that there are game users within 100 million households, representing more than $10 billion in sales, well above movie house revenue. Brand ad placement spending is projected by Nielsen to move from $75 million in 2005 to $1 billion in 2010.[19]

More than half of the respondents in a 2006 Yankelovich study said that advertising is "out of control." It may be time to ask: Is it really helpful for a brand to squeeze itself into every nook and cranny of buyers' lives just because they can? Are such brands making themselves more attractive, or just more irritating? Or, as *Business Week* has put it, "Push the brand too much, and viewers could resist the hard sell."[20]

In fact, ultimately it may be over-branded marketers who are the ones that have been had.

Brought to You by the People Who Brought This to You

When NBC announced its fall lineup for the 2005-06 season they pulled out all the stops. The previous year the network had been fourth out of the four major networks in delivering the valuable 18-to-49-year-old viewers that advertisers covet most highly, despite finishing first the year before that. Such are the ups and downs of network fortunes.

So, NBC launched a multimedia campaign in July 2005, which included meticulously embedded beauty shots of two new Mazda models in the promotions that were officially dubbed "NBC First Look Presented by

Mazda." The promotions were included in television commercials, a short film run before movies in theaters, a dedicated website, and CD-ROMs distributed to certain subscribers of Time-Warner's *Entertainment Weekly* and *People* magazines. Some of the pilot episodes for several new series were specifically re-shot to incorporate Mazdas into scenes with the stars, or just into incidental street scenes. The Mazda/NBC team also planned to hand out up to 2.5 million CDs using "street teams" in selected U.S. markets to generate buzz about the new Mazda models and the upcoming NBC season.

From the advertiser's point of view, the purpose of the program was to avoid the escalating costs of in-programming product placement. The other purpose was to make it nearly impossible for viewers to escape notice of who sponsored the programming (or, in this case, programming to come).[21]

Be Seen but Be Liked

In the buyer's world that lies ahead, it will be more important than ever for brands to not only be relevant and respected, but be as appealing as possible. The more that aggressive marketers feel they have to drive brands into buyers' lives, the more important it will be for them to make those brands as likeable as possible.

The only thing more difficult to resist than something irresistible is something that is also irresistible to everyone you know. When brands become more appealing, barriers drop, skeptics warm, and persuasion has a fighting chance. That can be a negative if the buyer is just being manipulated, but helpful to both marketer and the audiences if the company provides genuine offers and promises it intends to keep.

Those that we are most willing to follow—the leaders, the entertainers, the leading brands—all have to be likable in our eyes or we tend to pass them by; life is just too short and the list of options too long to put up with something that is less than likeable.

We go out of our way to patronize companies that seem to actually like the people who are their customers, such as Southwest Airlines, Trader Joe's, and Orchard Supply Hardware. A desire to be liked also prompts a good many companies to redirect their marketing to be more humorous (AFLAC), more light-hearted (MetLife's Snoopy spokesbeagle), more warm (United Airlines), and more human (IBM).

In the ideal, the brand delivers the whole package, both exceptional performance and an appealing personality that is based in genuine authenticity. A MINI

Cooper, for example, gushes all kinds of emotional benefits that make owning one more exhilarating than owning an ordinary vehicle. Some owners like them so much they name them, dress up their interiors, and talk to them as if they will talk back.

A Conversation

"So, I'm in my garage."

"This is Saturday?"

"Right, Saturday morning. And I'm trying to find my chain saw . . ."

"I haven't seen my chain saw in four years."

". . . and I hear this bloodcurdling scream, like somebody has been stabbed or something."

"This kind of thing never happens to me on Saturdays."

". . . and I run out front and it's my next-door neighbor's wife."

"She's been STABBED?"

"She sounds like she's been stabbed. But she's incredibly happy."

"Your next-door neighbor's wife has been stabbed but she's really . . ."

"Can I get through this, please? It turns out that my neighbor has surprised his wife with a brand new MINI Cooper."

"No kidding."

"Racing green, wrapped in a big red bow, for her birthday."

"This guy is setting a bad precedent."

"So I go out and congratulate her and for the next 25 minutes she tells me how much she is in love with this MINI, and all the while she's fondling it."

"Are we still talking about the car?"

"It was like . . . anthropomorphic."

"I used to feel that way about my chain saw."

Leave Them Liking You

One of the most likeable brands in America is actually two brands. Not that many years ago Budweiser was being eclipsed by more contemporary brands. Bud might have still been the king of beers, but many of its core constituents seemed to be drinking it out of habit. At one point its sibling, Bud Light, looked like a reaction to the pioneering Miller Lite instead of a strong brand on its own.

Then, in the mid-1990s, the Busch family decided to shake things up and prodded their ad agencies to create such memorable ad campaigns as the "Bud-

◆ What If? ◆

What if you established a "clutter" panel of customers and prospects that were interviewed regularly and asked to comment on the commercial clutter in their lives? What if you reevaluated your marketing communications programs specifically with an eye to reducing the invasiveness of the programs without reducing their total impact? What if you designed some research to see if doing so—and announcing that you were doing so—would have a positive impact on how customers and prospects viewed your company or brand? What if you approached your trade association with the idea of working with other groups to reduce, or at least stabilize, the amount of commercial clutter your industry is injecting into people's lives?

What if every variation of every form of marketing communications that you and your marketing colleagues unleashed on customers and prospects each day were exposed to you and your family every evening of every day it ran? Would you still have a family after the first week?

y-ser" frogs and "Whassup?" among many others, which garnered worldwide attention, lots of advertising awards, and reportedly spurred extraordinary increases in brand awareness, familiarity, and likeability.

The likeability of the advertising made the brands the talk of taverns and football parties. Today, Budweiser and Bud Light are among the most popular beers in the world, due in no small part to the likeability of their brands.[22]

Avis is another brand that is consistently likeable because its forty-year-old mantra of "We try harder" has the irresistible allure of the underdog. Avis has also created a consistently pleasant customer experience by obsessively analyzing every facet of the rental car experience and making it as easy as possible for the customer. In so doing, the brand has reinforced that its people do, in fact, try harder. Just as importantly, the people of Avis also project an identity that is inherently more likeable than category leader Hertz.

According to the loyalty measurement firm Brand Keys, Avis has surpassed Hertz in loyalty in many key U.S. markets, and outscored Hertz in the J.D. Power satisfaction studies. It's tough to beat: Great service wrapped in a likeable brand.[23]

Of course, the success of the Budweiser brands and Avis is due to many factors, but a likeable brand makes everything else work better. Brands must be seen to be sold, but they also have to be appealing when they're seen.

Creatively Presented Clutter

Target Stores used a clever hide-and-seek game with the Olympics logo police during the 2006 Winter Olympics in Turin. They managed to establish a presence at the Games, even though they had no plans to do business in Europe anytime soon and they were not an official sponsor (although they did sponsor several U.S. Olympians).

Using the sometimes controversial Olympics ambush marketing approach first perfected by Nike in the 1996 Atlanta games, Target wrapped their target logo around seven of the nine trains on the Bardonecchia line that were used to transport media and spectators to the venues. The stunt prompted European riders to spontaneously chant "Target! Target!" when they saw the trains approaching, even though most of them had no idea what Target was. [24]

Early in its corporate life, Virgin Atlantic battled to survive against the behemoth British Airways. Virgin positioned its brand as the likeable underdog that made people smile, pitted against the bullying giant that had owned the UK skies. Using advertising lines like "You never forget your first time," "Virgin, seeks travel companion(s)," and "Hello, Gorgeous," Richard Branson's upstart has become almost irresistibly likeable, particularly compared to what was then a stodgier British Air.

JetBlue is a brand that is doing everything possible to keep the likable cachet of a smallish underdog even as it seeks to grow into a big dog. While the company continues to use traditional media to get its message across, it is also reaching out with unexpected and more welcomed methods of telling the brand story.

Under a campaign banner called "Sincerely, JetBlue," the brand employed what's called "user-generated content." This included encouraging consumers to create their own JetBlue advertising, "story booths" where customers can record memories of their flights, and placing mini-journals on flights for passengers to jot down their thoughts about their flight experiences.[25]

There's clutter, and there's creative clutter. The latter may produce less resentment and more likeability. That could be the difference between irritated versus entertained customers.

*   *   *

The Communications Channel Strategy: Be There When They Want You There

Likeability has played a backseat role for too long in marketing. In the next marketing planning cycle, address the issue head-on, and watch the positive impact it has on business. Some specific suggestions:

1. Reconsider Your Brand's Likeability

Consider taking some preliminary steps to understand your brand's likeability:

❏ If the likeability of your brand is not being thoroughly explored in your ongoing tracking studies, consider conducting a stand-alone study that will help gauge the importance of likeability to drivers of choice in your industry, and the degree to which your brand has achieved what other brands have achieved in this important area. If you do not currently run tracking studies, this is a good opportunity to start, with a special focus on likeability.

❏ With those results in hand, conduct an audit of your current brand contacts (i.e., wherever the brand comes in contact with any constituencies), and determine where the brand's appeal could be enhanced.

❏ If likeability appears to be an important factor in purchases, consider re-casting your brand to put greater emphasis on its personality. If respondents don't admit to its importance in their decision making, have your research team devise indirect measuring devices to double-check the initial findings. For example, consider photo-sorting or anthropomorphic scenarios ("If the brand were a movie star . . .") that might get at buyers' actual need for likeability.

2. Learn from the Less-than-Likeable

Over the course of many workshops, this author has asked corporate audiences in Europe, South America, North America, Asia, and India the following question: "What do you think is the Microsoft 'brand vision'?" (i.e., what the brand hopes to become). Almost without exception, every group answered the same way: to take over the world. Nobody likes a bully and Microsoft's dominance and previous arrogant actions have reinforced that very image. This, despite the fact that founder Bill Gates and his wife were named "co-people of the year" by *Time* magazine in 2005 for their selfless giving of their time and financial contributions toward solving the world's health crises.

A few years ago it would have been unthinkable to consider Coca-Cola a brand anyone might dislike. One of the world's premier beverages and the most valuable brand in the world, Coke is enjoyed by tens, if not hundreds, of millions of people around the world. But the company has also made tough situations even tougher in recent years, such as during the 1999 recall and boycott of the brand's products in Belgium and elsewhere in Europe, when Coca-Cola headquarters fanned a flame by issuing a statement that there was no threat to public safety. (If it had been your child in the bathroom vomiting throughout the night, you would not have found that to be a very satisfying response.) The recall cost the company $66 million and contributed, at least to some small degree, to the eventual ouster of CEO Douglas Ivester.

Coca-Cola is also one of the targets of activist groups upset that sugared soft drinks are too readily available on elementary, middle school, and high school campuses. The uproar has led to cutbacks by all soft drink makers in their distribution of full-sugar beverages.

Coca-Cola is still the most valuable brand in the world and easily the best known branded beverage. But simply because a brand is strong does not mean it is invincible, especially if it is a beverage brand that finds itself entangled in matters that do not contribute to its likeability.

3. Plan for a Likeability Crisis
Then there are the love-me-hate-me brands that have something for everyone. Southwest Airlines is one of the most admired U.S. companies, but you'd never guess it when you hear the grumbling from businesspeople who have to pile into the planes without seat reservations. Martha Stewart attracts a significant percentage of the population while turning off others, some of whom were nothing short of gleeful to see Martha jailed for lying to prosecutors. Wal-Mart has been excoriated in small towns everywhere as purveyors of culture-cide and oppressors of the working downtrodden. Yet, it's still not easy on a Saturday morning to find a spot in a Wal-Mart parking lot.

The lessons from these and other companies are clear and suggest several actions:

❑ *Build your brand's likeability equity at every opportunity.* Even if your brand is designed for serious industries like health care or technology, every brand needs to be liked if it hopes to capture the emotional commitment of customers. In fact, it is such industries that most often need a likeable strain of awareness. Consider how your brand can achieve likeability within the greater context of your business.

The brand teams at M&M and Oreos plan their marketing to achieve that goal, as do their counterparts at McDonald's and Chili's. It's always about the product first, but the job of the product and the people who bring it to customers is made a whole lot easier when their brand is genuinely liked by one and all.[26]

❑ *Assume that the day will come when you will have to spend that equity, and plan carefully for that day.* Your goal should be to have established a brand that is so well liked that it is shatter-proof, even in difficult times.

Bank of America, Compaq, and Denny's have all fought through tough financial or business situations and all have fully recovered. Their customers and their potential customers are willing to forgive and forget if the company looks like it is trying to regain the respect and the likeability it formerly enjoyed.

❑ *Design future marketing programs with likeability as a major strategic goal.* Likeability can lead to stronger familiarity and affinity, but it's not likely to happen by serendipity. A brand must plan to be liked by methodically devising strategies that make it appealing, if not irresistible, to the right people.

4. Be There When They Want You There

Traditional marketing communications is being de-toothed, as chronicled in excruciating detail in books about the death of advertising, the impotency of direct mail, and the rise of anything that doesn't look like traditional marketing. In such a world, it is imperative that brands determine when and where their customers like to be contacted and do everything possible to be there when they want you there. That means that intrusiveness is not always useful, and can often be counterproductive. Be seen and heard, but not when your audience wants you to be out of sight.

You might consider auditing and assessing the degree to which the brand's marketing programs are seen as intrusive or welcomed into buyers' lives. Develop an "intrusion rating" for the various elements of the marketing program. Establish specific goals for how intrusive the brand should appear, and how its likeability can be used to defuse that resistance, making it more welcome in the eyes of the buyer. This approach can then be applied to specific media channels.

Throughout the Internet, we now see companies offering an "opt-out" option to customers and prospects. That approach is a direct result of the Net's history, which is based on providing alternatives to users, rather than mandatory directions. That same spirit can be equally liberating for traditional marketing situations, as more buyers want the option to opt out.

5. Choose Channels by Impact and Appeal

Media optimization has become a way of working for many companies, as they seek to find the most cost-efficient channels for their brand-building efforts. The criteria for such selections are usually based on gross cost, efficiency of delivery, and how well results can be tracked. But there are a number of other factors that could contribute important input to optimization analyses.

For example, consider analyzing the appeal of media channels, and address such questions as:

❏ How loyally do the channel's users return for more? How enthusiastic are they about what and how they learn about various brands through the channels? How credible does the channel appear to be to its regular users?

❏ When the channel is reaching its audiences, how ready are those potential buyers to buy? Again, this might be reported on a calibrated scale, ranging from a channel that buyers consider the best place to look for something to purchase, to channels whose audiences are not particularly thinking of buying, to channels where it is very unlikely that buyers will trust what is marketed there.

❏ Are there other players who have an influence on the viability of a marketing channel? Value-added resellers, for instance, can directly affect the appeal of a channel by encouraging or discouraging its use by customers.

❏ Finally, how likable is the channel itself? If customers find a television network or a newspaper overloaded with advertising and low on entertainment, it can have a chilling effect on its appeal. If bloggers enjoy the experience so much that they actually find the commercial content adds to that experience, the chances for friendly persuasion grow commensurately.

The blogosphere, in particular, offers opportunities for the marketer to selectively participate only where its presence is welcomed. It enables the brand to engage buyers, while not appearing to be an intruder, thus gaining the trust of its potential buyers. General Motors, L'Oreal, and Microsoft have created strong blogging presences that have opened up important dialogues with customers, and even made some friends who would not have been there if they had just been advertised at.

All of these measures could lead to an enhanced media channel selection process that evaluates how well the channel is contributing to the appeal of the brand. By including channel-specific questions in tracking studies or stand-alone surveys, channels can be more holistically assessed for their relevance, tactical strengths, and influence on the interest of the potential buyer. (See Figure 7-1 for an example of optimization factoring.)

Figure 7-1. Example of marketing channel assessments.

Capabilities	General Advertising	PR	Direct Marketing	General Online & Mobile	Blogging	Product Placement
Awareness-Generating Potential	Superior	Moderate-Superior	Narrow	Narrow, but growing	Variable	Poor
Ordering/Trial Potential	Poor-moderate	Poor-moderate	Superior	Moderate, but improving	Limited	Poor
Vehicle Quality Control	Variable	Variable	Variable	Good-Moderate	Limited	Variable
Vehicle Content Control	Good-Superior	Poor-Moderate	Superior	Good–Superior	Limited	Variable
Likelihood of Objectionable Intrusion	Variable	Low	High	Variable	Relatively High	Variable
Ability to Engage & Reinforce Brand Relationship	Variable	Variable	Moderate-Superior	Moderate-Superior	Moderate-High	Limited
Ability to Make Brand More Appealing/Likable	Good-Superior	Highly variable	Variable, but narrow	Variable	Moderate	Variable

6. Avoid the Turn-Offs

What your marketing programs say is critical, but how they say it could be just as critical. Avoid marketing channel turn-offs that lie in wait in the form of innocent-sounding sentiments:

❏ *We have to break through at all costs.* The insidious part of this argument is that it sounds like common sense. There is no point in marketing unless you are going to break through the clutter and be heard. But if "breakthrough" means breaking through whatever buyers use as a shield to protect themselves from marketing bullhorns, there may be a better way.

Marketing Channel Implications: It may be time to turn in your bullhorn for a scalpel. Use the creativity of your people and of your agencies' people to come up with inventive-but-likeable ways to "break through." How can you endear yourself to your buyers with appeal instead of pushing them away with volume? Where would they be *pleasantly* surprised to see you? (Hint: probably not when they're enjoying a commercial-free view, but where they might find it intriguing for your brand to pop-up.)

❑ *We don't need them to like us. We need them to buy from us.* Those two sentiments may be one and the same thing. Likeability is becoming more important by the day as marketers push harder on buyers and buyers grow weary of being the pushees. Certainly the message has to be relevant and credible, but the messenger and the brand also need to be welcomed into the world of the buyer, or the messaging just won't matter.

> *Marketing Channel Implications*: Likeability is the Rodney Dangerfield of brand attributes, but it is about to get a lot more attention and respect in upcoming years. Find out now how likeable your brand is; if it's deficient, find out how to fix it soon. It could make efforts to reach your audience a lot easier than is the case right now.

❑ *I know they keep raising the ante, but we can't afford to be outspent.* Sometimes it seems as if the "share of voice" is more important than the "share of market," particularly in exceptionally competitive markets. There is a natural tendency to match or beat what the major competition spends, just to keep your brand's head above water. But what's most important is not what your competition is spending, but what your "share of impact" is on your audience of choice, and to what degree just burying those people in more gross rating points or product placements is going to help or hurt the cause.

> *Marketing Channel Implications*: Try taking your eye off the competition for a few days and focus on what life is like at the "target's" end of your marcom campaign. Are you not getting through because the audience is on overload? Are you certain that injecting more commercial impressions into their lives is the best way to persuade them that your brand is a better alternative? Will you have to destroy the village to save it? Can you devise a marketing research instrument that will help you understand "share of impact"?

*   *   *

A Summary and a Few Questions

Marketers are taking every opportunity to market at every opportunity. There may be some serious push-back soon or, as in the case of some radio stations, they may find it beneficial to pull back rather than continuing to march deeper into buyers' lives. It is increasingly urgent for marketers to understand exactly how much their brands and their methods are actually liked by their audiences. It may be necessary in the near future to increase the priority of likeability in planning and tactics to ensure that cluttered communications channels don't seriously hinder a marketer's ability to persuade and convert.

To that end, here are a few specific questions to consider:

1. *How big an issue is commercialism and clutter in your particular industry?* Are you sure you have a good handle on the issue, or are you assuming that it is not a big problem because customers have not volunteered their points of view?

2. *How much do you know about what buyers think about overly intrusive commercial messages?* Has any of your past research probed into that subject, and if not, should it? Is it possible that you are losing favorability among your users, or even losing business because of these issues?

3. *Are you picking media channels because they're "hot," without regard for whether their audiences really want to be buried in marketing messages?* In the heat of competitive battles, it may seem prudent to spend all the money you've got wherever it will be used most efficiently. But what looks to be efficient according to audiences delivered may be less so because the audiences are weary of receiving more than they can take in.

4. *Are your marketing efforts more or less appealing than your competitors' based on how intrusive your programs are?* The same instinct that calls for aggressive message placement may also seek more impressions of any kind compared to competition. Consider whether all impressions are equal, and whether it might be preferable to seek greater "quality impressions" than competition, meaning impact that is more welcomed than resisted.

5. *How would your business be affected by trimming your media messages so that they appeared only when they would be welcomed by your customers?* Consider pulling together a "what if" plan that aligned spending around more welcomed marketing channels and messages. It may not be possible in your particular industry but, if it is, such a plan may be worth testing alongside a more conventional approach.

When customers and prospects start to turn down the volume, and conventional media don't seem to be breaking through, put your marketing messages where customers and prospects might actually enjoy hearing and seeing them. It may be the best way to break through in an age when breakthrough marketing is becoming more risky by the minute.

CHAPTER 8

Putting Trust Back into Value

It's Worth More if They Trust You More

You may have read about Roger Penguino. He's the guy who camped out for seven days in blistering heat before an IKEA store opening in Atlanta to get $1,000 in IKEA gift certificates. By the time the store opened there were 2,000 other inhabitants of "IKEA World" sweating in line right behind him.[1]

Every IKEA store opening is a cultural event that changes forever the surrounding population because it attracts people with a passion for genuine value, not just low prices. Those who shop at IKEA just want to get something that is actually worth what they pay for it. Few of them have ever heard of founder Ingvar Kamprad, but they would agree with his view that, "Expensive solutions to any kind of problem are usually the work of mediocrity."[2]

Kamprad has built the largest furniture chain in the world around a set of principles that have added new dimensions to the concept of value. IKEA stores are not just in the business of delivering value, they deliver value that is backed by practical integrity.

Value is good, but value that is buttressed by integrity is better because it guarantees that value is always there even when the price might rise. Building value with an integrity backbone tells the customer that they can expect to get a fair deal for a fair price, and that may be all that's needed to keep a customer for the long haul.

Value Is Everyone's Goal

A product's price is a limiter and filter. It defines for prospective buyers whether something is affordable and discourages those who cannot pay an absolute amount. Or it shoos away those who are suspicious of a price that is so low that it's too good to be true.

Value, on the other hand, is an enabler. In value, customers see the potential for opportunity. A sound value enables benefits to be received within acceptable cost parameters. Value empowers home seekers to become homeowners, car dreamers to become drivers, and clothes horses to join the fashion parade—all without feeling as if they sacrificed more than they got.

Value has more or less become a universal shopping goal. No matter how much money we make we want to get our money's worth. For example, there are approximately 180 million frequent flier accounts in the world, and a good many of those account holders are business executives who could certainly afford to pay for the air travel that they prefer to get for free.[3]

In good times and bad, a brand's value proposition can have a critical impact on its business performance. That's because, as Infosys co-founder N.R. Narayana Murthy once observed, "No one in life ever bought something because it was cheap. People want value for money. You must first be in an acceptable brand of quality and productivity—then you can talk about price."[4]

A value proposition defines the added value that your brand provides. Some of the most effective value propositions are those of leading low-cost competitors. Old Navy's proposition is about being hip without paying branded hip prices. 7-Eleven convenience stores are selling high-priced items for a good value, but the "quality" end of their proposition is convenience. Taco Bell is selling filling food for a price that doesn't empty your wallet.

The survey by the Grocery Manufacturers of America (GMA) mentioned in Chapter 3 also revealed that twice as many Americans would choose a brand that is high in quality and price versus one of average quality that is lower priced (57 percent to 28 percent). Interestingly, that 2002 survey was taken during the post-9/11 business recession when you might expect that most consumers would have turned into bargain price hunters.[5]

Consumers may not always do what they say they will do, but retailers think they had better be believed when it comes to value. A 2005 study of retailing executives by Capgemini U.S. LLC found that they are most concerned about two things: how to maintain low prices *and* how to deliver sufficient value in the form of convenience, variety of goods, and other benefits. These retailers believe that value is driving price, not the other way around, even in formerly price-driven sectors.[6]

Value Rules

Value is whatever the customer says it is, no more and no less. Price is the more visible half of the equation that customers use to assess value, while the benefit part of the equation is usually less concrete. The more meaningful value is, and the less important price alone is, the more likely that buyer and seller will be able to form a mutually beneficial partnership.

If an IT provider installs a computer system that yields revenue and productivity increases that exceed the leasing and installation costs of the system, the system is seen as a net value win for the customer company. The initial price of the system is certainly relevant when comparing alternatives prior to the sale, but price becomes much less relevant once the system is in, especially if its benefits are clearly exceeding its initial and ongoing costs.

The absolute costs have not changed, but the context in which the customer's assessment is being made has changed. The perceived value of the system has increased while the actual value has not. Likewise, if the system costs more than the benefits it delivers, then the anticipated value of the system is less than the actual value That's why overpromise can undermine the perceived value of any product or service in any industry.

Prior to and during its launch in 2001, the Segway Human Transporter received more free publicity than most new products, and its PR agency claimed their efforts achieved more than one billion media impressions.[7] Yet, all that hype wasn't enough to overcome the public's skepticism about the brand's value proposition; $5,000 was just too much to pay for something that wasn't really needed by most people. The founders sold only a fraction of the number anticipated, and the Segway turned out to be a product whose value was only appreciated by niche markets.

Value—or lack of it—can thus become a predominant feature that overshadows other significant benefits.

Priceless Value

When great value brands duke it out there is often a defining struggle for share of market that helps clarify which companies are most adept at adding more customer value to their value chains. The value showdown between Target and Wal-Mart is a classic clash between similar value propositions, with some implications about practical integrity.

Wal-Mart is the largest retailer in the world and is able to wield weight to drive supplier costs into the ground so that shoppers can enjoy low-low prices. Target, on the other hand, is taking the high-style route to sell its panache, knowing that shoppers expect relatively low pricing at their stores as well. One is a price-wise value proposition, the other is a value-driven value proposition.

Target—or "Tar-jay," as the cheap chic set call it—began to separate itself from the Wal-Marts and K-marts of the world a few years ago with more stylish inventory, upgraded stores, and significantly more elegant brand imagery in their advertising.

Wal-Mart's response has been to make some changes of its own, including opening its first upscale Supercenter in Plano, Texas in early 2006. Filled with such high-end niceties as a Kick's coffee shop with expensive coffee and snacks and a huge wine selection, the 203,000-square foot-leviathan is attempting to out-Target Target and lure in customers who may make a lot of money but don't necessarily like to spend a lot.[8]

Yet Wal-Mart's value proposition may be slipping in other ways. Professor Ken Stone of Iowa State University studied fourteen Wal-Mart stores as far back as the 1980s and found that local retailer sales declined by 25 percent within five years of Wal-Marts' opening, and that the share of total retail sales for department stores (predominantly Wal-Mart) had increased by 20 percent. At the same time, clothing, drug, jewelry, auto-parts, hardware, variety, and grocery stores in the area had lost from between 2 and 44 share-of-market points.[9]

That kind of impact on community businesses has led many communities to protest the building of Wal-Marts in their areas. Those protests, plus ongoing labor controversies, have made the total Wal-Mart value proposition a mixed bag of blessings and concerns (see Figure 8-1). Will that ever bother the army of Wal-Mart shoppers? It just might bother some, because today there are many more high-value alternatives to Wal-Mart than there were even a few years ago.

Zale and Signet: Customer-Defined Value

Zale Corp., and its flagship chain known for decades as "The Diamond Store," had a poor 2004 holiday season, and management became very concerned that they were fighting a losing battle for the low end of the market with Wal-Mart and other big discounters.

Management decided on a dramatic new strategy: move from a positioning of providing quality at low prices to a new quality stance that pushed higher margin jewelry. This precipitous shift was driven by Zale CEO Mary Forte, who had successfully marketed high-end merchandise at Federated Department Stores and Gordon's, an upscale chain within the Zale family.

The Zale brand wasn't nearly elastic enough, and the repositioning reportedly confused potential buyers and drove away existing customers

Figure 8-1. The possible dynamics of Wal-Mart value.

Value Enhancements	Value Suppressants	Possible Net Value Impact
Enables lower/middle class families to buy goods they otherwise couldn't buy.	Creates uniformity of tastes and purchasing that could homogenize taste.	Overall: Positive economic benefit for major segments of U.S. population, but not without costs to communities.
Stores create major new employment opportunities wherever they do business.	Employee compensation/benefits under fire. Also, may eliminate some jobs in local retail outlets.	Net employment gain, but employee compensation issues continues to simmer.
Adds significant tax base revenue to communities; generally results in improved infrastructures.	May have a negative impact on local culture and neighborhood shops and stores.	Communities usually need the tax base boost, but could they lose unique personalities in the process?

who counted on Zale for their inexpensive jewelry. The company endured an even worse holiday season in 2005, and the CEO was asked to leave.

In the meantime, UK rival Signet Group, which owns Kay Jewelers among other chains, was thriving. Signet stayed on course with its positioning of higher value at lower prices. By revolving their marketing efforts around a pure quality positioning ("Every Kiss Begins with Kay"), and by using funds from direct source savings to better train their people and bolster their marketing spending, Signet ultimately passed Zale on the left and became the largest jewelry-only retailer in the United States.

By the time Zale realized that it had misjudged the market, they were well into the holiday season of 2005. They tried to salvage the season by shouting discounts via "lowest prices of the season" banners, but same-store sales moved up only 1 percent, compared to a 5.5 percent gain for Signet.

It's a common misconception among even experienced marketers that the seller positions a brand in the buyer's mind. In fact, the seller can do no more than send cues into the marketplace; it is the buyers who decide what they will and will not believe. The "positioning" that takes place is all accomplished by the buyer in the mind of that buyer.

In the case of Zale vs. Signet, there were a whole series of complex dynamics that caused the events in the marketplace. But the most telling was that customers weren't ready to buy the repositioning of value that Zale was selling, and so they did not buy its jewelry.[10]

◆ What If? ◆

What if the value of your brand were directly related to how highly your customers rated your brand for honesty and integrity? What if your pricing was forced to float up or down based on an integrity futures market? What if your pricing policy was solely based on what customers thought was fair? What if the next time your competitor tries to lead with a price hike you release a marketing campaign that explains in detail why you are not raising your price because it would not be equitable to your customers? What if wherever your price is mentioned—on messaging, packaging, or elsewhere—you put a brief statement explaining why you think it's a good value?

What if you held community meetings in your marketing areas to explain your reasoning before you raised your price? Would you look forward to meeting with your customers, or find a reason to be out of town?

Price Discrimination vs. Price Discrimination

When does the word "discrimination" carry a good connotation? When it refers to the perfectly legal and ethical practice of price discrimination that involves segmenting customers by price accessibility. So, for example, we don't have any problem with seniors and students and kids getting into the movie theater for less than the rest of us. We're being discriminated against, but it's a benign form that offers discounts to worthy consumers and helps attract more business to the business.

And we're also generally fine with bulk discounts for bigger corporate buyers, and certainly with getting a lower price-per-unit for buying large bottles of detergent (as long as we don't dispense more per-use than we need just because it's on hand).

But price discrimination that potentially creates trust erosion where there was once value is price discrimination that is predatory. We see it in the extreme in price gouging of hurricane victims who have nowhere else to turn for food or fuel, and in illegal price fixing between competitors who fail to keep at arms length. We see it in anti-competitive predatory pricing when a company attempts to drive fair competition out of a market unfairly by taking a loss on a product or service simply because they can outlast their competitor.

This kind of price discrimination is marketing that kills value, not creates it. It is anti-integrity, which means that it will likely undercut short-term gains with more severe, long-term business erosion. If a business or brand can't make money the old-fashioned way—i.e., by legitimately competing for it—they do all of business a disservice by undermining the trust that others have built up.

Price discrimination that devalues is literally as old as recorded history, and it will outlive us all. We can only hope that consumers and business buyers will stay on the alert for real value and be able to recognize artificial value when they see it.

The Added-Value of Emotion

Marketing partnerships may sound like a formal business arrangement, but they can be as emotional as any relationship—because human beings are involved. According to William McEwen of Gallup Research, emotion is generally at the core of what most consumers are searching for. Even more, when a marketer can connect with a buyer's passion and pride, there are opportunities for a long-term brand loyalty. Once on board, confidence and brand integrity is how customers are retained after they have tried a brand for the first time.[11]

That is also true about business purchases. There is a mistaken belief that B2B purchases are devoid of emotion. In fact, there are no purchases devoid of emotion, including those in B2B transactions, because all purchases are made by human beings. By definition, no human being can act for purely rational reasons.[12]

In some industries, an emotion-laden partnership is one of the few things that differentiates and provides value, depending on one or more factors (see Figure 8-2):

❏ *How emotional is the product/service experience itself?* Rabid users of Cliché skateboards or BMX bikes may feel a powerful emotional attachment to those brands and products if they have made it possible to have wonderful experiences. Even a few business brands like Cisco or HP can generate strong positive emotions if their products perform consistently, or highly negative ones if, for example, laptops begin bursting into flames.

❏ *How much does it cost?* The high cost and involvement of an automobile warrant a strong emotional connection with the brand you buy. The original Mustang you drove in college, or the Accord you drive now, are laden with emotions that remind you of friends, loved ones, and moments that make up pleasant brand memories. Their value extends well beyond the purchase price and operating costs.

❏ *How often and how intense are the brand contacts?* A round of golf is inevitably filled with frustration and precious few moments of glory. No matter what kind of round you are having, it is never without emotion. A weekly game with your buddies may mean that you and

Figure 8-2. Likelihood of emotional value-added benefits.

Industry	Less Likely	Possible	More Likely
Consumer Packaged Goods	Customers seek function first	If product use has emotion linked to usage	--
Fashion	--	--	Everything about fashion connects to emotion in some way
Kitchen Appliances	Customers first want it to work well for a good price	If appliance reinforces status (e.g., HD TV)	--
Online Retailer	Channel is less involving than brick & mortar	Whatever emotion exists in offline may translate to online	If retailer is selling highly emotion-laden products (e.g., videogaming)
Automobiles and Motorcycles	--	--	Extension of identity
Enterprise Networking Software	Corporate buyers may focus primarily on specs	Users may be emotional about benefits (or lack of them)	--

your Callaway or Ping clubs form a value-added, emotional partnership, which some hackers terminate by throwing their partners in the nearest water hazard.

❏ *How experiential is the purchase process?* A coffee brand that's served at a gas station snack stand isn't likely to get high points for emotion compared to a cup at Starbucks, which is the quintessential experiential brand. A grocery store can be a largely emotionless place, except perhaps at the cash register, or if it happens to be a Trader Joe's where the shoppers are really customer-partners.

Because emotional connections can be so unpredictable, they may or may not be helpful to building a partnership with the customer. It depends on many factors, especially the decision set the customer has in mind when dealing with a particular category of product or service brands.

What the high-value brands are offering is a package with both emotional and rational value to the customer-partner. The interweaving of the two types of benefits can provide a complementary set of reasons for customers to come and stay with a brand, each of which can pinch hit for its counterparts when needed. So, when the price (rational) may seem a bit high for a Banana Republic shirt, the way the shirt makes us feel (emotional) when we wear it will help justify the price. When we're concerned that we may be buying a Nicole Miller coat that we really don't need (rational) but that looks great (emotional), the fact that it is on sale helps make it appear more practical (rational).

All of these issues can have a destructive impact on a brand's identity and a company's reputation among its constituencies. Such lapses can be caused by poor management or overzealous marketing or bad planning, but the result is always the same: Customers lose faith in something they had once trusted, and marketers lose brand value, usually followed by lost business. Although the overall integrity of the company may never be in question, the integrity of the value that it offers may be questionable (see Figure 8-3).

Figure 8-3. The dangers of brand value declines.

Brand/Company	What Happened
Dell	Dell's once-vaunted customer service failed to keep pace with customer needs and the company struggled to catch up with rivals by investing a reported $100 million to upgrade people and IT systems. In the meantime, Sony-made batteries in about 35,000 Dell laptops (as well as other brands' laptops) had to be recalled because of repeated incidents of spontaneous fireworks.
British Airways	It was poor customer service and declines in perceived value that opened the cargo door to major revenue declines and share theft by Virgin Atlantic, among others.
Nokia	The leading cell phone manufacturer thought it had a good grip on consumer tastes, but many of their designs were late to pick up on the "clamshell" rage, allowing key competitors to catch them in styling and performance.
Apple	Poor performing products in the face of Wintel dominance nearly killed the most authentic computer company of all in the mid-1990s. Only the return of tightly disciplined innovation demanded by Steve Jobs saved the brand and the company from the auction block.
McDonald's – U.S.	McDonald's sold U.S. kids and lost the vote of Moms, who couldn't relate to Ronald, and began feeling major guilt pangs about the impact of McD's menu on child obesity. As good as the chain's value prices were, they were undermined by real concerns by customers. Market capitalization fell $12 billion from 1999 to 2003, and prompted a comprehensive (and successful) renovating of everything from menus to stores to advertising.

A Conversation

"Hello . . . Hey, Jack, what's up? . . . Yeah, you're comin' in loud and clear . . . How was the flight? . . . the meeting? . . . you mean the meeting with the price guys? . . . Fine. It went fine . . . No, really, they're good folks, considering they aren't from our solar system. . . . Actually, we got along great until they started complaining about the price hike we're. . . . Yeah, they don't seem to believe in it. You know those guys, Jack. They said we should be looking at perceived value, yada yada yada, and I said they should be looking at the EVP's face when she starts beating us up about the bottom line. . . . Anyhow, we agreed to raise the price by 8 percent and mask it in the new service package. . . . It should work fine. The pricing test results came back and less than one-tenth of the sample noticed they were paying more. . . . I know, but nobody really looks at individual service fees. . . . Not to worry, with all the hoopla we're going to make about the new service package, nobody's going to make a big thing about higher fees. . . . Yeah, but everything is going up, so why not our prices? . . . OK, take care, Jack. And may your trip be free of service charges."

The Value of Integrity

A 2002 study among 6,000 consumers around the world found that they "demand honesty and respect from retailers and brand manufacturers more than they expect the highest-quality merchandise or the lowest prices."[13] Can we really believe that shoppers would pass up a bargain from a company with questionable integrity, especially now that we've found out that everyone lies? That's not clear, but integrity could very well become the final tie-breaker when buyers make their purchase decision.

The integrity of the seller has a lot to do with how the buyer views the value of what is being offered—not in the sense of deliberately misleading consumers, but in the sense that they must deliver the value promised or be suspect in consumers' minds.

K-mart and Sears historically emphasized price, but ultimately paid the price for underselling quality, eliminating any place for themselves among higher-value options. When the two companies merged in an effort to strengthen their joint value proposition, one retail analyst cracked that the 2005 merger might end up being ". . . akin to tying two drunks together and hoping that they'll be able to walk a straight line."[14] However that marriage works out, it was a shotgun wedding caused by being out-valued by the competition.

K-mart and Sears and Montgomery Ward and Alexander's and Woolworth's all were successful at one point until they were preempted by competitors that appeared to offer better values. None of them were ethically questionable in their dealings, but all have fallen away or fallen on hard times because they did not establish integrity of value.

When value is delivered, it usually comes in three forms:

1. Functional value meets the customers' needs for something that works on their behalf and delivers a concrete result. Whirlpool introduced a $400 KitchenAid Pro Line waffle iron, which defied the conventional wisdom that appliance buyers are most interested in price. Whirlpool reportedly can't make enough of them.[15]
2. Economic benefits of value are usually about pricing advantages or the nonpricing issues that positively benefit the customer from an economic sense, such as what is offered at Marshall's or Ross clothing stores.
3. Emotional value benefits deliver something intangible, often in the form of a psychological lift for customers. Both eBay buyers and sellers are gratified (and sometimes ecstatic) when an item is sold at a price for a better deal than either party would have gotten elsewhere.[16]

These value benefits can become even more compelling when value is fused to integrity. One of the great value integrity success stories in recent U.S. automotive history is that of Lexus, the luxury division of Toyota.

In September 1989, the Lexus LS 400 and ES 250 were introduced in the United States. Originally named Alexis—a moniker that was changed to avoid associating it with a scheming character on the then-popular *Dynasty* network program—the Lexus came on the heels of Honda's Acura line, but offering more upscale quality and at a more premium price. Lexus provided its customers with strong rationale for their purchases on three planes: economic, functional, and emotional (see Figure 8-4).

The Lexus value frame of reference had never been other Japanese makes, but the more expensive BMW and Mercedes lines. Here, against the gold standards in the industry, Lexus had a clear advantage in terms of reliability, durability, and lifetime maintenance costs, which is why it has been ranked as the #1 car line in reliability in the United States for eleven consecutive years, as well as having the fewest defects and perceived design flaws.[17]

Figure 8-4. The Lexus value triangle (U.S. only).

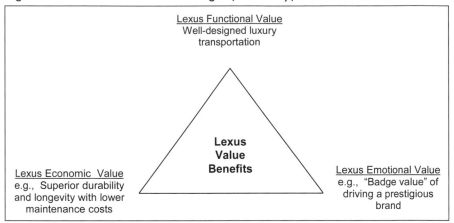

Put another way, the value of Lexus is demonstrated by its performance and price, but guaranteed by its integrity.

*   *   *

The Value Strategy: Trust Drives Value

To hear marketers and their customers talk, all anyone thinks about is price. But they're after value, whatever they say, and they're willing to pay for it more times than not, *if* the value is genuine.

1. Let Value Drive Price, Not Vice Versa

The first order of business should be to lock down the brand's specific value proposition statement, well before any other major strategic or tactical decisions are made. The marketing team should be able to succinctly and cogently describe why their brand offers a better value than alternatives for whatever price is charged. With the value proposition firmly in place, pricing strategy and tactics can be assembled with a stronger strategic base.

Second, consider using the value proposition as a central pillar of your business building efforts—*if* your brand or company has established itself as one of integrity of value. What at first may appear to be a need for a repositioning may in fact require a refocused value proposition.

Chevron is the second largest integrated U.S.-based oil company. In its extensive retail business, Chevron has been consistently advertising the virtues of its

Techron gasoline additive. Using Techron as the key reason for its premium pricing, Chevron and its independent dealers often ignore low-priced brands that fight for less profitable share points.

Chevron's determination to be the value-added competitor may seem self-limiting when fuel prices skyrocket. But Chevron sticks with its value-added proposition because the brand can make a persuasive case that a consumer's second-most expensive investment deserves and needs the Chevron edge, namely, their Techron gasoline additive. This focused value strategy also enables the company to promote other value-driven proof points, such as being the first to be named a "Top Tier Detergent Gasoline" by BMW, GM, Honda, and Toyota.

Chevron, like all of Big Oil, may always be distrusted by some because of its volatile pricing and improbably large earnings. But those issues notwithstanding, the company has definite value-added marketing strengths that enable it to market within a proven strategic superstructure, rather than responding to tactical opportunities that happen to come along.

There will always be temptations to veer from the value proposition. Competition will drop their price to gain revenue and/or share. Or the economy will hit a wall and prompt all competitors to consider making their brands more price-accessible. Throughout it all, the value proposition should be a steady compass—as much as the market will allow—that guides how the brand responds to these challenges.

Nike Provides Performance Value of a Different Kind

From its founding, Nike has always pushed the envelope in shoe design. More recently, led by chief designer John Hoke, Nike has embraced "sustainable design" as part of a company-wide initiative called "Considered." Hoke has his teams looking for designs that use less energy to make, contain less chemical content, and create less waste, such as shoes with snap-fit systems and organic cotton stitching.

For instance, Hoke asked his designers to create an ergonomic chair out of cardboard, using the restrictive art of origami, in order to stretch their minds into new places. The catch: The chairs had to hold up under a frenetic game of musical chairs.

Drawing inspiration from auto shows, museums, and other unlikely muses, Hoke's people are rethinking what new athletic apparel can be made of, and what options are out there that may be a small step toward a more stable environment. They could end up revolutionizing shoe design the same way Nike's marketing changed the way shoes are sold. These new environmentally friendly designs may not be the best revenue generators for the company, but they make it clear that Nike is thinking about and acting on the earth-wise concerns of others.[18]

2. Price According to How Customers Value Value

Many companies still use cost-plus or going-rate methods that are based on sellers' and the markets' perspectives, respectively, and they fail to take into account the most important factor in the equation: the customer's take on value.

The general consensus among pricing experts is that an "economic value to the customer" (EVC) model is one of the most sensitive and sophisticated ways to determine price. EVC takes into account customers' perception of value of the nearest substitutes for your offering, plus whatever they believe are your points of differentiation.

Points of differentiation that can help support premium pricing may come from anywhere. For example, an increasing number of industries and individual customers are beginning to have real concerns about the environment. Many are willing to pay more for products that have a minimal impact on our ecosystem.

A different form of EVC pricing is taking place at IKEA, which offers a unique shopping experience yielding inexpensive, distinctively styled, and good quality home furnishings that are, above all else, a solid value for those who seek value at the right price.

The $17-billion-in-sales company accounts for 5 to 10 percent of the furniture sales in every country in which it does business. Someone once estimated that 10 percent of the extant European population was conceived on an IKEA bed.

Shoppers at the IKEA kingdom look as if they are stuck somewhere between shock and awe as they wander through a unique brand shopping experience. As they envision how this lamp or that table will fit *perfectly* in the living room, it is real value that they see with their mind's eye, backed by the value of integrity that is uniformly offered to 410 million shoppers across the globe.

IKEA is where profit margins are a full 3 percentage points ahead of Target's, and that's despite *lowering* prices 2 to 3 percent every year. IKEA is, in short, a place where it seems downright unreasonable to walk out the front door empty-handed.[19]

In some economically challenged countries, an IKEA outlet is a symbol of how far they've come. In the United States and Europe, it may be a sign of where we are all going.

3. Use Value to Cement Trust

One of the common traits of the companies we've been profiling is that they consistently deliver what their customers consider to be a *superior* value, regardless of in which price brackets they operate. Herman Miller, Patagonia, Infosys, In-N-Out Burger, Timberland, Kiehl's, John Deere, and Trader Joe's are in very different businesses . . . and yet, in the same business: making their customers' money accomplish all that their customers need it to do, if not more.

Every one of their products and services is worth a premium, whether or not that customer is charged a premium. Every one of their products and services rarely fails to be seen as the right value for the right price. They each enjoy the fierce loyalty of their customers because competitors simply can't match their ability to deliver superior value.

Any number of other companies and their brands are struggling to find a value proposition that is both meaningful to customers and unique enough to provide differentiation. Gap, Inc.'s brands, for example—including Gap, Baby Gap, Old Navy, Banana Republic, and Forth & Towne—must differentiate themselves from one another as well as from their competition. This is very tricky business since each of the brands must also deal with the vicissitudes of fashion changes while juggling offerings that provide an edge against constantly evolving competition. It's essentially a game of three-dimensional chess.

Companies that have created trust through superior value have committed to their value propositions on all levels. Marriott has gained significant footholds in several different value niches, and always by promising and delivering quality at whatever price point is right for that segment.

Marriott's Fairfield Inn properties promise Marriott's consistent quality at low prices. Their Courtyard by Marriott hotels are distinctively businesslike, and weary road warriors are sure to get exactly what they expect at the end of a hard day, at a price the accounting department can live with. And Ritz Carlton—referred to by Marriott as its "partner" to lift it above its more plebian properties (but owned almost entirely by Marriott)—is at the top of its class in amenities and value.

Value leaders build trust by making the most of what they are, and by not trying to be what they aren't. Motel 6 is positioned as good quality at bargain rates. There's no room for stretching that brand into the moderate accommodations sector of the market, and their parent company, Accor, would be crazy to try. By strategically staying close to home they strengthen their hold on their share of the low-price tier.

One company that has long understood the link between trust and customer value is Deere & Co., marketers of the John Deere brand. This $20 + billion corporation with 45,000 employees worldwide is more than 167 years old, and it still runs its operations as the founder had in mind, based on "quality, innovation, integrity, and commitment."

John Deere's origins are as a company of Midwestern U.S. straight-shooters, and value seeps into every part of their business. Value is reinforced in everything from their unparalleled product quality to their excruciatingly careful protection of what they consider their most valuable asset: their brand. The company is steadfast in its determination to market the highest quality products in a manner that melds integrity with success.[20]

4. Head North on the Chain

Procter & Gamble has built a whole cadre of keystone brands by investing sufficient time and money to understand the exact nature of the benefits that consumers were seeking. In so doing, they pioneered new forms of value-added benefits encased in superior brands.

When P&G advertised Pampers to young mothers in the 1970s, they sidestepped the guilt that a "convenient-for-mom" positioning might have generated among such women whose own mothers had used washable cloth diapers. Instead, Pampers advertising talked about the genuine benefits to the baby (the "stay-dri lining"). When they marketed Joy dishwashing liquid as a "good reflection on you," P&G reminded customers that clean dishes were more than hygienic, they were another way to communicate that those who lived there ran a well-maintained home. More recently, P&G's Scope was positioned not just as a mouthwash, but a love-enabler that lets users "get close."

Some critics have suggested that such psychological appeals were manipulative and triggered unnecessary purchases. Although that point is debatable, it is clear that P&G doesn't just market brands at their face value but digs deeper into their worth (equity, resulting from trust) within a household, even in what other companies saw as commonplace categories.

Other examples of brands that used brand trust to move up their industry's value chains: Starbucks became the best place to spend the morning, not just a place with the best coffee. Harrah's moved from a casino chain to an entertainment community that nurtures its past and future customers and offers them a never-ending series of incentives to return. Michelin transitioned from just being a premium quality tire brand to a symbol of safety reassurance, thanks to a baby-in-the-tire graphic that burned itself into the memories of millions of family tire buyers. McKinsey & Co. became a firm of C-level mentors, not just management consultants.

Value propositions are encompassing integrity because the perceived value of a company in the eyes of customers is directly tied to how much they can trust that company and its brands. How much is a business customer saving by switching to a lower-priced overnight delivery service when packages are lost or way-laid? How valuable are bargains at an outlet apparel chain when the clothes don't make it past the third washing?

Value has become an important pillar in the practical integrity that successful companies and their brands are offering to their constituencies.

5. Avoid the Turn-Offs

An astonishing number of marketers manage to chip away at brand value by making decisions that undermine customer trust. These are cautionary tales that can be helpful guideposts for marketers who could potentially make the same mistakes on any given day:

❏ *Inflating marketing claims can lead to value deflation.* Simple exaggeration—sometimes referred to as "hype"—may not have all that simple an impact on brand identities. Truly ordinary toiletry brands will not attract the opposite sex and may lose their luster when romance fails to appear. Ready-to-eat cereals that are supposed to help you lose weight had better taste good because their dietary benefits may fall well short of the mark. Online network protection programs that promise security and fail to stop a just-crafted computer worm are unlikely to get credit for all the viruses they did stop.

   Value Implication to Consider: If the value gained is less than the value lost when exaggerations come home to roost, stick to the facts. If you consistently stretch the truth or flat-out de-ceive, either your people or your customers will rebel, at which point things could get ugly.

❏ *Camouflaging pricing can make your value disappear.* Price promotions are supposed to be incentives to purchase, but some marketers treat them as an opportunity to obscure true price/value relationships. For example, a group of electronics retailers settled with government in-vestigators after the FTC said that they had claimed that consumers could get a computer for less than $300. In reality, the actual cost exceeded $1,000 because it required a fees-laden service contract with an Internet service provider. Tough-to-read advertising "mice type" revealed that some consumers would require additional long-distance charges to connect to the Internet.[21]

   In the summer of 2004 the three largest U.S. wireless companies agreed to a 32-state consumer protection settlement surrounding al-legedly misleading ads and confusing contract disclosures in their cutthroat business. The industry leaders agreed to provide more accurate service coverage maps, extend the time for consumers to back away from an agreement, and clarify the terms of those agreements. Consumers also got back their activation fee, and disclosures in ads were clarified and boosted in prominence.[22]

But to this day, if you go into some wireless stores to buy a phone, the price printed in extra-large type under the phone may be for new subscribers only. If you're buying a replacement phone as a current subscriber, you have to look extra hard to find your price, in much smaller type, and it may be two to three times greater than that for a new subscriber.

Now none of us are going to give up our cell phones because the major carriers are throwing eye tests at us. But in a world already fraught with well-founded skepticism, when we discover that what is promised is not always delivered, it makes us that much more likely to keep searching for alternatives, as Quixotic as that search may be.

Value Implication to Consider: The negative impact of a hidden value flaw will never be forgotten by the customer who discovers it. You can count on that person telling ten more. Avoid the temptation to roll out a great deal with a Catch-22 that may instead catch some caustic headlines.

❏ *Product "improvements" had better improve the customer's view of brand value.* Fifteen years ago, Samsung Electronics specialized in products that you bought if you couldn't afford Sony. Now one of the world's most innovative companies, Samsung has built isolated incubatory hideaways where its top thinkers come up with extraordinary new products that bring meaningful value to the Samsung brand. Performance-driven designers, engineers, and planners are locked away in Samsung's Value Innovation Program (VIP) centers, where they must stay until they solve the problem at hand. One of their most important functions is to draw "value curve" schematics that identify product attributes and their potential value to the customer.[23]

Value Implication to Consider: Any change to a popular brand or product may do far more damage to a value proposition than standing pat, even if the competition is closing the differentiation gap. If innovation is critical to your business (and it probably is), redirect your best minds toward the task of creating the best value in the industry, not just the best whiz-bang technology.

❏ *Frequent discounting may communicate that the brand doesn't know its own value.* Brands from U.S. automakers, some beverages, and aging technology solutions can temporarily stimulate trial of the products but permanently undermine their value in the minds of buyers who are interested in quality over price. Attracting bargain hunters in order to make some quarterly revenue hurdles is not going to help build a brand with low revenue-per-user customers. Just ask General Motors how much sustainable revenue can be generated from discounting.

That company has been hemorrhaging money for years because of escalating costs and a struggle to build cars that can compete head-on with the likes of Toyota and Honda. GM's response to falling sales has been to create temporary and hollow sales bumps with such promotions as the "Employee Discount" program in 2005.

The program significantly increased revenue compared to previous periods, but it slashed profitability. When by the spring of 2006 the Japanese brands had steadily achieved a record 40 percent share of vehicles sold in the United States, GM and other U.S. brands had fallen to near-record lows.[24] To date, GM has repeatedly lowered prices but skill struggles to establish value.

> *Value Implication to Consider:* Keep your eye on the ball, in this case, the high-profit segments that tend to steer clear of brands that cheapen themselves with excessive discounting. There's no such thing as "brand" versus "retail"—it's all about the brand, no matter what the message is. Reducing price sends the wrong message to high-integrity users.

❏ *Seeking fatter margins through product or service slippage may only marginalize the brand's equity.* Perceived product/service dilution can kill the enthusiasm of even the most devoted customers. In 2001, Staples office supply stores were receiving eight complaints for every one compliment. In order to keep profits up, service had been allowed to slide, and with it, revenue and share growth. Value, customers told Staples, did not necessarily have to do with lower pricing as much as finding an easy buying experience.

The company turned around its fortunes by focusing on how easy it can be for small businesses to get what they want at Staples, and they created an emblematic "Easy Button," supported by several years of strong advertising and promotion. By 2005, Staples was earning 18 percent higher income and had outperformed Office Depot by most measures. The value Staples had lost was regained and then some.[25]

More recently, major players like Dell, Home Depot, and North-west Airlines dented their brand equities when they cut back on customer service funding in order to improve the bottom line. The impact on business from the customer service problems encountered by these companies is difficult to measure, but it's undeniably there or Dell would not have invested $100 million to fix their CS problems. Each of these companies has inadvertently spawned anti-marketing sites (*dellsucks.net, homedepotsucks.org,* and *northwestsucks .com*). One market analyst asked the right question: "When a customer is actively marketing against you, where does that show up on a P&L?"[26] The answer is that the impact of customers marketing against you shows up in all the wrong places—as gross revenue declines and unplanned promotion expenses needed to counter negative buzz, all of which affect the bottom line (see Figure 8-3).

> *Value Implication to Consider:* You can't fully understand the value implications of quality slippage unless you understand the nature and scope of the value you offered to begin with. Consider running a stand-alone research study that dimension-alizes how valuable your brand and product is to your users. Using that data, carefully test quality adjustments before implementing.

*   *   *

A Summary and a Few Questions

Value has been elevated from a synonym for cheap to a significant driver of choice in most, if not all, industries. An integral component of value is the integrity of the brand or company offering it, integrity that can be bolstered by the right strategic moves or squandered by the wrong ones.

By creating and supporting the right value proposition, the brand deemphasizes pricing issues and focuses on the value-added benefits that are enhanced by a strong integrity of value. This enables the brand to move up the value chain and become an even more important factor in the lives of customers and prospects.

Some additional questions to consider:

1. *Have you fully explored the meanings of value in your industry? For your own business?* Have your research studies included questions that at-

tempted to quantify the value of value to your customers? Do you know how value stacks up against other drivers of choice in your industry?

2. *How well does your company or brand deliver on the three core benefits of value: functional, economic, and emotional?* Do you outperform competition in each of these benefit areas? Is one weaker than the others and is it a vulnerability for the brand? What steps could you be taking to shore up deficiencies in the eyes of your customers?

3. *What are the dynamics of your brand's value?* Are there positive and negative aspects to your value proposition that are netting out as a loss in perceived value? Is it having an impact on the way in which customers are viewing your brand?

4. *Are value issues driving your price?* Or are you still pricing according to your own value (e.g., cost-plus pricing), or according to what you see happening in the marketplace (e.g., market-driven pricing)? Have you made an attempt to fully understand the economic value to the customer of your company's offerings and pricing? Do you know how you stand versus your competition in terms of customer-perceived value?

5. *How can you use your price/value strategy to improve your customers' views of your integrity?* Are there some price/value moves you could make in the marketplace that would reinforce the reputation of your company as a seller of great integrity? Are there opportunities for you to lead your industry in value initiatives that could enhance your perceived leadership in providing greater value to buyers?

Good, if not great, value is mandatory in today's marketplace. High-integrity decisions are the best method of achieving value in a skeptical world. Part Three will demonstrate how to fold that integrity into all aspects of a marketing program.

PART THREE

MAKING IT HAPPEN

CHAPTER 9

Integrity Team Building

Convince Your People and They Will Convince the World

I n the late 1920s, a millwright at Herman Miller died. Founder and CEO D.J. DePree was a young manager who walked to the man's house to personally deliver condolences to the widow.

The millwright's widow thanked D.J. for coming, then invited him into the parlor with some other guests. After a while, the widow asked if it would be all right if she read some poetry. She returned a moment later and read a few poems aloud, and D.J. commented on how beautiful the poetry was. It was her late husband, the widow replied proudly, who had written the poetry. As Max De-Pree, D.J.'s son, wrote sixty years later, "Many of us at Herman Miller continue to wonder: Was he a poet who did millwright's work, or was he a millwright who wrote poetry?"[1]

They tell that story at Herman Miller to this day because it reminds everyone that management is about working with whole persons, not "employees." You are expected to bring your whole person to work, and those who work with you are expected to respect all of that person, including what you are most proud of outside of company walls.

Marketing with practical integrity can only be a reality when the people who make, sell, distribute, and market products and services make integrity an important part of what they believe in and do, each and every day they do it. Practical integrity can thus become part of who they are, both at work and elsewhere.

When Companies Become Their Brands

Commercial brands have been around for hundreds of years, but they began to gain momentum with the blossoming of the industrial revolution in the nineteenth century, and rapidly picked up pace following the widespread growth of radio and television. Yet it wasn't until the latter half of the twentieth century that brands began to reflect more than what was portrayed in just a slogan or logo.

Gradually, entire companies began to take on the characteristics of their master brands. The VW Beetle was a practical little car that looked funny, sounded funnier, and had a heritage linked to Adolf Hitler. But inexplicably it became a symbol of youth, independence, and rebellion against what most Americans drove and believed.

Visa was a handy plastic card that could be used from time to time when you were low on cash. But thanks to persuasive advertising campaigns that showered the country with countless impressions of pleasurable places to go and eat and spend, Visa began to represent what we all wanted but needed help to afford.

The next stage in brand development, the one we are experiencing right now, took shape when more companies became centered on their company-wide brands. These "masterbrands" encouraged their people to "live the brand" in all that they do. Corporations like Starbucks, IKEA, Nokia, and Dell were seen as companies whose brand was impossible to separate from the organization itself (see Figure 9-1).[2]

Today, masterbranded companies are more common than ever because managements have discovered the value of rallying their people around a single brand, which to some degree is a reflection of the organization's culture. For some companies, like those we have been profiling in this book, living the brand means adopting the practical integrity tenets that have built the business over time; that's when a company is making the most of its assets through higher marketing standards.

Figure 9-1. The evolution of company-wide brand development.

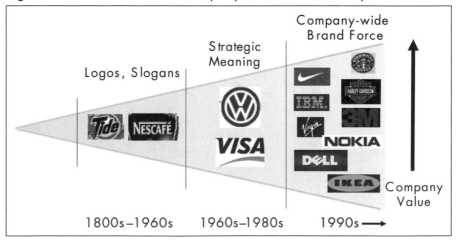

Timberland: A Company of Unrepentant Do-Gooders

The Timberland Company, a New Hampshire–based footwear and apparel manufacturer, generates revenue approaching $2 billion. According to its website, Timberland offers "the consumer a company to believe in and get involved with . . . our employees a set of beliefs they can stand behind . . . the community help and support at all times . . . [and] shareholders a company people want to buy from and enjoy working for."[3]

In its Path of Service program, Timberland gives each employee forty hours of paid time off every year to serve communities on company time. The company annually organizes its global "Serv-a-palooza" events that sponsor good works around the world. On that day, the worldwide offices of Timberland are closed so that all 5,600 employees can help out where help is needed, generating more than 50,000 person-hours of labor in twenty-five countries. Timberland even calls up many of its vendors and asks them to lend a helping hand.

It's all part of what the company management calls "doing well and doing good." Although some cynics consider such well-publicized corporate service to be self-aggrandizing, the extraordinary commitment of the Swartz family, which has a controlling interest in the company, certainly seems genuine enough.

The people of Timberland like to use the phrase "Make It Better." By that they mean they seek to make better products and a better world in which to enjoy them. Jeffrey Swartz, Timberland's president and CEO, embarked years ago on a path that he calls "boots, brand, and beliefs." He once put it this way: "As a company we have both a responsibility and an interest in engaging in the world around us. By doing so, we deliver value to our four constituencies: consumers, shareholders, employees and the community."[4]

While no one, including Timberland, is claiming that their corporate social responsibility efforts are the reason for their success, apparently they don't get in the way of their selling, and they may be a positive factor in their healthy growth. The company's revenue increased nearly 30 percent between 2001 and 2005, right through a U.S. economic slowdown, and full-year net margins have consistently been in the 8 to 10 percent range. The Timberland stock price has also far outperformed the S&P 500 during that time, although changing fashion trends have put increasing pressure on the family-owned company.[5]

Proud and Proud of It

Staff members must be proud of the work they do if they are to do work that makes the company proud. When the pay is not right or the hours are too long, it is pride that keeps people pressing on. When the company is doing well but management wants to stretch to a higher plane, it is pride that often supplies the juice for that extra effort. The companies that have a culture based on practical integrity are the happy recipients of a series of bonus benefits that feed staff pride, above and beyond however else they may be compensated, including:

❏ *Quality Made with Integrity.* Companies operating with practical integrity are, by necessity, creating products and services of higher quality. Their people tend to have an infectious passion that floods a work environment and is injected into every project or end-product.

The integrity built into Herman Miller's products can be at least partly attributed to what is known there as "The Frost-Scanlon Plan." Joseph Scanlon was in charge of labor-management relations in a steel mill in the 1930s and later became a professor at MIT. There, Scanlon worked with Dr. Carl Frost, who adopted many of Scanlon's views about how to create a positive working environment.

Frost went on to teach at Michigan State University and helped businesses in the region—including Herman Miller—to put the Scanlon Plan into operation during the 1950s.

In a nutshell, the Scanlon Plan calls for the relationship between management and workers to be based on a covenant instead of a contract, which gives the workers a strong sense of pride and ownership in what they produce. It involves participative management and gain sharing among all involved; it becomes an environment that encourages innovation and commitment because all reap the rewards.[6]

When properly channeled, personal pride can create products that have the best possible chance of protecting a brand's or company's integrity. The people of Herman Miller prove that as a matter of routine.

❏ *Personnel Benefits.* There are also very real personnel benefits to practical integrity. Morale is generally strong, and camaraderie becomes a common currency because it is bonded with a strong sense of integrity.

The people of Timberland tend to be civic-minded individuals who want to give back to their communities. They feel doubly blessed to be working for a company that is so committed to the same causes that it provides paid leave for 40 hours a year so that their people can perform the services they want for the people who need them the most. The morale is high because the people of Timberland feel like people of integrity working for people of integrity.

It's the same feeling that permeates companies like Deere & Co., In-N-Out Burger, and Whole Foods.

❏ *Recruiting Benefits.* Quality people are attracted to a company because quality persons are already there. The company's people believe that they are working for a place of integrity that treats them with the dignity they deserve. Pride in integrity also provides a powerful system of self-improvement and a recruitment process that identifies quality prospective employees.

Individuals who apply for jobs at Kiehl's in New York or at Patagonia in Ventura, California do so knowing that they may have a chance to work for a company with unfettered integrity. In many cases it is the reason they apply, and in all cases it has a definite impact on why they stay as long as they do.

Also, their emphasis on integrity makes it easier to spot the candidates who just might not fit in.

A Conversation

"Robert? Hi, I'm Kristin. Please, sit down."

"Nice office."

"Thanks. So, I read your resume. What has brought you to us?"

"Well, I've always heard good things about this place."

"That's nice to hear. What things?"

"Sorry?"

"What good things have you heard?"

"Oh, ah, that you respect the people who work here . . . and . . . you know . . . things."

"Uh-huh. So . . . your background is in corporate communications . . . and you've had one-two-three positions in seven years. So, why did you leave?"

"Which one?"

"Any of them."

"Well, I have very definite points of view about corporate communications. It seems to me that corporate communications should be a cheerleader."

"Uh-huh. And if the company makes a mistake?"

"Hey, I mean, every company steps into it once in a while, so why focus on the negative? Let's face it, we're all . . ."

"Human?"

"Exactly. I mean, people have enough bad stuff in their lives, we don't have to add to it by spending their valuable time chewing over something they can't do anything about, if you know what I mean."

"I'm beginning to."

"It just seems like you build your rep on the good news, so push the positive, is what I always say. I invented that line . . . 'push the positive.'"

"I bet you did. Well, it's been great talking with you, Robert. I'll hang onto your resume and we'll give you a call if we ever have anything that might fit your . . . ah . . ."

"Background?"

"Exactly."

Fostering a Place for Integrity

Companies that practice practical integrity often are very careful to recruit people who reflect the organization's values, and yet want to be given enough freedom to make their own contributions.

Patagonia senior executive Rick Ridgeway tends to hire people with the right values system and train them for particular positions, rather than finding people who may be qualified for a job but who are not prepared to commit to Patagonia's views on the environment. "We start with people who have a passion for our values that want to be here because they know what we stand for and for what we live for. We can teach them the rest . . . For the most part, we don't have to look for them, they find us."[7]

As part of their orientation process at Patagonia, the new associates receive the company mission statement—which is discussed frequently throughout the company—and meet personally with legendary founder Yvon Chouinard, who speaks to them about the philosophy of the company and his book, *Let My People Go Surfing*. If an employee at Patagonia has an issue about what is being sold or how it is being marketed, that employee is listened to and his or her comments are taken seriously. The individuals at Patagonia are empowered by the company itself, and by its environmental mission.

W.L. Gore is another company with strong values that center on encouraging individuals to find their own way of contributing to Gore's strong heritage of innovation. The company accomplishes its product development feats with a unique organizational structure that has little organization or structure. The Gore associates literally work on whatever they think has merit and are most likely to help the company succeed. In that way, they are always passionate about their work because their work is always something that they have a passion for. That passion generates a strong sense of product integrity.

The entrepreneurial atmosphere is further nurtured by what Gore calls their "flat lattice" organization, with few titles or reporting relationships. As one sales leader put it, "You don't tell anybody at Gore to do anything." Instead of bosses each associate selects a "mentor," and groups are run by "sponsors."

The work teams are kept small and agile and run by consensus. Committees decide on personnel issues for each associate, such as evaluations and merit raises, and that includes the compensation of Bob Gore, the CEO and son of the founders. The company encourages people to communicate through one-on-one discussions rather than via memo or e-mail. Each associate spends at least 10 percent of his or her time thinking about new ideas.[8]

The Gore people operate their organization—which largely operates itself—on the basis of four principles: fairness to one another, freedom to encourage others, the opportunity to make and keep commitments, and collaborating with other Gore associates whenever the company's reputation is involved.[9]

The closely-held company does not release earnings information, but its revenue base approached $2 billion in 2006 and has been growing at a rate between 9 and 18 percent in recent years.[10] Those are integrity-driven financials—the most rewarding of all.

Healthy and Skeptical

Marketers have to respect the customer's right to choose, including the right to walk away. They also have to be respectful of the customer's right to products that deliver what's promised, value that is exceptional regardless of absolute price, and honesty in how products and services are marketed.

If that respect really does exist, it needs to be embraced not just in the marketing department, but throughout the company. And not just in the company mission statement, but in the way that staff members think and talk about their customers. To make that happen requires some strong standards and a strong sense of accountability.

Every company of any size has some sort of quality control team. They are paid to be observant, curious, critical, and meticulous in examining products or services for flaws. They are, in short, professional skeptics. But critical thinking should not be confined to the QC team.

It is a healthy and prudent practice for employees to deputize themselves as quality lookouts in their own work. That doesn't mean that they should turn into cynics who assume the worst, but there's no reason why they can't be simul-

◆ What If? ◆

What if your company were to produce videos that asked tough questions about what your company is and where it needs fixing? What would the videos focus on? Would your management endorse the project? Quietly encourage it? Or kill it before it got going?

Do you think it would be healthy or hurtful for your company to interview employees about their views (maybe anonymously?) about the company and share it with everyone else? What would most of your staff talk about? Would it be something you'd be willing to share with outsiders? How could the work of the company—including the marketing team—be enhanced by such an experiment?

Could it possibly bring your people together more in support of the company? What if your management took the feedback the wrong way if the company were criticized in the video?

taneously candid and supportive. Not long ago, we saw an interesting experiment in doing that very thing in one of the world's largest industrial corporations.

Beginning in mid-2006, Ford Motor Company launched some highly visible—and high-risk—efforts to build credibility among its own people, and among any of the public that cared to listen in. At a time when everything was going wrong at Ford (see Chapter 4), management decided to roll the dice and tell its employees—through open online documentaries—that it was time to face some bad facts and rally around the company and the brand.

As of this writing, Ford has launched 27 of a planned 50 weekly online short films called "Bold Moves. The Future is Ford." The series started as a no-holds-barred dose of straight talk about Ford's business situation ("This is a company that could really go down"), past internal mistakes ("Rip out the BS and political posturing"), and the need to move ahead with renewed momentum or face a very uncertain future ("We must change or die"). Gradually, the series episodes morphed into self-sell pieces that attempted to pump up employees with the good news about a company in bad times, but they still include candid assessments from third parties.[11]

Ford's previous management had made it clear that one of the company's biggest challenges was convincing its own people that Ford was getting better. Apparently the company decided that it was time to put up or shut up . . . publicly. And not long after the campaign launched, William Ford, Jr. also put his job where his money was and stepped away from the CEO's office to make way for new management.

A Motivated Staff: Marketers' Best Friends

There are enormous differences between a marketing program that is planned and executed without the commitment and support of the company's staff, compared to one in which company staff enthusiastically endorse what is being sold and how it is being marketed.

That is the kind of difference that is found at the 550 Wawa Food Markets in the mid-Eastern United States, where buyers come back because of the friendly staff who go out of their way to remember customer names and their favorite brands. Employees at one Wawa store closed its doors and decorated the store like a chapel to host a wedding ceremony for a couple who had first met in the aisles of the store.

They do things like that at Wawa because the people who patronize the place love it and because it comes naturally to the people who work there. Most importantly, it's part of the company's culture and what the brand stands for in the crowded, competitive convenience store market.[12]

Author Jim Collins and his team, in researching companies that had moved from good to great, discovered that "The old adage 'people are your most important asset' is wrong. People are not your most important asset. The *right* people are." [Italics his][13] Part of what makes people "right," Collins explains, is the ability to foster an environment in which the truth can be told with impunity.

Marketing is one part of a company that puts that trait to a test. If a strong state of integrity exists it should be celebrated inside a company, not taken for granted. Employees should be reminded regularly of customers' faith in them as honorable people, who will treat customers as they themselves would like to be treated. That is the case among the counter staff at Kiehl's, the store staffs at Trader Joe's and Wawa Markets, the engineers at W.L. Gore, the IT people of Infosys, and the designers of Herman Miller.

Focusing marketing efforts on internal employees is relatively rare because there is an understandable tendency to concentrate on the battle with external competitors and market forces. But as the companies profiled in this book have proved, the fastest and most reliable engine of external success is through internal commitment. That is just as true, if not more so, when it comes to a commitment to practical integrity.

Rationalizing "Acceptable" Customer Deaths

Companies that periodically pay lip service to integrity but fail to make it an operational driver are sending the very signals that could doom their best marketing efforts, not to mention the company as a whole. One extreme example is a medical device manufacturer whose faulty quality control forced it to recall or issue safety notices for 88,000 heart defibrillators and 250,000 pacemakers, after the death of a 21-year-old patient.

The company commissioned a twelve-person panel of outsiders, which ultimately lambasted executives when they found that the company had wrongly depended on statistical projections rather than medical counsel. According to documents filed in a lawsuit against the company, executives allegedly projected that some patients might die as the result of short circuits, basing their projections on statistical analyses, but they found those fatalities to be "acceptable."

To whom were these deaths "acceptable?" To the families? And what about those who worked for the company at the time? How did those employees feel about such a revelation? How did those allegedly responsible for calculating such ghastly statistics rationalize working for a company that reportedly marketed a device with "acceptable" deaths among its customers?

The company in question was ultimately sold, along with an estimated $2 billion in possible legal liabilities. For obvious reasons, the management at the acquiring company subsequently decided to phase out the original defibrillator brand name.[14]

That's what's called an "unacceptable" loss in net brand equity.

Integrity Starts (Where Else?) at the Top

For integrity to be practical, it needs to be codified in behavior, not just in standards. The people of a company need to believe that the company *should* be one of integrity, that it *can* be one of integrity, and that they can be a part of making that happen. Although company employees are often ready to follow in that direction, they are rarely willing to lead until they are given a vision of what the company should look like, and until they see evidence of the endorsement, if not the personal involvement, of management in integrity issues.

In the 2005 *Fast Company* survey of mostly U.S. businesspeople, first mentioned in Chapter 1, 95 percent of the respondents said "yes" or "absolutely" when asked, "Do the ethics of the CEO play a meaningful role in the way the business gets done?"[15]

Today's successful CEOs often see themselves as motivators of their people, as opposed to the command-and-control autocrat model of years past. They are frequently encouraging if not pushing their staffs to stretch for the tough goals. The company's people need only try harder, think things through more thoughtfully, and dig deeper for that last ounce of determination, to achieve business gains for the organization and personal gains for themselves.

But that view appears to be evolving to include some important limits. Based on a 2005 worldwide survey of executives from 365 companies, researchers from Booz Allen Hamilton and The Aspen Institute concluded that:

❏ Ethical behavior is a core component of company activities

❏ Most companies believe values influence two important strategic areas—relationships and reputation—but do not see the direct link to growth

❏ Most companies are not measuring their "ROV" (return on values)

❏ Top performers consciously connect values and operations

❏ Values practices vary significantly by region

❏ The CEO's tone really matters[16]

This is a major change from even a decade ago and encourages observers to believe that ethical issues are finally being taken seriously by managements. It may be some time before integrity is directly tied to revenue gains, but there is little question that actions lacking integrity can have a negative impact on topline performance.

Most importantly, the Booz Allen/Aspen Institute finding that the top performers are connecting values and operations bodes well for the future of companies that succeed at that, including in their marketing operations. The study also confirms that, like most other issues, the CEO's demeanor can have a profound influence on how everyone else in the organization treats any issue, and especially when it relates to the ultrasensitive issue of integrity. The CEO's personal involvement can also have a similar impact on how the marketing is conducted and monitored for adherence to practical integrity.

BP: Are They Really Green?

With 2005 earnings of nearly $27 billion on revenue exceeding $295 billion, BP is the largest integrated oil company in the world. Along with the rest of Big Oil, BP is regularly accused of adding to the planet's pollution while simultaneously helping to remove its atmosphere.

In 2004, for instance, BP reportedly produced more than 85 million tons of greenhouse gases, nearly a 2 percent increase compared to the previous year. And, as environmentalists are quick to point out, the company increased its oil and gas extractions in 2004 for the 12th consecutive year.[17] It didn't help BP's cause when a pipeline breech some believe the company should have caught pumped 267,000 gallons of thick crude oil across two acres of Alaska's Prudhoe Bay.

On the other hand, according to its prominent CEO, Lord John Browne, BP is spending $8 billion over several years on alternative fuel energy solutions. The company also claims to have reduced its own carbon emissions by 10 percent below 1990 levels.[18]

In addition to its environmental efforts, warts and all, the company has publicly positioned itself as "Beyond Petroleum," focusing a spotlight on environmental crises and incorporating the concept of "green" into its core organizational values.

Some environmental organizations are applauding BP's efforts, and loudly. At the World Economic Forum in Davos in January 2006, Corporate Knights, Inc., a Canadian-based nonprofit group focused on corporate responsibility tracking, named BP as one of its Global 100—companies that they believe are operating in the most sustainable way in the world.[19]

The company has not announced that its environmental stance has generated specific business gains. However, it has been suggested that BP is creating an internal environment that attracts and fosters young people with environmental concerns. That may yet pay concrete dividends if some of these recruits apply their passion to finding environmentally friendly solutions that deliver both pride and profit.[20]

That benefit alone might make it worth the effort if its 100,000 employees become an army of believers.

*   *   *

The People Strategy:
Build a High-Integrity Team

1. Integrity Audit: Time for Candor

A candid internal integrity audit can quickly yield a workable list of challenges and shortcomings that could help create more powerful marketing efforts, as well as better align programs in other groups of the company. Below is a short list of suggestions that could guide marketing leaders in marshalling internal forces on behalf of marketing efforts, and serve as an important step in building a stronger, more persuasive marketing program.

❑ *Find out if your company's own people believe your marketing claims.* If not, where are they themselves unconvinced, and why? Whatever their number, your employee force is a better judge than the marketing team alone about what is credible and what is double-talk, however cleverly executed. Discover what they think, use what they think, and verify whether their views are representative of the larger base of prospects.

❑ *Consider assessing your marketing team members' personal integrity.* Are they fundamentally honest? Do they understand the line between aggressive marketing and deception? Or do they have wobbly values that are actually cynical and reflect a "whatever-it-takes" attitude?

❑ *What actions has the company taken in the past to avoid marketing integrity problems?* Were issues anticipated or reacted to when they became a problem? Was there a system in place to process the marketing integrity problems, or was it handled on an *ad hoc* basis?

❑ *Analyze what has happened if/when your competition has operated with questionable integrity.* Did your (or would your) company or brand respond in kind or be willing to suffer business consequences by not following suit?

2. Follow the Values

Be certain that your marketing programs reflect the most admirable values of the company . . . or the best values of customers, regardless of company values.

Company values, almost by definition, have become charmingly idealistic and hard to argue with. In some ways, the entire purpose of values is to establish almost unrealizable goals so that the staff can never stop stretching to reach them. The question is, how closely do your company's marketing programs match those values?

Consider laying the values and the marketing program elements side-by-side and carefully comparing how they match, or appear to be out of synch. What steps would be necessary to ensure that any discrepancies did not happen again?

At Gap, Inc., all vendors must be approved by its Global Compliance team before any orders can be placed. Those compliance standards have become more stringent in recent years because of the need to crack down on labor rights violators that might be among its suppliers. Gap is also using competition between its vendors to help upgrade offshore working conditions. The company is measuring the progress made by vendors with an integrated scorecard. That scorecard is then employed to compare vendor responsiveness—and the vendors know it—which creates a healthy competition to increase standards. Gap, Inc. officials also hope to get all of their vendors to the top two tiers of performance on the scorecard as soon as possible.[21]

Such awards and vendor certification approaches could easily be adopted by all marketing departments to ensure that the work they produced met the highest standards of integrity.[22] This approach is even more effective when an organization receives accolades from outside agencies—especially when the company had been criticized for its practices in the past.

Returning to Gap once more, the company received widespread praise in 2004 and a Social Reporting award from *Business Ethics* magazine when it released its first Social Responsibility Report, which systematically diagnosed where it had succeeded and where it had room for improvement in managing its offshore sourcing vendors. "[The report] really raises the bar," said David Schilling of the Interfaith Center on Corporate Responsibility. "It's in the category of pioneer work."[23] This kind of rigor in reporting can be a very public way of demonstrating how closely the company's actions match its values. The same sort of approach can also be applied to marketing initiatives, if integrity issues are relevant to the work being done.

3. Encourage Healthy Skepticism

Encourage your marketing team to foster a healthy skepticism about product claims, to continuously be on the lookout for overpromises and flawed offerings, and to catch integrity lapses before they become public.

Skepticism among customers and prospects is something to be concerned about. A robust skepticism within the marketing team itself is a valuable aptitude because it offers an early test for the viability of claims. No one knows better where the skeletons are buried than the marketing staff. Use that knowledge to filter out specious claims, counterproductive exaggerations and any programs that your customers themselves would reject if they were given the choice.

4. Conduct Integrity Pretesting

Many companies routinely run marketing claims by focus groups or through quantitative research to be sure that they are relevant and compelling to prospective customers. In the same way, test the integrity of your marketing programs before they are launched. That research should also include questions about the credibility and trustworthiness of the message and the brand that carries it. It's far better to run into skepticism before a launch than after a program is already in the marketplace.

Once a full audit with these kinds of questions has been completed and analyzed, the company will have a strong understanding of the role of integrity in the day-to-day operations. Just as important, a roadmap can be assembled for strengthening the company's integrity actions in marketing and beyond.

5. Lead from the Top, but Look to the Middle

Cricket is as much a passion as a sport in India. Good tickets to good test matches are often hard to get. That's why several years ago some Infosys marketing staff in Bangalore were overjoyed to be invited by a vendor to the most important test match of them all, India versus Pakistan. The invitations even included spouses and guests, with full access passes to all VIP facilities over the five-day match.

Their spirits fell quickly, though, when their manager asked whether the cash value was over a certain modest amount. Yes, they responded, probably sensing what was coming. "Then," replied the manager, "you'll have to return the tickets." The junior staffers were not a happy bunch. "Where do you draw the line?" continued the manager. "If a gold chain costs as much as these tickets, then why not begin accepting jewelry? Once you slide the rule a bit on a given occasion, it becomes easier to slide it the next time around."[24]

As in the Infosys story, middle managers can often have a more frequent and profound influence on how workers handle integrity than does management. This was confirmed by the results of a 2000 Ethics Resource Center survey that found more workers feel pressure to adhere to ethical standards from their supervisors than they do from their top management.[25]

Here are some suggestions for involving both your management and your mid-level managers in marketing integrity:

❑ *Establish a marketing integrity initiative that is publicly endorsed by senior management.* Start the ball rolling for this by creating a presentation to senior management that emphasizes the importance of the marketing team building and maintaining the company's reputation as an integrity-driven organization.

❑ *Develop a periodic marketing integrity review, conducted by marketing managers, as part of their ongoing presentations to management.* Systematize integrity audits that demonstrate how well (or poorly) the company's marketing programs are adhering to integrity standards, and what steps are being taken to improve the company's performance in this area.

❏ *Promote a marketing integrity awards program that annually celebrates the marketing individual who best exemplifies the concept of marketing integrity.* Arrange for members of the senior management team to present the award within the marketing department.

These programs can and should be endorsed by senior management, but administered by middle managers who are likely dealing daily with marketing integrity issues.

The Southwest Employee Auditions

It's no secret that Southwest Airlines is one of the best-run companies of its kind (and it has this author's vote for one of the best U.S.-based brands around). But *Business 2.0* magazine included Southwest as the place that holds one of the "best kept secrets of the world's best companies." The "secret" is that applicants at Southwest don't really interview for potential jobs, they audition for them, much of the time without knowing they're being evaluated.

Starting with an applicant's first call to the company to obtain an application, the manager taking the call immediately starts noting anything special that stands out about the person, including some things that aren't necessarily positive. If they're flown in for an interview, they carry specially marked tickets that alert crews along the way, who make notes of how friendly and steady they seem to be.

In order to gauge how other people respond to them, each one is asked to give a brief talk. Not only is the speaking applicant evaluated, but how well the other applicants respond to that person is also noted carefully.

The Southwest audition "secret" is probably partly responsible for the airline's industry-low turnover rate and low customer complaint levels. More to the point here, the people of Southwest understand that they are the living, breathing personification of the carrier's brand, and they live it as well as any service company in the country.[26]

6. Find the Right Manager

Every major corporation now has compliance officers who track and encourage integrity. For example, Gap, Inc. has given integrity awards to its employees for the last several years, usually awarded to people who have performed with integrity in challenging situations and gone the extra mile to communicate integrity and ethics in their work.

But organizational integrity is about much more than putting the right policies in place. It's about having the right mentality when hiring, training, and leading your people. The position of "ombudsman" has been created in many news organizations in recent years, ever since the spate of plagiarism and fictionalized stories began plaguing more and more city desks. The ombudsman's role, among other things, is to challenge writers and editors about the accuracy of what they write. It is a check-and-balance system that is a necessary integrity checkpoint.

That is even more the case in news companies like the *New York Times,* where the 1,200-member staff still consider their product to be the "paper of record." The best ombudsmen are both supportive and skeptical, and it makes for an end-product that is more likely to reflect the highest standards of integrity.

Because marketing can have such a huge impact on a brand's equity, there may be a need for a sort of ombudsman—perhaps called a "marketing integrity manager"—whose job is to make sure that all marketing is accurate and honest. The role of this type of manager should be a supportive role, not that of a police officer peering into others' work in search of violations, which would probably not be helpful.

This manager should be a respected individual who can nonjudgmentally motivate the marketing team to stretch to the highest possible standards, encouraging individuals and teams to do the right thing—for the sake of the brand and the business, if nothing else. The integrity manager could suggest alternatives, share best practices, and find creative ways to reward integrity when it is demonstrated.

7. Build Transparent Integrity

We spend most of our waking hours on the job and devote more time to our colleagues than to our families. Sooner or later, we form some connections with the people we work alongside; if we're fortunate, the group or entire company has a sense of community. Practical integrity is the perfect glue for such a community. It is rooted in what every company ought to do, driven by what every company needs to do, and guided by what the customer wants us to do.

Herman Miller publishes a booklet about company values that have been a part of the company's way of working as long as anyone can remember. One section in particular makes it clear how important transparency is:

> Transparency begins with letting people see how decisions are made and owning the decisions we make. So when you make a decision, own it. Con-

fidentiality has a place at Herman Miller, but if you can't tell anybody about a decision you've made, you've probably made a poor choice. Without transparency, it's impossible to have trust and integrity. Without trust and integrity, it's impossible to be transparent.[27]

One community-based business that has done all of the above in unique ways is eBay. The company offers a working template for practical integrity, both in how it operates and how its people support its operations.

eBay is a thriving community of insiders—some of whom even work for the company. The king of the online auction sites now has a market worth exceeding Bloomingdale's, Macy's, Sears, and Toys 'R Us combined. The company is a go-between, but instead of just serving as a faceless conduit, the people of eBay also create communities of sellers who depend on the company and its operations to help them make a living.

The feeling is mutual, according to CEO Meg Whitman, who believes that the people of eBay don't work for the company; they work for the buyers and sellers on eBay, sometimes called the "ultimate economic democracy."[28]

One of the extraordinary things that sets eBay apart is the institutional premise that people can be trusted. The management of eBay, inspired by the instinctive idealism of its founder, Pierre Omidyar, established a "community values" code that, in this case, includes those who do business with eBay. Its first tenet: "*We believe people are basically good.*"[29]

Omidyar once said that eBay actually established its idealistic community, not really out of idealism, but because it seemed to be a practical way to offset the natural human tendency to assume the worst about people.[30]

Omidyar and CEO Meg Whitman don't force the eBay community's values on its people, but let it spread organically like in distributed networks. An important part of that process is peer-to-peer sharing, which is all held together with the values of the company that are lived as much as they are talked about.

Like most companies, eBay is a community of individuals who openly resist what they know to be unethical, who initiate whatever they can to urge ethical behavior, and who raise an integrity issue when it might otherwise be ignored. In fact, eBay has come to be an example of a practical integrity monitor for the rest of us who have something to buy or sell.

*   *   *

A Summary and a Few Questions

As more companies recognize the value of building company-wide masterbrands, they are also beginning to see the tangible benefits of their people having pride in the integrity of the organization. There is an opportunity for the staff to exercise some healthy skepticism about the work of the company, particularly as it relates to external marketing. A motivated, informed staff can be the marketer's best friends because they will daily demonstrate the value of the company that is also represented by the marketing programs.

The tone for a company's ethics and values are set by management, and so it is with the integrity that is practiced by the marketing team. But the middle managers are also important as practitioners and guides for younger staff on marketing integrity issues.

Some additional questions to consider:

1. *Are the people who design and implement the marketing for your company whole persons of integrity?* Are they able to look higher up in the company and see people of the same or greater integrity? Has anyone ever even asked those questions before? Practical integrity is as much about what marketers and their colleagues believe in as it is about what they do.

2. *How would your own people rate the integrity of your marketing programs?* How would they assess the integrity of your product development? Do they believe that your integrity as a company and a brand is adding to the value of your value proposition? Do they believe your marketing communications are honest and straightforward?

3. *Are you helping your HR department hire people of high personal integrity?* The first line of defense for integrity is in the hiring process. A properly trained HR team not only finds the best people in terms of conventional qualifications, they also know how to identify the ones who will contribute to the values of the organization. What could your team be doing to assist HR in finding applicants who are ready and eager to practice practical integrity?

4. *How could you be clearer and more aggressive in communicating to your people the need for practical integrity in everything they do?* Is integrity a tacit understanding in your marketing department, or an unbreakable rule? In what creative ways could you be even clearer with your team that if it doesn't pass the integrity sniff test, it doesn't make it out of the room?

5. *How might your people help your industry as a whole to increase the quality and frequency of employing practical integrity?* Are there opportunities for you to become a leader of integrity in your industry? Can you develop programs or communications that would encourage stronger adherence to integrity guidelines? Can your trade organiza-

202 · MAKING IT HAPPEN

tion or other industry groups be a vehicle for pushing for more integrity in marketing communications and other marketing channels?

Integrity was bred into many of us at an early age. For those who received such an upbringing, it is not likely they will ever forget what integrity is all about. Unfortunately, that does not necessarily mean they will always act on their instincts, for the reasons we have discussed in earlier chapters. Regardless of the staffs' backgrounds or the business situations in which they operate, practical integrity is a discipline that can be held accountable for its impact, as we will see later in Chapter 11.

CHAPTER 10

Benchmark Against a New ROMI

Achieving Return on Market Integrity

W arren Buffett began his storied business career at the tender age of six when he bought six-packs of Coca-Cola from his grandfather's grocery store and resold them as individual bottles for a tidy profit of 5¢ per. Now worth in the neighborhood of $45 billion, Buffett has said more than once that it takes sixty years to make a reputation and sixty seconds to lose it.

General Re, a troubled reinsurer that Buffet's Berkshire Hathaway company had acquired, was issued a subpoena in January 2005 in connection with possible insurance improprieties. When he heard about the subpoena, Buffett sent a memo to his managers and his board. It read in part: "Berkshire can afford to lose money, even lots of money; it can't afford to lose reputation, even a shred of reputation. . . . A small chance of distress or disgrace cannot, in our view, be offset by a large chance of extra returns."[1]

In other words, no matter how much revenue might be generated from what Buffet called "playing around the edges," that revenue can never be worth the loss of a company's integrity. In the near future, it appears more likely than ever that the integrity of a company or a brand will even more directly contribute to its return on investments.

The Rise of ROMI

By one estimate, the average tenure for chief executive officers is 54 months, while the average tenure for chief marketing officers (CMOs) is less than half that.[2] That disparity is not likely to change anytime soon, given the demand by management for CMOs to deliver higher revenue with less spending, and to prove the worth of every marketing investment, often before the investment is made.

Return on Market Investment (ROMI) became a hot topic about a century after some marketing exec was first asked to justify his budget. Delivering ROMI is now a pervasive and difficult challenge because there is no widespread agreement on how it should best be measured, or even if it really can be measured at all with any consistency.

Nevertheless, marketing accountability is seen by senior marketers as critical to delivering effective marketing, according to a 2005 survey of marketing executives by the American Marketing Association (see Figure 10-1).

As a quick reminder, the simplest formula for ROMI looks like this:

$$\text{Return on Market Investment} = \frac{\text{Gross Margin} - \text{Market Investment}}{\text{Market Investment}}$$

ROMI can be expressed a number of ways but is usually reported as a percentage. So if a company spends \$1 million for a marketing program that generates \$5 million in gross revenue with a 30 percent gross margin, then the company has achieved a ROMI of 50 percent:

$$\$5M \times 30\% = \$1.5M - \$1M = \$500K \div \$1M = 50\% \text{ ROMI}[3]$$

It's one thing to define ROMI, it's another to successfully calculate it. For one, the term "market investment" may not only refer to out-of-pocket costs such as advertising media, but must also take into account all of the other funds of the company that are put at risk, such as the value of the work hours needed to plan and run the program or the costs of the supporting corporate systems allocated to help get the program out the door (i.e., overhead).

Figure 10-1. Benefits derived from marketing accountability.

SOURCE: American Marketing Association, presented by AMA and Aprimo, 2005, accessed September 24, 2006 at: www.tmcatoday.org.

In addition, the static ROMI formula describes the costs and yields of a marketing program at a single point in time. Marketing programs almost always deliver an impact over a given period. That return influences, and is influenced by, the company's gross margin, the lifetime value of customers, and other financial factors that measure value movement over what may be a series of years.

But by far the most difficult challenge for marketers is attributing specific revenue gains to marketing alone. What starts out as a purely empirical calculation quickly gets down to some subjective factoring that must take into account revenue movement due to sales efforts, market changes, economic conditions, competitors' responses, and a bevy of other variables.

All of this is made even more complicated by the fact that marketing investments are often not considered true "investments" in the same way that capital spending or even salesforce hires are viewed. More often, they are considered unavoidable costs of doing business that are easier to cut than to justify. (Did you ever try to explain the long-term value of an "investment" when management can only think of it as a "cost?")[4]

There is a way to help management better understand the value of marketing investments: Help them to see that it may have a positive impact on a company's or brand's overall reputation, which in the long run may be an important influence on both short- and longer-term business performance.

A Different Kind of ROMI

The integrity of a company or brand is really what the customer is buying in the long run, because it guarantees that the company will deliver on its product or service promises. Measuring the positive impact of integrity requires getting a fix on a special kind of return to the business, which could be called a Return on Market Integrity.

The calculation for Return on Market Integrity would simply be a variation on traditional ROMI approaches, specifically:

$$\frac{\text{Return on Market}}{\text{Integrity}} = \frac{\text{Integrity-related Revenue} - \text{Marketing Integrity Investments}}{\text{Marketing Integrity Investments}}$$

❑ Marketing integrity investments might include prorated research costs that relate directly to tracking how well the company/brand is respected, trusted, and relied upon by its customer base.

❑ It might also include staff costs for those whose primary task is building and maintaining brand integrity.

❏ Legal and related costs might be involved because they ensure that all messaging and programs are in line with the company's integrity policies and values.

❏ Even prorated production and media costs behind any efforts specifically designed to demonstrate the brand's integrity might also be included.

Of course, like traditional ROMI, this calculation requires knowing how to attribute revenue to integrity-related actions, and how to integrate whatever impact integrity has on return on investment to the broader marketing investments made in support of the brand. But even if it meant making a significant number of assumptions, it could be a start toward quantifying the importance of integrity to the brand and the company.

Why Integrity Is a Return Worth Measuring

Why even bother to calculate Return on Market Integrity? Because, all other market factors being equal, practical integrity can be a force that may increase return-on-marketing investment. Here's why:

❏ *Measuring the impact of integrity can help marketers learn some key reasons why customers may remain loyal, leading to increased profitability.* Commitment is the difference between buying and believing, between purchasing out of habit and investing in something that you count on. We buy because we need or want; we commit to companies and brands that have treated customers as trusted partners, proven their credibility, offered value with integrity, and marketed their products and services honestly.

The 90 percent of Infosys customers who return year after year are there for one major reason: They can count on Infosys to deliver what they promise because they believe in the company's integrity. The customers who tell their friends about Patagonia, Timberland, and John Deere are sharing good experiences about good companies—not just about those companies' products, but about the kinds of companies they are and the way that they do business.

Practical integrity is a powerful bond that can garner strong loyalties because customers know they are dealing with a company that is distinctive in a way that is relevant and meaningful. If at all possible, that bond needs to be quantified.

❏ *Similarly, tracking integrity impact may yield new ways to attract more new customers than if the company had not adhered to such standards.* Any marketing program will perform more effectively and efficiently if it is built on provable claims about proven products and services embodied in brands that people trust.

Kiehl's Since 1851 is still operated like a neighborhood apothecary, which means that the people of each store have a personal stake in what they sell. The products they serve and the service they provide are uniquely superior to so many other alternatives, and customers return because they know authentic integrity when they see it. Women and men see and hear so many half-truths when it comes to health and beauty aids that they are irresistibly attracted to truth-telling when they find it.

In these skeptical times, integrity can be a powerful draw for some disillusioned buyers who are looking for a new place to land; getting a firm fix on the impact of integrity may facilitate that conversion.

❏ *Measuring Return on Market Integrity may help build strong competitive strategies that could provide an edge in the marketplace.* A competitor may gain some ground over the short term by stretching the truth or endangering its brands' equity, but this is an arena where what goes around tends to come around. Staying on course with practical integrity will pay for itself in the long run because those without such integrity will ultimately be flayed and fried by customers, regulators, or watchdog groups. As we discussed in Chapter 5 about "disruptive integrity," companies that stand out as high-integrity organizations can often enjoy competitive advantages, as has been demonstrated by Whole Foods, Apple, and Intel in their respective industries.

❏ *By regularly evaluating integrity performance and its impact on the financials, a company may also be able to reduce or eliminate unforced integrity errors, which have cost other companies major brand equity and sales declines.* There can be no more disheartening use of precious marketing funds than having to deploy them to correct mistakes of judgment and integrity.

In 2003, Americans woke up to discover that their supposedly safe mutual funds investments were less safe and considerably more risky than they had been told. A long litany of well-known mutual fund companies and major financial services companies were pulled into the muck as it became clear that billions of investor dollars had been risked in shady sales and money manipulation schemes, none of which were revealed in marketing communications. Upwards of $10 billion were yanked from the funds by angry investors, and the violators spent tens of millions on advertising apologizing for their transgressions.[5]

Marketing monies will not need to be diverted for corrective advertising or public relations defensive stands if a company stays true to mores driven by practical integrity. That requires that the company always have a good grip on the state of its integrity and its impact on the business, to the extent that is identifiable.

Equity Impact

There is absolutely no guarantee that companies that practice practical integrity will avoid some embarrassing situations in the future. Hewlett-Packard, for one, has historically been a company that has operated with exceptional integrity, but that ethos did not prevent members of its management from allegedly making serious ethical mistakes when investigating an information leak on its board of directors in the fall of 2006. On the other hand, when CEO Mark Hurd promised a congressional subcommittee that such an integrity breech would not happen again, his promise may have carried a bit more weight because of the company's 68-year record of spotless integrity prior to the scandal.

The probability of companies that employ practical integrity making serious integrity errors is much smaller than that of other companies, because they are committed organizationally and culturally to honesty and candor. That makes an enormous difference in how they create their products and services and how they market them to their customers.

Looking at it from another angle, how can practical integrity *not* have at least a moderately positive impact on business and therefore make it easier to market, especially given the well-documented rise in consumer and business customer skepticism and doubt? Whatever return a brand or company enjoys, whatever success it has in moving revenue with its marketing programs, that success will be enhanced—possibly dramatically—by a known reputation for practical integrity. Figure 10-2 suggests how that impact might play out.

COMA: The Costs of Value Lost

Management will never stop wanting more short-term revenue to be generated from marketing because many executives see it as marketing's reason for being. But remember that executive managers are always looking at both sides of the

Figure 10-2. Impact of equity-building actions on business.

	Example Indirect ROI Measures	Example Direct ROI Measures
Equity Building Business Actions	Gains in: All awareness levels All positive customer attitudes Perceived brand/company integrity	Gains in: Distribution Orders Revenue/volume Lower acquisition costs Customer lifetime value
Equity Eroding Business Actions	Declines in: Top-of-mind awareness "Right for me" and other key attitudes Perceived brand/company integrity	Declines in: Customer retention rate Revenue/volume Long-term stock price Revenue/cost ratios New acquisition rate

balance sheet, which is why the single most common move by a new CEO is to cut costs. Such actions are a signal to stakeholders and Wall Street that swift action can and will be taken to improve financials.

Marketers have an opportunity to feed that need by reminding management of the flip side of marketing impact: not just what can happen when marketing is supported but what is likely to happen when that support is substantially cut or eliminated. If marketing's most common role is to generate new revenue, a less common—but just as critical—role is to protect the company's assets. That's where a new four-letter acronym might describe this side of marketing accountability: COMA, or Costs Of Marketing Atrophy.

A "coma" is a sleep-like state of unconsciousness, which is an apt description of many marketing programs that are eviscerated by budget cutbacks or neglect. The term "atrophy" refers to a wasting away of some part of the body, usually because of a lack of exercise and/or sustenance; it is also a pretty good summary of the impact of malnourished marketing programs.

For some companies, brand atrophy is only one cutback away. The undermining of a brand's assets may begin when costs must be cut somewhere and, rather than trim more tangible assets like salesforce personnel or capital investments, management cuts all or part of the marketing spending because it is hard to quantitatively defend, or because several components of the marketing program may be more difficult to justify than others and their support is pulled before the CMO can effectively demonstrate their value to the marketing mix.

COMA attempts to quantify the real costs that a brand or company incurs when its marketing programs are reduced or eliminated. When that happens, not only is the opportunity for new revenue lost or diminished, it also raises the cost in terms of endangering what can be the company's most valuable assets.

COMA can create a decline in total brand/company equity, expressed as a percentage, which is the net brand equity following losses due to marketing atrophy:

$$N = (G + S) - D$$

Where:
N = Net Brand/Company Equity
G = Gross Brand Equity
S = Savings from Marketing Reductions
D = Brand Equity Loss from Impact of Marketing Atrophy

To take a simplified example, if a company estimates that its gross brand equity is $1 billion and it normally spends $10 million in marketing to sustain that equity, then cuts that marketing to $1 million, it may turn up (save) $9 million in cash. However, if that move results in share and/or revenue loss that reduces its brand equity in that same time period by, let's say, 3 percent ($30 million), then the resulting net equity loss would theoretically amount to about $21M:

($1B + $9M) − $30M = $979M (or − $21M versus previous equity level)

In this scenario, then, management would appear to be saving $9 million, but the brand's equity would be losing several times that amount.

A Conversation

"Laura, I can't help you."

"You've got to help me, Mac."

"It's not that I don't want to, but you're asking me to ignore opportunities to reduce costs."

"Look, Mac, all I'm trying to do is help us to look beyond the short-term cutbacks and see the big picture about what's happening to our brand equity."

"They don't pay me to do the big picture. They pay me to cut back spending."

"But don't you ever worry that all these cutbacks are hurting, not helping?"

"Never. I take great pride in my cutbacks."

"I understand, and you're very good at them. But here's a chance to show management that you have some creativity."

"I resent that, Laura. I'm very creative."

"I didn't mean it that . . ."

"I'm a very creative person. After work I'm a completely different guy."

"I'm sure you are, Mac."

"And at work I'm creative, too. Just not with my cutback reports."

"And why not with your cutback reports?"

"Because cutbacks enable us to slide more to the bottom line."

"But what if we slide so much to the bottom line that we no longer grow?"

"I'm not concerned with growth, Laura."

"Yeah, I get that."

The Impact of COMA

How are the costs of marketing atrophy identified and tracked? In much the same way as ROMI, but the effects may be more easily spotted, depending on the characteristics of the industry involved. As with ROMI, the impact may fall into indirect and direct clusters of findings over short- and long-term time frames.

The immediate COMA impact may include short-term declines in top-of-mind awareness (usually the first to erode), waning familiarity with brand details and news, and the beginnings of trial or reuse slippage. Similar declines in harder business numbers then follow, including early volume and revenue downward movements (see Figure 10-3).

Can such a broad concept as gross brand equity even be measured accurately over time? That's a question that Interbrand, the premier brand valuation experts, answers frequently. The most accurate way to know the real value of a brand is to sell it. But since most brands are far too valuable to part with, the methodologies used by Interbrand and other valuation companies are the best indicators we have. (See interbrand.com for more information on the Interbrand valuation process.)

To whatever degree the marketing team is successful in assigning hard numbers to these values, it may very well shift management discussions from turning up marketing savings to recognizing the net equity loss the company may suffer. That process may require getting management's agreement to some going-in assumptions, but it may be well worth the time and effort if the end-product is

Figure 10-3. Impact of COMA on business.

	Immediate Impact	Sustained Impact
Indirect Impact on Business	Immediate top-of-mind awareness decline Early negative attitude shifts Usage rate decline Early drop in trial levels	Major total awareness declines Significant attitude loss Loss of usage edge vs. competition Major trial/retrial losses
Direct Impact on Business	Initial volume softness Inability to sustain share of market Initial inventory rise Softness in distribution or reseller support	Major volume/share declines Major, costly inventory back-up Widespread sales support pull-outs

a consensus that short-term expense savings could have an unacceptable impact on the company's total worth.

In the End, It's About Nutrition

One of the reasons why this all relates to practical integrity is that it too, like marketing spending, could have a short- or long-term impact on brand equity. That's because both marketing support and practical integrity act like nutrition for the brand body.

We can eat junk food for years, or fail to exercise, or even smoke, and still keep moving through our lives. But sooner or later, our body pays the price. On the other hand, feeding our body nutritious food may not pay dividends immediately. But we usually reap some reward down the line when we feel better, and sometimes live longer.

Such is the case with investments in brands. Those investments in terms of marketing spending or establishing practical integrity may not yield next-period revenue gains, but they will increase the likelihood of dividends somewhere down the road.

As we discussed in Chapter 4 about the Ford brand valuation decline, it appears highly likely that brand equity is affected by credibility declines, among other factors. Depending on the industry, cutbacks in marketing spending may do the same if the momentum of a brand is dependent on keeping awareness or familiarity elevated, particularly compared to competition.

Spending support alone is not likely to add to the perceived credibility or integrity of a brand, particularly if the spending is used to just hammer away at buyers in ways that irritate rather than persuade. However, if the brand has messages that reinforce its integrity-based promises, retaining spending levels will likely reduce COMA, and boost credibility, which can lead to stronger business performance.

Given the difficulties of identifying and describing Return on Market Investment, there are no guarantees that marketers will always be able to use Return-on-Integrity or COMA calculations as justification for proceeding with their programs. Yet, the more forces they can harness to increase the probability of delivering traditional ROMI, the more likely they are to get the needed approvals to do what they know is necessary to support their brand and their company.

*   *   *

The Metrics Strategy: Benchmarking Against a New ROMI

It's a handy excuse: We can't measure the impact of a marketing program whose re-

◆ What If? ◆

What if your marketing team adopted a nutrition perspective in everything they did? What if the metaphor of a brand requiring long-term nutrition for the business to be healthy were the primary rationale given for funding and other support? What if the team created an elaborate but persuasive model of the business as the "body" of the company, sales as the working parts, and marketing as the source of fuel?

Would it be possible to propose that, as is true for poor nutrition, the impact of cutbacks in marketing can't be detected right away, but will surely be felt down the road? Could the competition be positioned as threats to health that can only be combated over the long-term by providing nutrition to the business on a consistent basis? Might past company downturns be tied back to decisions that led to "malnutrition"?

What if you just experimented with the metaphor and tried it out in a meeting or two to see if it might (finally) be a credible way for non-marketers to understand the critical nature of marketing support?

sults are muddied with sales efforts, competitive counter-offensives, price promotions, and so on and so on. In a perfect world, all such variables would be frozen. Since the world is not perfect, the marketing manager must find a way around its imperfections.

1. Get a Grip on COMA

If a marketer can sort out variables by likelihood of influence on Return on Market Integrity, it may be helpful in determining the sensitivity of the brand, company or industry to integrity issues.

In the example in Figure 10-4 a marketer may spot a group of variables that *might* influence the ROMI calculation, but only a relatively few that are *likely* to do so. This exercise could be a good first step that leads to more quantified analyses of variables that may have an influence on conventional ROMI, and/or the Return on Market Integrity.

Tracking COMA, like tracking ROMI, may require assigning values for indirect factor declines and mingling them with hard data from traceable softness in the marketplace. For example, if you can find even a directional correlation between awareness loss and attitude shifts and business declines, then you may be able to state with some certainty that declines in these two indicators happen too frequently to be entirely coincidental. Similarly, if share of market trends tend to head south within six to twelve months after marketing spending declines, that may be sufficient to indicate a link, particularly if there have not been any other major changes in the marketplace during that time.

When such changes do take place and disrupt your ability to read links between marketing levels and performance, it may be time to set up a controlled test area. If the revenue from one or two isolated areas can be dampened without harming the overall business performance of the brand or company, isolated markets are often the best way to demonstrate the dependency of business performance on marketing support.

Although brands in some industries are less immediately sensitive to marketing cutbacks or integrity controversies, COMA can rapidly accelerate once it has begun. This is because competition may take advantage of their higher share of voice, or because top-of-mind awareness declines may trigger a cascade of drops in familiarity, then usage. Or attacks on a brand's or company's integrity may have an influence far beyond the bounds of the marketing programs.

The other half of the COMA story is the additional investment needed for a brand or company to recover from a marketing cutback or from controversy stemming from its perceived integrity. When a brand suffers a major cutback in spending or a serious slam on its reputation, the impact may be a function of several factors, including how frequently that class of product/service is re-

Figure 10-4. In-market variables by likelihood of influence on Return on Market Integrity.

Variable	Potential Influence	Reason for Influence	Influence Factor (Probability)	Type of ROMI	Value Index (100 = Average)
Major competitive price reduction	Competitive share gain	Price sensitivity of industry	75% chance of significant influence	Return on Investment	130
Rogue salespeople use "incentives" to sell in new product line	Significant externally, if discovered. Internal morale killer.	Could undermine company's integrity with all customers	90%	Return on Integrity	110
Marcom messaging found to be deceiving	Significant	General skepticism of buyers	75%	Return on Integrity	135
Pending strike by service workers	Potentially serious, depending on outcome	Strike would shut down services after marketing investments would largely be committed	100%	Return on Investment	150
Product recall	Very serious, depending on scope	Recall would undermine trust in brand	80%	Return on Integrity	140
Economic downturn	Modest due to relative inelasticity of industry	Industry is relatively stable regardless of economic conditions	50%	Return on Investment	75

purchased, competitive activity levels, or the sensitivity of the industry to marketing spending.

2. Build an Integrity Impact Report

An integrity impact report could be built much like marketing mix optimization modeling, which is a series of multivariate regression analyses that identify the optimum combination of marketing elements to achieve performance goals. A similar approach could be used to determine the relative impact of integrity and related reputation issues on business performance.

Many companies track the views of their customers about product quality, level of customer service, and other standard evaluative measures. What if those companies also asked about the impact of integrity on their customers' views and actions? Admittedly, most customers would probably say that they are very interested in the integrity of a company they buy from. Yet if the company probes deeply into customers' readiness to act if integrity issues arise, it could yield some very valuable insights.

For instance, if customers believe that product durability or customer service treatment is related to the integrity of the company or vice versa, such findings could be helpful in the planning of future initiatives in those areas of the company.

Marketing "dashboards" that track both in-market performance and integrity issues can provide special perspectives on what is happening in the marketplace. If a company is seeing business declines and there are no significant general market or competitive factors at work, that company's user base may be losing faith in what the company is promising. The company's brand could be suffering from equity erosion because of a lack of credibility, or a declining relevance due to disinterest. Integrity speaks directly to the first issue, and indirectly to relevance because it could be a sign of a deeper loss of trust that emerges first as apathy.

Gap, Nike, and Starbucks, among many others, have all taken significant PR hits for controversial sourcing practices in the past. It's difficult to say to what degree sales were affected by rising consumer concerns, but the negative publicity and ongoing blog discussions about alleged abuses by company vendors could not have helped selling efforts.

As of this writing, however, each of these companies has invested millions to better understand where violations exist, to eradicate or significantly alter human rights abuses, and to much more closely monitor offshore suppliers. All three companies would probably be the first to admit that they have a long way to go before the problems are fully solved, but their efforts are being noted by customers and prospects and should have a positive impact on their credibility and respect among buyers and prospects.

Also, a properly aligned marketing dashboard will be highly sensitive to push-back from customers who no longer have faith in the company's brand. These are more than attitude checks; they are probes into the beliefs of customers that can erupt at any time into a domino effect in the marketplace and an eventual departure of even longtime users. If some of the troubled companies we've chronicled earlier in this book that experienced major brand equity declines had maintained such a dashboard, they might have been better able to predict and manage the storms that engulfed them.

3. Integrate Integrity into ROMI

A number of companies have incorporated the concept of Return on Integrity into their sales efforts, usually referring to post-Enron financial integrity or corporate values initiatives.[6] But a Return on *Market* Integrity requires linking practical integrity measures with business performance. This kind of Return on Market Integrity would address three issues:

1. *How are marketing efforts influencing purchase patterns among customers and prospects?* This seeks to understand how customers are responding to marketing in real time.
2. *How are customers and prospects responding to the way that the marketing is being directed at them, and how is that affecting their purchase decisions, if at all?* Assuming that the product performance and the competitive environment would remain roughly at the same levels over time, this could be one of the most accurate projections of how likely they would want to maintain a long-term affiliation with a brand.
3. *How does the customers' or prospects' view of the integrity of the company influence the efficiency of the marketing programs?* If a brand or company is respected as a practitioner of integrity, it is likely that fewer marketing dollars are going to be required to prompt a sale, while the opposite is true of less respected brands.

The addition of integrity factors may present new challenges in terms of statistical rationale, but it also could significantly enhance the impact and internal sellability of marketing efforts. That especially would be the case if this new integrity-sensitive business environment has made management more concerned about integrity issues throughout the organization.

*   *   *

A Summary and a Few Questions

Return on Market Investment (ROMI) is tough to nail down in any business, but marketers are getting better at calculating the impact of their marketing investments. Another angle to ROMI that marketers might want to consider is the cost of marketing atrophy, or COMA. By understanding how much is lost in brand equity or other business measures, management may get a better understanding of the full liability marketing cutbacks can create. What may also help the cause is to consider a brand's Return on Market Integrity, because it could have a real impact on how the brand and company are viewed by customers as they make their purchase decisions.

In addition, consider these questions:

1. *Do you have the tools necessary to gauge your Return on Market Integrity?* Are your current marketing research instruments flexible enough to credibly track and analyze the impact of integrity on your business, either positively or negatively? Are you able to identify specific variables and "freeze" them in order to read the ongoing return of your marketing programs? How might tracking buyers' view of the integrity of your brand or company assist in the calculation of total ROMI? What modifications would you have to make to better address integrity issues? If an integrity crisis erupted, would you be ready to track its impact on business performance?

2. *Have you ever assessed your COMA, i.e., the amount it costs you if and when your marketing programs begin to atrophy for whatever reason?* Are you able to provide management with a quantitatively sound analysis of how your marketing programs have been damaged by either cutbacks in support or integrity-harming events? If you began tomorrow, how quickly could you get the capability to address these challenges before you have to do so reactively?

3. *Would the environment in which you work help you or hinder you if you determined how best to use integrity to increase conventional ROMI?* Is there a willingness in your organization to 1) discuss marketing integrity issues and 2) do something to rectify any shortcomings? Is your organization more likely to wait for integrity problems to crop up before doing something about integrity challenges?

4. *What specific steps should you consider taking to help your organization become better at quantifying the impact of integrity on your business?* Would it make sense to incorporate integrity analyses into your ongoing marketing analysis work? If so, how would you go about it, and how would you gather support of the rest of the marketing team to build enthusiasm for the initiative?

Marketing integrity, like everything in marketing, must have a positive impact on business results. In our last full chapter, we will explore how to motivate the people of a company to plan for, and train, integrity throughout the organization.

CHAPTER 11

Preparing for a Better Way to Market

Integrity Planning and Training

Marketing communications executive Adam Hanft wrote a piece in 2004 for *Inc.* magazine in which he pointed out:

> We are now entering a cycle where ethical accountability will shape the way companies will be judged and valued. This isn't ethics as ornament, as the accessory of the moment, but as a new systemic force and reality.[1]

Marketing teams will play a crucial role in this new era of ethical accountability, but only if they can integrate programs like practical integrity throughout their marketing planning and training.

To that end, the remainder of this chapter will provide 1) a guide for building a marketing plan based on practical integrity, and 2) a suggested approach for training a marketing staff in the application of practical integrity to their individual roles on the team.

*   *   *

The Integrity-Based Marketing Plan

To help illustrate how all of marketing planning might be affected by integrity issues, the following is a marketing plan outline, highlighting typical plan components in *italics*. Following each subsection are suggestions for where and how integrity could be integrated into the plan, and how it could play an important role in the marketing of a brand or company.

Marketing Plan Executive Summary

Purpose and Scope of Document

This opening section is where the marketing team can lay out the overview of their marketing plan. The role of integrity in marketing programs could first be discussed here. For example, integrity could be positioned as the guiding principle of the Plan.

In companies like Patagonia, Timberland, and Herman Miller, integrity is central to their business values and marketing approaches. This is the section of the planning document where that kind of core commitment might be reaffirmed. If integrity has not yet been discussed explicitly in marketing planning documents, this preview of the Plan could underline the importance of integrity in all future marketing programs.

Recap of Key Elements (Including Recommendations)

Each of the key components laid out in the sections that follow are previewed briefly here, including recommendations that are impacted by practical integrity. For instance, this summary could point out how the entire Plan has integrity goals and strategies interwoven throughout it, and that they serve as one of the strategic adhesives for the full marketing planning process.

Marketing Situation

1. General Business Trends

❑ *Economic Issues:* How current or pending economic conditions in the marketing areas are likely to have an impact on customer or competitive actions.

❑ *Social Issues:* How the brand may be affected by social trends such as fads or social movements.

❑ *Governmental (Where Applicable):* How current or pending legislation or regulation may influence or even dictate certain marketing decisions.

Each of the trends discussed in this section of the Plan may be affected by practical integrity issues. That might include tough economic times that make it that much more important to provide an honest value to customers, such as what IKEA claims to provide. Or it could focus on buyers' need for a brand that they can trust in a highly competitive industry with many claims and counterclaims, such as the enterprise software or automotive markets. (Or tough times might also tempt the marketing team to try questionable tactics in order to generate more business during a difficult economic period.)

If governmental regulation is a major issue in the industry, this is also where the Plan could deal with the nature and extent of the regulation. (A stronger emphasis on integrity within the marketing plan might help staffers to avoid situations that might cause government regulators or watchdog groups to take an undue interest in your programs.)

2. Industry/Category Trends

❏ *Current Business Situation:* What are the key marketing metrics for the company, business unit, and brand?

❏ *Trends versus Previous Periods:* How do current business conditions compare to past experience?

❏ *Forecast of Future Trends:* Given all of the above, what are the most likely future business performance trends for both the short and long term?

The industry trends and broader circumstances that have an impact on marketing can also have a direct influence on integrity issues. For example, in an industry rocked by scandals, such as the mutual funds sector a few years ago, an explicit integrity-related benefit promise could have been a point of differentiation (although not a claim that would be wise to market aggressively). If an industry appears to be untainted by such troubles but customer retention is a problem for other reasons, such as is the case in the travel industry, credibility claims might help create a superior positioning for a company or one of its brands.

In addition, the ongoing outcry against misbehaving business leaders in general could suggest a need to more aggressively market a company's values as evidence of its trustworthiness. Explicitly claiming to be a company customers can trust may not reduce skepticism (in fact, it may raise it), but more subtly integrating integrity discussions into marketing outreach might have a positive impact over time. Just one caution: Don't even do that if there is any danger that pending actions by the company could be seen as less than transparent.

3. Competitive Environment

❏ *Definition of Competition:* What is the competitive set comprised of, including nondirect competition such as customer abstention?

❏ *Current Status of Key Competitive Brands:* What are the key facts about competitors that may have the greatest impact on the brand?

❏ *Likely Movement of Competitive Brands Given Expected Category Evolution:* How will competitors adjust to changes in the marketplace?

❏ *Audit of Current and Future Threats to Existing Brand Franchise:* Is the company under greater threat from its inability to make its numbers, or from its loss of current customers, or both?

As has been proven repeatedly by such companies as Trader Joe's and Deere & Co., strong integrity values can be a key competitive advantage. The integrity actions of such companies can 1) provide the headquarters staff, salespeople, or retail force with greater credibility as they promise benefits to prospective customers; 2) strengthen marketing communications with claims that are based in provable facts rather than empty hype; 3) fortify customer service morale and performance with evidence of the company's integrity-based actions; and 4) enhance pricing, distribution, and other marketing-related initiatives in order to reinforce the company's commitment to keeping its promises.

Marketing Plan

1. Business Objectives

❏ *Specific volume/revenue/share/profit/other goals, as applicable.*

❏ *Breakout of goals by brand or organizational segments.*

❏ *Profitable revenue is gains or similar objectives.* While integrity may not play a direct role in generating revenue, it has an important contributing role as a possible reason for trial (as in the case of the Timberland customers who admire that company's community service work), as an aid to retention (as with Kiehl's customers who keep coming back because of the integrity of their products and people), and as a builder of employee enthusiasm and productivity (as at W.L. Gore and eBay).

2. General Marketing Strategy

❏ *Source(s) of Business.* This could include, for example, expanding the current user base, and/or attracting new users, and/or increasing customer usage rates.

❑ *Overall Marketing Strategic Approach.* This might include building top-of-mind awareness and initial trial of a superior product that is likely to persuade onetime users to consider habitual use.

❑ *Competitive Strategy.* For example, this could be maintaining performance superiority regardless of impact to bottom line (with limits).

Companies that are considered more reliable and more credible by their existing customers have more marketing strategy options available to them than companies that may not enjoy such reputations.

When a company like Infosys sees 90 percent of its growth coming from existing customers, it is free to launch business development strategies to reach out to new customers, confident that their current user base is relatively secure because of the company's solid reputation for integrity. Or if the company chooses to drive deeper into its current customer companies, its practical integrity will also serve as a door-opener and reinforcement of the Infosys identity.

Alternatively, the stronger the integrity reputation of a company like Infosys, the more likely the company will be able to compete successfully against the world-class competition in its industry, such as IBM and Accenture. A reputation for integrity can help level the field against quality competition, even those much larger in size, and enable the company to pursue a marketing strategy that seeks to build global share of market.

3. Focused Marketing Strategies

❑ *Customer Partnering*

- *External Partnering:* Comprehensive descriptions and thorough analysis of external customers and prospects, segmented by real and potential importance to short- and longer-term business performance.
- *Internal Partnering:* A similar analysis for all internal partners, including management, middle management, and rank and file staff.

In this skeptical age, integrity can be an effective stimulant of initial interest for new prospects and a driver of choice for ongoing users. Integrity might be a key user issue in the food business, for example, because we rely on food companies to ensure the safety of what we put in our mouths. In contrast, integrity may be less inherently top-of-mind among apparel customers, but it can rise to the surface when outsourcing labor relations or other controversial issues are taken into account in the purchase decision.

4. Brand Platform

❏ *Brand Positioning.* What the brand promises, as understood by the customer, relative to competition. Should also include an analysis of optimum proof points.

❏ *Strategic Persona and Values.* The human-like characteristics of the brand, including the values the brand stands for.

❏ *Brand Attitude (Where Applicable).* What customers think the brand thinks of them.

❏ *Value Proposition.* The value provided to the customer-partners, in their own view.

There are several places in the brand platform strategies where integrity may play a pivotal role. The brand positioning, for example, might include integrity as part of the central promises, thus providing points of superiority over competition. Or, it could serve as one of the strategic proof points as a reason to believe overall benefit promises. Integrity is implicit, for instance, in the positionings of Patagonia, The Body Shop, and Johnson & Johnson.

Integrity could also become strategically integral to the brand personality, which might convey how dependable or trustworthy the brand and product are. Integrity might also become a key component of the brand value proposition because it would guarantee the values provided by the brand.

These platform points of entry for integrity are very important to a company like Trader Joe's. The company's self-described role as "purchasing agents for the consumer" is affirmed by its reputation of integrity in its product delivery and its value proposition. Similarly, product integrity—in both the conventional and practical integrity definitions—plays an important role in the positioning of John Deere tractors, which are sold under the proposition that "Nothing runs like a Deere."

5. Identity Distribution (Including Internal Identity)

❏ *Brand Contact Opportunities.* What are the entry points for the brand into the lives of the customer-partners and the company's own people?

❏ *Redistribution of Contacts.* Is there a need to look at redistributing brand contact points?

Exactly where and how a brand comes in contact with customers could have practical integrity implications if, for example, the brand is seen as intrusive and, as a result, may not be seen as all that likeable.

How a marketer markets is becoming a much more important issue than in the past. How the brand spreads its messaging needs to be considered within the context of when and how customers want to be contacted. And when the contact takes place, is it done in a way that cloaks the brand's involvement, or is it clear to the buyer that someone is trying to sell something? These issues should be discussed in detail in this or other sections of the Plan.

6. Integrated Sales/Brand Strategy

❑ *Mutual Goals of Brand Marketing and Sales Programs.* What are the common goals that these two critical groups can rally around? In what other ways can sales and marketing collaborate to form the basis for a more integrated working environment?

❑ *Integrated Channel Strategies.* How can marketing create more integrated approaches to existing and future channels?

Often one of the most difficult relationships for marketers to maintain is with their own sales department. This part of the Plan would speak to how the two teams' efforts could be more productively integrated. It offers an opportunity for marketing management to clarify the integrity values it is incorporating into the Plan, and how they hope to have those views supported and reinforced by sales actions, and vice versa.

Note: This should *not* be presented to sales as a commentary on the integrity of salespeople or their operations, but rather as a point of consensus around which the two departments can come together.

When Lou Gerstner arrived at IBM in the early 1990s, the integrity of both the IBM brand and company operations was in question—not ethically, but in the sense that they were no longer bolstering the integrity of the IBM reputation. The needs of customers were often being ignored. Gerstner rejuvenated the historical hallmark of IBM (customer service) and in the process reestablished the company's commitment to an integrity that requires that promises made be promises kept.

7. Pricing Strategy and Value Proposition

❑ *General Pricing Approach.* For example, will the pricing strategy be leading the competition or following it, demand-driven or according to pre-set tiering, or based on historical trends? To what degree will it approach pricing from the customers' perspective (e.g., Economic Value to the Customer [EVC] pricing)?

❏ *Situational Strategies.* How will the brand maintain positive value perceptions among its customers? How will the company defend its value properties against competitive inroads?

Overall, pricing strategy should deal with pricing as an indicator of value rather than as a tactical tool to undercut competition, including competitive pricing. It should also be considered much more than a per-unit revenue promise; it is the telegraphic way to communicate how much the buyer-seller partnership is valued.

FedEx is a master at adding profitable services that shine the spotlight on benefits, supported by concrete features, and which emphasize value-added benefits instead of price points. They were among the first to install dedicated computer ordering and tracking in their customers' shipping departments in the 1980s, enabling customers to participate in the supply chain process (and reducing FedEx costs in the bargain).

FedEx also continuously updated its software to add more value with each transaction. They provide ultra-dependable overnight and same-day delivery. Their computer tracking has never been beaten. They tend to cost more than their competition but are perceived as a superior carrier that provides top-drawer service when nothing else will do.

All of these features reinforce the value of FedEx, but it is their integrity that they bring to the business that seals its value proposition.

8. Field Marketing Programs

❏ *Strategies*

- *External Customer-Partnering (Targeting) Strategies.*
- *Advertising, Sales Promotion/Merchandising, Distribution, Online, Mobile, Direct Marketing, Public Relations Programs.*
- *Creative Strategy.* What the brand promises and what proof points and personality will be conveyed (based on positioning and strategic persona).
- *Spending (Media) Strategy.* What criteria will be used to determine spending, and what will be used if/when the spending budget is cut back or increased.

❏ *Tactical Plans.* The specific programs that will be executed in the marketplace.

The external marketing tactics are the only marketing touch points for most customers. Marketing plans that are supported by practical integrity are based on delivering what is promised with unerring consistency. That, in turn, puts significant pressure on the creators of the marketing messaging to avoid over-promise, which can undermine whatever integrity equity exists.

Some examples of tactical elements that could be driven by a company's integrity strategies:

❏ *Product.* Offering only products and services that perform so superbly that they generate their own marketing momentum, above and beyond formal marketing efforts.

❏ *Price/Value.* Employing pricing at wholesale and retail levels that reflects the company's commitment to provide fair and equitable value, and which discriminates only on a legitimate basis, such as legitimate cost differences rather than customers' ability to pay.

❏ *Marketing Communications.* Fielding only those communications that have been repeatedly checked for accuracy and clarity. Also, ensuring that the communications channels used are building positive awareness among prospects, not annoying them.

❏ *Sales Promotions.* Full, money-back guarantees that validate the reliability of products sold and the integrity of the company to back up its claims.

9. Internal Stakeholder Strategies

❏ *Internal Marketing Planning.* A mirror image of the external Plan in structure, internal marketing treats company staff as prime customers.

❏ *Messaging Strategy.* Delivering messages that will best motivate internal staff.

❏ *Message Channel Strategies.* The specific channels to be employed to reach internal staff effectively, yet helpfully.

❏ *Tactical Plans.* What will be executed in the internal marketing of the brand or company, such as streaming video and other electronic communications. Every major corporation provides employees with video presentations of management talks, etc. This is also an opportunity to include specific discussions of integrity planning and actions. Hewlett-Packard, for instance, provides regular online training for their employees on what they call Standards of Business Conduct (SBC). Their SBC programs could easily be adapted to include applying practical integrity to all marketing efforts.

❏ *Printed Materials.* Companies that still distribute old-fashioned "house organs" could consider adding a regular feature on how the company markets and performs in general with integrity, or an ongoing FAQ on integrity issues.

❏ *Online (E-mail, Proprietary Communications System, Intranet).* BP, for example, provides on its website opportunities for both employees and outsiders to track the company's environmental efforts, and even to evaluate their effectiveness (see bp.com, "HSE tracking tool").

❏ *One-on-One and Group Meetings (Management Brown Bag Lunches).* These are opportunities for management to discuss integrity issues, and for company staff to raise points about questionable company practices.

As discussed in Chapter 9, the company staff members are the first line of customers. They may be insiders, but they have strong expectations that their company will deliver for them, not just for the external customers. The integrity that is spotlighted in the internal marketing efforts must be at least as strong proportionately as its counterpart that drives the external marketing programs.

10. Metrics and Measurements

❏ *Measurement Strategies.* The measurement strategies that will guide the tracking of the marketing programs, including:

- Pre/post-measurement strategies
- Ongoing tracking strategies
- Return-on-Market Integrity calculations, as feasible

❏ *Programs.* The specific research program that will be used to determine whether goals were reached by the various marketing programs. This should include internal stakeholder research:

- Research instruments and methodologies to be used
- Attitude and awareness tracking studies
- Periodic market checks
- Customer/nonuser panels

This is the place in the plan where Return on Market Integrity, a particular kind of ROMI, can be defined and explained. In addition to more conventional marketing metrics, integrity returns can provide some key indicators of such measures as trust and reliability to the metrics that are tracked surrounding the marketing programs.

This may require some pioneering research innovation to craft a research tool that will identify key integrity issues and performance. The project could offer the research teams a chance to be creative about how to probe into areas that may not have been explored by the company in the past.

11. Logistics and Costs

❏ *Specific Logistical Actions.* How and when will the Plan be implemented:

- Near-term projects that must be completed to fully enact approved strategies (beyond the tactical plans listed above), prioritized by urgency and importance
- Specific timetable with responsibilities and methods of accountability

❏ *Budget.* How will the marketing programs be funded and accounted for:

- Itemization of costs
- Source of funding
- Contingency planning if funds are significantly reduced or increased

It is important that integrity-related marketing actions complement and enhance other marketing plan logistics, not encumber or otherwise interfere with them. For example, a company that launches a sweepstakes promotion does not require any additional effort to be sure that the program is run honestly and with customers' needs foremost in mind. In the same way, integrity elements of the Plan should not add significant additional cost—unless the marketing team is promising additional revenue due to efforts in that area.

Plan Summary

As a part of the Plan's final wrap-up, the marketing plan summary might also include a recap of integrity efforts that have been integrated into the marketing programs and how they are expected to enhance the planned programs across the board.

Most larger companies have a full array of codes and policies that deal with ethics, compliance, and what the company considers right and wrong. For the

◆ What If? ◆

What if no major marketing recommendations could be issued unless they discussed the impact of the proposals on the company's integrity reputation? What if all future marketing plans began with a statement about how critical marketing integrity was to the organization? What if the head of marketing led a review of all work during that period, with the specific goal of assessing how well it demonstrated the company's integrity (in addition to its other business-building goals)? What if each senior member of the marketing team was in charge of facilitating one session per year with new employees, regarding the importance of marketing integrity?

What if the marketing department proposed to the rest of the company that it organize a series of company-wide brown-bag lunches, led by well-known business leaders, to discuss the state of integrity in American business?

marketing team, it will be an integrity-driven marketing plan that speaks most persuasively about what the brand and company stand for, and what they must do to protect its integrity reputation.

The right plan will help the internal staff to support the company's actions on behalf of practical integrity, and provide a detailed guide about how practical integrity can become an important component of all marketing initiatives.

*   *   *

Practical Integrity Training

Training the Individual and the Team

Honda's success in the 1970s in the United States was followed up a decade later with its announcement that it was introducing the Acura luxury brand, and there were more than a few skeptics. True, Honda had made superior quality, durable small cars. But to leap into the American luxury market—even with a "stealth branding" strategy that cloaked the Honda parentage—was stretching credibility. The car was a fine product that lived up to Honda's reputation, but without specifically relying upon it.

When Honda and Toyota later announced in the mid-1980s that they were introducing luxury car brands, there were some serious doubts about their ability to deliver what they promised. Skeptics could be found even after both companies' successful Acura and Lexus introductions. It turned out to be a nonissue.

Some traced Honda's and Toyota's success all the way back to the revolutionary manufacturing methods introduced to Japanese industry in the 1950s by famed U.S. consultant W. Edwards Deming.

In his seminal work, "Deming System of Profound Knowledge," the pioneer consultant maintained that "the first step (toward more productive change) is transformation of the individual." Deming understood that radical and positive change in production methods (and, we can assume, in other company activities) must start with the individuals accepting their responsibility to contribute to that change.[2]

With that change, a number of Japanese companies began manufacturing products that generated their own marketing propulsion, fueled by, among other things, a merging of company integrity and the personal integrity of its people that was built into every car.

That was a genuine revolution in the training of individuals in an industry. It is that sort of innovative thinking and commitment to positive change that should form the foundation for the integrity training in a company, although obviously on a much smaller scale.

Training That Is Administered Once, but Replenished Frequently

The stand-up comedienne Phyllis Diller once remarked: "What's the point of making a bed? You just have to do it all over again six months later." That, in a nutshell, is what corporate training often turns out to be—apparently necessary at the time, with results that rarely stick, and which often has to be repeated for reasons that are never clear.

As we discussed in Chapter 9, if a company's staff is going to convince customers and prospects of the merit of their brands and organization, they are going to have to be convinced themselves. In a company that is fully driven by integrity throughout its organization, its marketing team members might never need to undergo practical integrity training. They may have already forged mutually beneficial customer partnerships, always built products that marketed themselves, promised only what they could deliver, and already created communications whose claims were beyond reproach.

For other companies that are just trying to make their numbers but are inadvertently hurting their cause by ignoring practical integrity, there is a better way to go about marketing products and services, and it may require training for it to be done right.

Training Goals

Practical integrity offers a company's staff or brand team something real and persuasive to rally around and implement. Most companies will not grossly violate any laws, but they may not be marketing with accuracy or candor, either. Practical integrity training can help the marketing team to understand the benefits of becoming known as a company with unimpeachable integrity.

Although training should be customized to each company, here are some possible training goals that might be a good starting point:

❏ *To understand where the company performs with integrity and where it could improve.* Both what is "practical" and what represents "integrity" will vary greatly by company, industry, sector, and specific marketing circumstances. Any training initiative should first be clear about these definitions. Regardless of the industry, however, integrity training should be grounded in honesty, equitable value, and promise-keeping.

❏ *To appreciate the powerful influence marketing tools can have on all constituencies inside and outside the company.* Marketing staffs routinely employ marketing "weapons" whose power and influence are not always understood, much less appreciated. Practical integrity training can help to clarify how major marketing tools can be used to reinforce a company's or brand's commitment to integrity-based marketing.

❏ *To learn how to refine and redeploy their marketing programs* so that they can build a stronger business, driven by the company's integrity and the high-integrity manner in which its brand(s) is marketed. Training could provide a forum for marketing staff to work through how specific implemented or planned programs might be refined to better reflect the commitment to practical integrity.

Training Leadership and Participants

Practical integrity training should be personally endorsed by the company CEO, ideally with that person launching the kick-off session. From that point forward, the senior-most marketing officer should be overseeing the work of the participants, with one of the senior marketing staff members actually responsible for the training implementation.

Practical integrity training is one of those subjects with relevance at all levels of an organization, so it might be best to simply mingle senior and junior members of each marketing team within a given integrity training session. However, care must be taken not to allow the senior members to dominate the conversations. Consequently, when the participants break out into groups to discuss some key issues, the group facilitators and recorders should never be senior marketing personnel.

Because marketing touches so many different units in a company, it also may be helpful to have representatives from other departments of the company involved in the training as well. For example, individuals from product development, sales, supply chain/distribution, customer research, and other units could be invited to attend, with a reminder that it is their input that can often have a major impact on the company's dealings with integrity issues. A representative from human resources should also be a participant, since those staffers need to be aware of integrity challenges as they are recruiting new employees and counseling the current staff.

Finally, the company's marketing communications and research providers might also be actively involved in this training. These companies and individuals are representing the company in their field work and planning and they could very well inadvertently damage the brand's equity through their actions.

Training Channels

Here are some suggested channels to consider that would keep practical integrity on employees' radar screens:

- ❏ *A full marketing integrity workshop.* The best training of this type begins with a half- or full-day workshop that immerses the participants in the background, components, and recommendations for implementing practical integrity in their work lives (see Appendix D for a prototype script for an integrity training workshop).

- ❏ *Online "teasers," reminders, and tune-ups via the company intranet.* An intranet offers simple, inexpensive opportunities to send daily or weekly messages to staff that remind them of the tenets of practical integrity. It might also make sense to stream brief videos through the intranet to provide updates on the issues from management. These can be used as teasers that prepare and motivate the staff before undergoing practical integrity training, or as follow-up.

- ❏ *Annual awards programs that celebrate acts of integrity in the marketing ranks.* Integrity awards are becoming more common in the corporate world, but they tend to focus on traditional integrity issues. It may be helpful to establish practical integrity awards that highlight proactive marketing actions. The scope of these might go beyond simply acting with integrity and include proactive product, pricing, and marketing communications initiatives that contribute to the company's general reputation.

❏ *Brown-bag lunches where the CEO, CMO, and other executives discuss why marketing integrity is so critical to the company-wide mission and business performance.* Integrity is on the minds of all C-level execs these days, and these informal get-togethers are ideal places to discuss the issue within the context of marketing.

❏ *Guest speakers who discuss what other companies are doing in the integrity area, including best practices.* Best practices in practical integrity is a topic that can be presented with real credibility by representatives of noncompeting companies and other experts who have insights and experiences to share.

Example Integrity Training Content

Here are some suggestions about the specific topics that might be included in integrity training, along with a brief rationale for each:

❏ *The Power in (and Slipping from?) Our Hands.* What impact do our marketing tools have on the marketplace, and where and why are we in danger of losing some of that impact? What is happening out there that might be undermining our efforts to sell our products and services? How are our customers and prospects changing in ways that give us less control and make it more difficult to be relevant in their daily lives? What steps must we be taking to catch up with habits and practices that are threatening to marginalize our businesses?

❏ *The Lynchpin Importance of Marketing Integrity.* If the past five years have taught us anything in business it is that integrity is an issue that influences customers, and often in negative ways. Everyone in a company must be persuaded that integrity is no longer just a guideline for clean living, but a growing demand by the public that can have an impact on businesses of all types in all parts of the world.

❏ *Understanding Practical Integrity.* Is "marketing integrity" a contradiction in terms? What does it really mean, and why is it critically important to the company as a whole? How does "practical integrity" have a direct bearing on delivering the numbers? The respect it garners may be the key to customer loyalty and increasing customer lifetime value.

❑ *The Scope of Responsibility.* Why practical integrity is everybody's business because it involves everybody's job. Practical integrity touches every major operation of a company—sales, marketing, manufacturing, product development, supply chain, finance, and HR. Practical integrity is about integrating all of the contributions made by the staff into a more persuasive story for prospects throughout the marketplace.

❑ *Incorporating "Living Integrity" into Our Everyday Marketing Work.* Marketing integrity must be lived, not just learned. The exercises for the participants in training are designed to integrate marketing integrity principles and practices into their daily work so that practical integrity becomes reflexive instead of burdensome. Part of this process will be personally committing to some marketing integrity principles. (To test yourself, take The Marketing Ethics Quiz in Appendix E.)

Example Training Exercises

Every company has its own set of marketing situations, competitive pressures, and industry environments. Any marketing integrity training needs to take those unique circumstances into account and include whatever content is most appropriate. The following are some example exercises that may be useful to include in training sessions:

❑ *Express Your Brand's Integrity.* Create a "graffiti wall" where participants can write and draw their impressions of what integrity means in the context of the marketing of their brand or company. This technique worked successfully for BP a few years ago as it seeded among its people the new name and mission of the organization formed by the merger of Amoco and British Petroleum.

❑ *The Job Architect.* Give participants an opportunity to redesign their jobs to be more integrity-centered, including suggestions for being compensated for specific integrity programs or acts of integrity. This author has had good luck training individuals in technology companies by offering them opportunities to redesign how their daily work is conducted.

❑ *A Day in the Life.* Use a video or written narrative to portray a day in the life of participants and show how a greater emphasis on marketing integrity might change the way they work. eBay and Southwest Airlines, among many others, have helped their staffs to better understand their customer types by producing high-quality videos that profile key customer partners.

❑ *Integrity Jeopardy.* Use a light-hearted quiz show format with a serious message to ask training participants questions in the form of integrity scenarios. The other participants are the "judges" who decide which response reflects the best possible marketing integrity solution. This author successfully trained mid-level managers in a professional services company with this approach.

❑ *Fact or Fiction?* Have participants tell stories of business situations that teach valuable lessons about marketing integrity. At the end of each story, the other participants vote about whether the story was fiction or nonfiction, and why it has relevance to the company.

❑ *Integrity Nightmares.* Ask several participants to create "nightmare scenarios" involving the compromising of the company's or brand's integrity. The rest of the participants debate about possible solutions and the short- and long-term impact of each. This technique has been used successfully—sometimes in the form of "war games"—to work out the best approaches to restoring customers' faith in a company's integrity.

Training Practical Integrity Trainers

To help perpetuate the practical integrity way of working, a small number of trainers should be appointed and trained in how to train others. Some key characteristics to look for in a trainer are:

❑ Does he seem to have a strong sense of personal integrity, and is that the general view of him by others in the company? Also, does he have a sincere interest in integrity issues, particularly relating to marketing?

❑ Is the prospective trainer among the middle or senior-middle managers who have sufficient experience to make their observations credible in the eyes of training participants?

❑ Is she well respected by others and has she demonstrated a positive influence on peers?

❏ Is the prospective trainer articulate and does she speak persuasively in formal and informal settings?

❏ Does he have any experience presenting or facilitating group discussions? Is he an attentive listener and genuinely interested in others' views? Does he enjoy teaching or mentoring, and has he demonstrated that interest in other settings in the company?

❏ Has she displayed strong (but not necessarily unquestioned) loyalty to the company?

Trainer Guidelines

Keep in mind that each training group may have its own set of specific needs and work circumstances that may require customizing the training approach accordingly. However, the following general guidelines may be helpful to trainers:

❏ *Learn the training material quickly and thoroughly.* The participants must believe that you are well versed in the material. It is not necessary to literally become a "practical integrity expert," but it is important for you to be sufficiently familiar with the material that the participants can rely on you to either answer a question immediately, or promise to obtain an accurate answer and respond within a few days of the training.

❏ *Recognize that your participants are at different levels of understanding and enthusiasm about integrity training.* Try to determine as early in the training day as possible how much interest and experience the participants have with practical integrity so you can adjust your approach to their interest and aptitude levels.

❏ *Conduct training that is as interactive, fun, and engaging as possible.* Participants do not want to sit and listen to one-way communications about any subject, particularly about integrity. Involve them using continuous Q&A that is interwoven throughout the program. Make use of the suggested exercises and games, and add your own versions once you have become comfortable with the training routine. Help the participants feel as if they are contributing to the success of the day. Training is education, and most people don't have the desire to go back to the classroom. Change that perception by making it clear as early as possible that this training will be fun, not work.

❏ *Employ as many real examples as possible.* Prior to the training, obtain several examples for each of the points you will be making, using well-known brands and companies. Work with the participants within the context of as many case studies as possible to show how practical integrity works in real-world situations.

❏ *Emphasize the need for future commitment in word and action.* Take time to underline the importance of a commitment to marketing integrity. Help them understand that they must *personalize* their approach to practical integrity, that is, incorporate the brand into their daily routine so that it becomes part of who they are as a company staff member. Consider asking them to sign an informal commitment to always perform their jobs with practical integrity.

Integrity marketing planning and training are the disciplines that will sustain and build upon the company's ability to drive practical integrity throughout the organization. They can be used as a potent tool to help your people to compete more effectively in the marketplace. It may require some hard work and commitment, but the payoff for the company, its people, and its other constituencies can be positive growth and protection against some of the challenges that lie in the path of every company.

CHAPTER 12

A Final Thought

Many years ago, I served in the U.S. Army Reserve. One day our commandant, alarmed at the number of Army Jeep accidents his troops had experienced, asked a driving expert from the California Highway Patrol to visit our unit to provide special instruction to those of us with aggressive driving habits.

Midway through our training the CHP officer was asked, "How do you know when you are going too fast around a curve?" The answer, the officer replied, can be found in the seat of your pants. When you feel your tail end sliding a bit because of centrifugal force, you're probably driving too fast.

When we are in danger of violating our own sense of integrity, we feel a similar tug, although not necessarily in the same place. The trick is to actually pay attention when we get that internal warning that we may be going too fast around the curves. In life, we might call that feeling a pang of "conscience." In the commercial world, we call it good business.

I have a friend who has worked with some of the biggest marketers in the country, and who has not always felt good about the work he did. One day, over coffee, he said to me: "What I need—and I think a lot of other people need—is a better way to do marketing. A way that we can be proud of." It was a goal of this book to provide at least one approach to that challenge.

When I'm not consulting, I teach strategic marketing to MBA students. This is one of the last things I say to my classes at the end of a course:

> There will always be people who stretch the truth in marketing, or promise more than they can deliver, or push their messages into people's lives where they are not needed or wanted. There will always be people who assume that they can be less than honest because they think buyers expect marketing to be less than honest. There will always be people like that, but, ladies and gentlemen, you do not have to be one of them.

The future holds extraordinary opportunities to contact and persuade buyers through imaginative channels, using inventive new appeals via mind-stretching technology. But at the receiving end of all that creativity and innovation will be a lot of skeptical people with more command-and-control tools and less patience for business behaving badly.

As you struggle to market successfully in this skeptical world, it may be helpful to remember that there is nothing more practical than marketing with integrity.

APPENDIXES

An Example Integritometer (Software Company)

G *oal:* Keep the promises we make, and make only promises we can keep.

Example Project	Example Customer Promise	Example Benefits Delivered *as Perceived by Customers**	Discrepancy Between Promises and Delivery	Integrity Rating
Desktop Software, v.2	Delivered w/o bugs by Q1 '06.	Delivered Q3 '06	6 months delay due to debugging	2 of 6 Poor
Call-back Service Calls	24-hour call-backs	Less than half made within 24 hours	Major customer satisfaction declines	3 of 6 Below-par
Money-back guarantee	Money back, no questions asked	All requests honored	None	6 of 6 Superior
Communications Program	Frequent innovation	Last wholly new product: Q4 '05	Significant fall-off	2 of 6 Unacceptable
Aggregate for all programs	**"Superior service and innovation"**	**Believe we over-promised and under-delivered**	**Significant total discrepancy**	2 of 6 Poor

*Based on research or other methods of verification.

A Few More Marketing Malfeasance Stories

The following are additional anecdotes based on true experiences. They have been altered slightly to clarify points and to protect the identity of all parties involved. However, the substance of the anecdotes have remained intact.

True Story

Often I played the game of reducing per unit usage in order to keep pricing up and increasing profits. A couple of times, a new package was actually larger, but the consumers got less for their money. My rationales included the fact that the new usages were clearly shown and a belief (still held) that people are smart and will make decisions that are good for them. I recently noticed that a major detergent brand changed the size of their cap, which virtually guarantees that more liquid will be used. This is similar to increasing the flow rates from toothpaste and shampoo.

True Story

Over the past several years, a certain yellow-pages directory publisher has been extending the life of its many directories after they had been distributed. For example, the life of a yellow-pages directory is twelve months. This company leaves the directory on the street for up to fifteen months and bills the advertiser for the extra time that the old directory is still out there. The notification of the extension typically arrives at the advertiser's office unexpectedly, after the book has been on the street for six or nine months. While the company won't admit it, the reason it extends directories is either: a) to move revenue from one year to another for financial reasons; or b) the local sales force has not achieved its goal so the publisher keeps the local canvas going for another one to three months. This violates the understanding with the national advertiser who paid in advance for twelve months of exposure.

True Story

The president and marketing guy of a media company came to an advertising agency and said they could take over buying. They would guarantee the same rates that the agency was quoting clients (i.e., clients would be billed the same rate, which already included the agency's mark-up), and they would also give the agency a share of their profits. This latter deal would be a private relationship that clients would never know about. (The ad agency president rejected the offer.)

General Observations from a Food Expert

The food industry is ripe with examples of what I feel is questionable marketing. Products are positioned as containing "no" cholesterol or "no" trans-fats, for example, although they are still high in total fat content. Products that contain only small amounts of calcium are promoted as containing calcium (implying the content is significant), while the actual amount is insignificant. I see this as taking advantage of naïve consumers by playing on a current hot topic to promote sales. It bothers me too when products that never contained fat are suddenly touted as containing "no trans-fats." Although none of the information is false, it is clearly taken out of context.

True Story

A certain company officer:

- ❏ Was always having us redefine the category when we made trade presentations in order to make our shares looks better. This has included leaving off entire brands because "they were on their way out."

- ❏ Intimidated suppliers to cover our purchasing mistakes by accusing suppliers of not communicating properly, using the threat that they would lose the business if they argued too much.

- ❏ Used stock photos off the Internet to depict our end-product, even though it bore no resemblance to the real thing, arguing that it was only supposed to be a serving suggestion.

- ❏ Falsified product ingredient labels to avoid using terms that sounded less flavorful.

True Story

A young advertising agency executive was on his first commercial shoot and was told by the production crew that they could not get the client's product to operate the way that the storyboard specified. It seemed that the major claim and positioning line of the product was not in sync with what really happened when it was put to use.

The agency executive insisted that the commercial shooting proceed as best as possible with no tampering with the product. A few minutes later, he was told that he had an urgent phone call from his office. He left the set to take the call (which wasn't urgent) and returned to the set a few minutes later.

The product performance shot had been completed (in record time) and the crew had moved on to the next scene. It was only during the viewing of the edited spot that the young (and painfully naïve) exec realized that the product demonstrated had been staged and shot while he was off the set. Neither the client nor the agency had any inclination or money to reshoot the shot.

True Story

A newish marketing director, manic and insistent on putting his own mark on the company, was not satisfied with the direction a carefully and professionally managed ad account review was taking.

On his own initiative, he cobbled together a group of ad execs from small NYC "boutique" shops (read small, struggling, and fading one- or two-person agencies, holdovers from an earlier era) and helped them with a proposal intended to short-circuit the review process. But I had to take a stand when I read in the fine print of the proposed contract that one of the old ad execs was in line to make as much as 10 percent of an approximately $50M ad budget as a "finder's fee" for cobbling the group together.

I confronted the marketing director, who denied any knowledge of this "finder's fee." I told him that trashing my reputation was one thing, but that I would not go along with defrauding my employer. Either those old cronies went, or I went . . . to the bank attorneys and auditors. The cronies went, followed shortly thereafter by the marketing director.

True Story

The director of marketing for a major tobacco company would routinely scrutinize all research and development data related to the health hazards of the company's products to "filter" the data in ways that would minimize application of newly established guidelines requiring full disclosure prior to advertising approval.

True Story

A U.S. multinational client wanted to advertise heavily a certain skin-softening ingredient in a new foam bath product. When the claim was analyzed, it was clear the amount in each container was about the size of a teardrop and would do little to soften anyone's skin. The marketing firm was instructed to proceed anyway and the campaign had a full run.

Word of Mouth Marketing Code of Ethics

The following is the current draft of the Word of Mouth Code of Ethics, issued by the Word of Mouth Marketing Association (WOMMA). Note that, as of September 2006, this code is still in draft form and the version below is posted on the organization's website (womma.org) for public and member comment.

The WOMMA Code*

Summary

1. Consumer protection and respect are paramount
2. The Honesty ROI: Honesty of Relationship, Opinion, and Identity
3. We respect the rules of the venue
4. We manage relationships with minors responsibly
5. We promote honest downstream communications
6. We protect privacy and permission

Purpose

WOMMA members believe this Code is a foundation for an ethical, prosperous industry. To survive and succeed, word of mouth marketing must earn the trust of consumers by protecting their right to open, honest communication.

The WOMMA Code establishes guidelines when planning and executing word of mouth marketing campaigns. Its purpose is to help define best practices, unacceptable practices, and baseline rules of the road. It is a tool for ethical marketers to understand where the lines are drawn and how to do the right thing. Word of mouth that occurs naturally through the process of serving and satisfying customers isn't addressed here, because it is fundamentally genuine.

This is a work in progress. Word of mouth marketing is a new profession, and we are still in the formative stages of this new relationship with consumers. The environment is changing rapidly, the rules are unclear, and ethical practices are still being defined. We will continue to improve the WOMMA Code as the practice of word of mouth marketing evolves.

This is a code that WOMMA members choose to live by. We hope all ethical marketers will do the same.

The Code

1. *Consumer protection and respect are paramount.*
   We respect and promote practices that abide by an understanding that the consumer—not the marketer—is fundamentally in charge, in control, and dictates the terms of the consumer-marketer relationship. We go above and beyond to ensure that consumers are protected at all times.

2. *The Honesty ROI: Honesty of Relationship, Opinion, and Identity.*

   Honesty of Relationship

   ❏ We practice openness about the relationship between consumers, advocates, and marketers. We encourage word of mouth advocates to disclose their relationship with marketers in their communications with other consumers. We don't tell them specifically what to say, but we do instruct them to be open and honest about any relationship with a marketer and about any products or incentives that they may have received.

   ❏ We stand against shill and undercover marketing, whereby people are paid to make recommendations without disclosing their relationship with the marketer.

   ❏ We comply with FTC regulations that state: "When there exists a connection between the endorser and the seller of the advertised product which might materially affect the weight or credibility of the endorsement (i.e., the connection is not reasonably expected by the audience) such connection must be fully disclosed."

Honesty of Opinion

❏ We never tell consumers what to say. People form their own honest opinions, and they decide what to tell others. We provide information, we empower them to share, and we facilitate the process—but the fundamental communication must be based on the consumers' personal beliefs.

❏ We comply with FTC regulations regarding testimonials and endorsements, specifically: "Endorsements must always reflect the honest opinions, findings, beliefs, or experience of the endorser. Furthermore, they may not contain any representations which would be deceptive, or could not be substantiated if made directly by the advertiser."

Honesty of Identity

❏ Clear disclosure of identity is vital to establishing trust and credibility. We do not blur identification in a manner that might confuse or mislead consumers as to the true identity of the individual with whom they are communicating, or instruct or imply that others should do so.

❏ Campaign organizers should monitor and enforce disclosure of identity. Manner of disclosure can be flexible, based on the context of the communication. Explicit disclosure is not required for an obviously fictional character, but would be required for an artificial identity or corporate representative that could be mistaken for an average consumer.

❏ We comply with FTC regulations regarding identity in endorsements that state: "Advertisements presenting endorsements by what are represented, directly or by implication, to be 'actual consumers' should utilize actual consumers, in both the audio and video or clearly and conspicuously disclose that the persons in such advertisements are not actual consumers of the advertised product."

❏ Campaign organizers will disclose their involvement in a campaign when asked by consumers or the media. We will provide contact information upon request.

3. *We respect the rules of the venue.*

   We respect the rights of any online or offline communications venue (such as a web site, blog, discussion forum, traditional media, live setting, etc.) to create and enforce its rules as it sees fit. We never create campaigns or encourage behavior that would violate or disrespect those rules.

4. *We manage relationships with minors responsibly.*

   ❑ We believe that working with minors in word of mouth marketing programs carries important ethical obligations, responsibility, and sensitivity.

   ❑ We stand against the inclusion of children under the age of 13 in any word of mouth marketing program.

   ❑ We comply with all applicable laws dealing with minors and marketing, including COPPA and regulations regarding age restrictions for particular products.

   ❑ We ensure that all of our campaigns comply with existing media-specific rules regarding children, such as day-part restrictions.

5. *We promote honest downstream communications.*

   Recognizing that we cannot control what real people say or how a message will be presented after multiple generations of conversation, we promote the Honesty ROI in downstream communications. In the context of each program, we instruct advocates about ethical communications and we never instruct or imply that they should engage in any behavior that violates the terms of this code.

6. *We protect privacy and permission.*

   We respect the privacy of consumers at all times. All word of mouth marketing programs should be structured using the highest privacy, opt-in, and permission standards, and we comply with all relevant regulations. Any personally identifiable information gathered from consumers through their participation in word of mouth marketing programs should be used only in the confines of that particular program, unless the consumer voluntarily gives us permission to use it for other purposes.

Example Integrity Training Workshop Script

G*oal:* To obtain input and reach consensus on key issues related to applying practical integrity to all marketing planning.

Time	Discussion Topic	Tools
9:00–9:15AM	Agree on Workshop goals, agenda, guidelines, and deliverables. Overview of current state of integrity in organization.	Agenda, Slides
9:15–9:45	Agree on Business Objectives and how integrity can affect their delivery. • Describe the marketplace: • What are the key events and trends in marketplace that are integrity-related? • What is our assessment of current integrity issues that will influence the future marketplace?	Flip-charts, Market Schematic
9:45–10:15	Our Customer-Partners: • Who are they? What do they want? • What can we do to meet their needs with more integrity than our competition? • How can our integrity be helpful in gaining and holding new customer-partners?	Flip-charts

Time	Discussion Topic	Tools
10:15–10:30	Break	
10:30–11:00	Our Competition: Who/what could prevent us from achieving our business objectives? • The competition we should be most concerned about, short-term and long-term. • Discussion of competitive strengths and vulnerabilities. • What have the competition (or we) done in the past to hinder or help our integrity?	Flip-charts, Competitive Slides (if needed)
11:00–12 noon	Strategic Positioning: Defined and discussed • How is our positioning impacted by our integrity record? • How could we strengthen our positioning with greater emphasis on integrity issues?	Flip-charts, Slides
12–12:30 PM	Lunch	—
12:30–1:45	BREAKOUT and REPORT-OUTS: Discuss optimum benefit promises impacted by integrity.	Flip-charts
1:45–2:15	Reaching Consensus: • The optimum benefit promises and candidate proof points.	Flip-charts
2:15–2:45	Brand Persona and Values: • How would you describe our brand as a person? • Visualization exercise. What kind of "personality" should the brand convey? What kind of integrity values?	Flip-charts Visualization Exercise
2:45–3:00	Recap and Discussion of Next Steps	Review Flip-charts

APPENDIX E

The Marketing Ethics Quiz*

1. *Promises Not Kept:* You run a research firm and recently sold a proposed industry study to a group of clients based on the guarantee that you'll be conducting interviews with 100 industry influentials. Because of timing and logistical difficulties you only complete 75 of the interviews. But you're still going to lose a ton of money on the deal. You priced the study too low to begin with and it ended up absorbing more time than you had projected. Your clients, those who bought the study, have already pre-paid, and they like the results even though you fell short of the guaranteed interview count. You choose to remain silent and don't proportionally rebate your clients for the shortfall. Right or wrong?

2. *The Refund Not Refunded:* You're flying to meet a client in another city. At the last minute you decide to extend the trip to visit a second client while you're on the road. The deal is that your clients always rebate you in full for travel expenses. You bill both clients for the full, return airfare from your city to theirs in spite of the fact that you were able to secure a multi-city, discounted fare and in the process made money on the deal. Right or wrong?

3. *The Money-Back Guarantee:* Your sales literature very clearly states that a dissatisfied customer is entitled to a full refund or credit irrespective of the reason or the cause. You do a job for a client but, because of contributory negligence on both sides, as well as lack of clear definition and cause of the problem, your client chooses to pay you and let the matter drop. You believe that you went above and beyond the call of duty in addressing the client's needs. But you still don't offer a refund. Right or wrong?

*Excerpted from "The Marketing Ethics Quiz: How's Your Conscience?" *The Alf Report*, www.thealfreport.com, May/June 2003.

4. *The Plane Crash:* You're the marketing director of a major airline. One of your planes crashes because of airline negligence. You know that you have to expose the airline's insurance representatives to the next of kin as soon as possible in order to negotiate quick settlements. The longer the delay, the greater the risk that a class-action–suit attorney will get to them first and force protracted litigation, which in turn will result in higher settlement costs. It doesn't feel right to force a confrontation with the next of kin at their greatest moment of vulnerability but you do it anyway. Right or wrong?

5. *The Name Dropper:* You and I meet for the first time. During the meeting you ask me to provide names of friends and associates, people who might be prospects for your product or service. You subsequently write them a letter and in the opening paragraph you mention that the referral came from me. The problem is, you did it without my permission. When I gave you the names, I neglected (and you deliberately failed) to mention the issue. Right or wrong?

6. *The Fake RFP:* You're the head of a young, aggressive advertising agency and you'd love to know how your competitors package and present themselves. So you fake an RFP for an imaginary account that's up for review, send it out, and specify that responses be mailed to a blind postal address. Your competition wastes precious time responding to a fictitious request for proposal and you gain valuable insights into your competitors' psychology and marketing technique. Right or wrong?

7. *Fresh from the Faucet:* You're in the bottled-water business. Unlike your competitors' products, your water doesn't come from nature's source. No gurgling springs for you. You take good old-fashioned town water, distill it, treat it, and package it with a fake, natural-sounding name, together with label artwork resplendent with waterfalls and bubbling brooks. A classic case of the reality not matching the perception. But it's great marketing. Right or wrong?

Notes

Introduction

1. Herring, Hubert B., "A Company's Ethics Do Concern Shoppers (or So They Say)," *New York Times* (online), January 29, 2006.

2. "A Crisis of Confidence: Rebuilding the Bonds of Trust," 2004 Yankelovich State of Consumer Trust report, presented to 10th Annual Fred Newell Customer Relationship Management Conference, Chicago, Ill., June 2–4, 2004.

3. "Consumers Want Some Respect from Marketers: Study," *Promo* magazine (online), April 20, 2004.

4. Kleiner, Art, "Daniel Yankelovich: The Thought Leader Interview," *Strategy + Business* (online), publication of Booz Allen Hamilton, Inc., Fall 2005.

Chapter 1

1. Friedman, Thomas, *The World Is Flat: A Brief History of the Twenty-First Century* (New York: Farrar, Straus and Giroux, 2005).

2. Based on estimate of 694 million online users in May 2006 by comScore Networks, www.comscore.com/press/release.

3. Source: Nielsen/Net Ratings, 2005; and Ian Davis and Elizabeth Stephenson, "Ten Trends to Watch in 2006," *The McKinsey Quarterly*, March 8, 2006.

4. Abate, Tom, "Generation M: Are we so immersed in media brine that it's become an environmental health hazard?" *San Francisco Chronicle* Magazine, January 1, 2006, p. 6.

5. "2005 Marketing Receptivity Survey" (Topline Report), Yankelovich Partners, April 18, 2005, p. 3.

6. "Marketing Accountability Study White Paper," American Marketing Association, April 2005, p. 4.

7. See World Economic Forum report of Gallup survey at www.weforum.org.

8. Alsop, Ronald, "Ranking Corporate Reputations: Tech Companies Score High in Yearly Survey as Google Makes Its Debut in Third Place; Autos, Airlines, Pharmaceuticals Lose Ground," *Wall Street Journal*, December 6, 2005, p. B1.

9. "'Integrity' Tops Web Dictionary's Lookups," The Associated Press (online), December 10, 2005.

10. Morgensen, Gretchen, "Are Enrons Bustin' Out All Over?" *New York Times* (online), May 28, 2006.

11. Sources: U.S. Department of Justice: "Corporate Fraud Task Force Fact Sheet," August 9, 2006 and August 29, 2005; and "FBI Financial Crimes Report to the Public," May 2005.

12. Farrell, Christopher, "The Other Side of Adam Smith," *BusinessWeek* (online), November 15, 2002.

13. Nocera, Joe, "A Tussle, of Sorts, Over Organics," *New York Times* (online), July 15, 2006.

14. "Why Trust Is Important: A look at the consequences of lost trust in the business world," Edelman 2006 Annual Trust Barometer.

15. Staff Report, "Integrity Matters," *Fast Company* 98 (September 2005): 52.

16. "Improper Accounting Practices Tops Marketing Chiefs' List of Ethics Concerns Facing U.S. Business," public relations release (online), IDG publishing, August 30, 2004.

17. "The Big Picture—Ethics," *Business Week* (UpFront), June 19, 2006, p. 13.

18. Tyler, James M. and Robert S. Feldman, "Deflecting Threat to One's Image: Dissembling Personal Information as a Self-Presentation," Basic and Applied Social Psychology, 27(4), 2005, pp. 371–378.

19. See: Godin, Seth, *All Marketers Are Liars: The Power of Telling Authentic Stories in a Low-Trust World* (New York: Portfolio, 2005).

20. "Corporate Ethics and Brand Purchasing" (white paper), Millward Brown online site, accessed January 24, 2006.

21. Vogel, David, "The Market for Virtue: The Potential and Limits of Corporate Social Responsibility," Washington, D.C.: Brookings Institution Press, 2005, pp. 30–31.

22. Drumwright, Minette E. and Patrick E. Murphy, "How Advertising Practitioners View Ethics: Moral Muteness, Moral Myopia, and Moral Imagination," *Journal of Advertising* 33, 2 (Summer 2004).

23. *Note:* Parts of this section are based on: Lynn B. Upshaw, "The Trouble with Food: Ethics and Integrity in Food Marketing," *Advertising Express* (India), November 2005.

24. "A Crisis of Confidence: Rebuilding the Bonds of Trust," 2004 Yankelovich Consumer Trust Report (Executive Summary), June 8, 2004.

25. The "Gross Equity" column is based on Aaker, David A., *Managing Brand Equity: Capitalizing on the Value of a Brand Name* (New York: The Free Press, 1991), p. 17.

Chapter 2

1. From Kiehl's mission statement company website, www.kiehls.com, accessed June 13, 2006.

2. "The Greenhouse," Herman Miller Corporate Factsheet, provided by the company, undated.

3. Phone interview with Kris Manos, Herman Miller, Inc., March 28, 2006.

4. Phone interview with Mark Schurman, Herman Miller, Inc., March 28, 2006.

5. Bryan Dozeman, *Sales Insights from a Herman Miller Watercarrier* (New York: iUniverse, Inc., 2006), p. 38.

6. From "What We Believe," Herman Miller website, accessed April 1, 2006.

7. "Woods says he'll return to Tour for U.S. Open," *ESPN.com*, May 30, 2006, with additional material from *Bloomberg News* and *The Associated Press*.

8. Karmali, Naazneen, interview with N.R. Narayana Murthy, "India 1999" Symposium, New Delhi, India, January 2000.

9. From "Reflections of an Entrepreneur," speech by N.R. Narayana Murthy to Wharton School of Management, as published in *The Times of India,* June 20 and August 10, 2001.

10. Results from 2006 Brand-comm survey of 545 Indian business students published in: "Narayana Murthy, most admired biz leader," *rediff.com,* May 12, 2006; and from *Hoovers* online, Infosys profile, accessed July 23, 2006.

11. Phone interview with Aditya Jha, Infosys global brand manager, December 22, 2005.

12. Rai, Saritha, "Plan to Set Aside Jobs for Poor Stirs Protest," *New York Times* (online), May 16, 2006.

13. Friedman, Thomas L., "Race to the Top," *New York Times* (online), June 3, 2005.

14. "Corporate Fast Facts," Infosys company publication, 2005.

15. From Infosys corporate social responsibility factsheet, "Infosys: A Corporate Citizen," 2005.

16. "Focusing On: Software Application TCO: Company Business and Marketing," *Software* magazine (online), February 2000.

17. Friedman, Thomas L., *The World Is Flat: A Brief History of the Twenty-first Century* (New York: Farrar, Straus and Giroux, 2005), p. 7.

18. Trader Joe's website, accessed February 20, 2006.

19. Olson, Elizabeth, "Sunday Money: Spending: The Growing Cachet of the Store Brand," *New York Times,* November 27, 2005.

20. Lewis, Len, *The Trader Joe's Adventure: Turning a Unique Approach to Business into a Retail and Cultural Phenomenon* (Chicago: Dearborn Trade Publishing, 2005), p. 45.

21. Associated Press, "Trader Joe's targets 'educated' buyer," Seattle Post-Intelligencer.com, August 30, 2003.

22. Sarkar, Pia, "The tao of Trader Joe's devoted fans meet online to swap news, stay connected," *San Francisco Chronicle* (sfgate.com), June 6, 2006.

23. McGregor, Jena, "Leading Listener: Trader Joe's," *Fast Company,* October 2004, p. 82.

24. Armstrong, Larry, "Trader Joe's: The Trendy American Cousin," *BusinessWeek* (online, European Edition), April 26, 2004.

25. From 2002 interview at Pepperdine University, accessed on February 14, 2005 at www.gbe.pepperdine.edu.

26. From Patagonia website, www.patagonia.com, accessed June 28, 2006.

27. Ibid., accessed March 30, 2006.

28. Chouinard, Yvon, *Let My People Go Surfing: The Education of a Reluctant Businessman* (New York: Penguin Press, 2005), pp. 141–155.

29. Witt, Louise, "Retailer Gets Out the Green Vote," *Wired News* (online), September 24, 2004.

30. Phone interview with Rick Ridgeway, Patagonia, Inc., January 27, 2006.

31. From Patagonia website, www.patagonia.com.

32. Hoover's online, accessed June 26, 2006.

33. Vilaga, Jennifer, "Profitable Player: Kiehl's," *Fast Company* 99, October 2005, p. 55.

34. Sullivan, Deirdre, "Kiehl's executive reveals secrets of guerrilla marketing to fashion club," *Wharton Journal* (online), April 10, 2006.

35. Phone interview with Cammie Cannella, and with Shannon Cooney, a vice president of public relations, June 13, 2006.

36. Company website and Cammie Cannella, ibid.

37. Vilaga, Jennifer, "Profitable Player: Kiehl's."

Chapter 3

1. Wind, Jerry et al., "Courtyard by Marriott: Designing a Hotel Facility with Consumer-Based Marketing Models," *Interfaces (The Wharton School)* 19:1, January/February 1989, pp. 25–47; and "Courtyard by Marriott Reaches 100,000-Room Milestone with Opening of 218-Room Hotel in Moscow," *prnewswire.com,* Marriott, Inc. online public relations release, December 4, 2004.

2. For a full discussion of this perspective, see Tim Kitchin's essay in: Ind, Nicholas (ed.), *Beyond Branding* (London: Kogan Page, 2003), pp. 72–83.

3. Baishya, Dipayan, "Marketing guru extols value of brand awareness," *Economic Times,* July 6, 2005.

4. Lewis, Len, *The Trader Joe's Adventure,* pp. 80–81.

5. From IKEA–UK website (www.ikea.com/ms/en_GB/), accessed August 26, 2006.

6. Telephone interview with Kris Manos and Mark Schurman, March 29, 2006.

7. For a more complete discussion of partnering in B2B markets, see Fred Wiersema, *Customer Intimacy: Pick Your Partners, Shape Your Culture, Win Together* (Santa Monica, Calif.: Knowledge Exchange, 1996), pp. 99–120.

8. Sumit, Mitra, "Money Machine," *IndiaToday* (online), November 8, 1999.

9. Aaker, David A., *Managing Brand Equity: Capitalizing on the Value of a Brand Name* (New York: The Free Press, 1991), pp. 162–163.

10. Kranhold, Kathryn, "Client-Satisfaction Tool Takes Root: GE Embraces Measurement of Customers' Experience; Winning Back 'Detractors,'" *Wall Street Journal,* July 10, 2006, p. B3.

11. Janoff, Barry, "Study Indicates Marketers Can't Gauge Consumer Needs," *Adweek,* November 8, 2001; and "Accenture Survey Finds That Customer Loyalty Can Be Lost in a Click: Internet Challenges Companies to Re-think Customer Relationships," International Communications Research report (online), accessed via www.icrsurvey.com, December 21, 2005.

12. "Brand Loyalty High Among American Consumers: New Grocery Manufacturers of America (GMA) survey," GMA press release, June 13, 2002.

13. Goetz, David, "A toast to Maker's Mark: Popular brand brought into Jim Beam's fold, could gain global clout," (Louisville, Ky.) *Courier-Journal,* March 4, 2006.

14. Harrington, Ann, "Who's Afraid of a New Product? Not W.L. Gore," *Fortune,* November 10, 2003.

15. Faber, David, "Ten Things You Didn't Know About eBay: CNBC Special Report looks behind the scenes of global online marketplace," from transcript of CNBC program, January 29, 2005.

16. Phone interview with Rick Ridgeway and Eve Bould, March 6, 2006.

17. Magee, David, *The John Deere Way: Performance That Endures* (Hoboken, N.J.: John Wiley & Sons, 2005), pp. 74–80.

Chapter 4

1. DePree, Max, *Leadership is an Art* (New York: Doubleday, 1989), p. 74.

2. Arndt, Michael, "Built for the Long Haul: Premium Quality is what has kept Paccar trucks on a 67-year winning streak," *BusinessWeek,* January 30, 2006, p. 66.

3. Ponemon, Larry, "Building Trust in Your Organization: The top 10 most trustworthy companies and what you can learn from them," Darwinmag.com, June 2004.

4. "A Crisis of Confidence: Rebuilding the Bonds of Trust," 2004 Yankelovich State of Consumer Trust report, presented to 10th Annual Fred Newell Customer Relationship Management Conference, June 2–4, 2004, Chicago, Ill.

5. Peters, Jeremy W. and Michelle Maynard, "Lofty Promise of Saturn Plant Runs into G.M.'s Fiscal Reality," *New York Times*, December 2, 2005.

6. "The Worst American Cars of 2006," *Forbes.com*, July 20, 2006.

7. Welch, David, "Saturn's Second Liftoff?" *BusinessWeek* online, April 12, 2006.

8. Paine, Lynn Sharp and Kim Bettcher, "Recall: Bridgestone Corp. (Abridged)," *Harvard Business School* case 9-306-020, July 20, 2005.

9. Shirouzu, Shirouzu, "Toyota May Delay New Models to Address Rising Quality Issues," *Wall Street Journal,* August 25, 2006, p. A1.

10. George, Chris, "Welcome to In-N-Out: In-N-Out is the envy of the entire industry. What's their secret?" *QSR* Magazine, July 2004.

11. Narrative provided by anonymous marketing executive at a major, unnamed packaged goods company, February 1, 2006.

12. In-N-Out Burger website (www.in-n-out.com); and Hawn, Carleen, "The In-N-Out Burger: The In-N-Out burger is giving McDonald's a run for its money," *Fast Company*, September 2003, p. 36.

13. "Loyalty study: Subway, Wendy's top ad rivals," *Nation's Restaurant News*, August 4, 2003.

14. "The Quest for the Ultimate Fast Food Has Ended," *EOpinions.com*, June 6, 2000.

15. Thompson, Stephanie, "'Deadenbacher' Creeps Consumers but Drives Massive Traffic," *Advertising Age* (online), January 22, 2007.

16. Cassidy, H., "This Shoe's One Cool Cat," *Brandweek*, October 20, 2003; and O'Brien, K., "Focusing on Armchair Athletes, Puma Becomes A Leader," *New York Times*, March 12, 2004; and "Stars of Europe, Managers," *Business Week*, July 7, 2003, and Hoover's online, July 2004.

17. Theodore Kinni, "Pride Goeth Before a Profit," *Harvard Business School Working Knowledge* (online), September 29, 2003.

18. Breen, Bill, "Can Microsoft Finally Kill All the Bugs?: Viruses, flaws, and worms, oh my!" *Fast Company* 75 (October 2003): 82.

19. Kaihla, Paul, "Best Kept Secrets of the World's Best Companies," *Business 2.0*, April 2006, p. 89.

20. "Best Managers of 2003: Yun Jong Yong," *BusinessWeek* (online), January 12, 2004.

21. Payne, Cindy, "W.L. Gore & Associates: A case study," *Foundation for Enterprise Development,* June 1998.

22. From Patagonia website, www.patagonia.com, accessed April 4, 2006.

23. Patagonia customer letter published in *Mountain Gazette*, republished in the Fall 2005 Patagonia catalog, p. 47.

24. As quoted (among many other places) in Christiansen, Clayton M., Scott Cook, and Taddy Hall, "Marketing Malpractice: The Cause and the Cure," *Harvard Business Review*, December 2005.

25. Another valuable approach to benefit mining has been called "means-end chain analysis." The method refers to a linking of benefits, product attributes, and values. See Vriens, M. and F. Hafstede, "Linking Attributes, Benefits, and Consumer Values: A powerful approach to market segmentation, brand positioning, and advertising strategy," *Marketing Research*, October 1, 2000.

26. Kelsey, Dick, "Gates: Computing Advances this Decade Will Outdo 90s," *Washtech*

.com, November 12, 2001, as quoted in Youngme Moon, "Microsoft: Positioning the Tablet PC," *Harvard Business School Case*, rev. January 6, 2003, p. 1.

Chapter 5

1. From "The Quotations Page," www.quotationspage.com, accessed August 23, 2006.

2. Staff report, "The *New York Times* Scandal Recalls Glass Episode," *Forbes.com*, May 20, 2003.

3. Johnson, Linda A., "Scientific fraud found at Bell Labs: Star researcher fired for falsifying data," *Seattle Post Intelligencer*, September 26, 2002.

4. Morrison, Blake, "*USA Today* reporter resigns after deception," *USA Today* (online), January 13, 2004.

5. Strupp, Joe, "The Jayson Blair Affair, Three Years On," *Editor and Publisher*, May 15, 2006.

6. Whitman, Janet, "Tribune Posts Charge and Finds More Errors in Circulation Data," *Dow Jones Newswires/Wall Street Journal*, July 16, 2004, p. A11.

7. Lemonick, Michael D., "The Rise and Fall of the Cloning King," *Time*, January 9, 2006.

8. Ivry, Sara, "Plagiarists Exposed, Then Explored," *New York Times*, January 20, 2006.

9. "Crisis of Confidence: Rebuilding the Bonds of Trust," 2004 State of Consumer Trust Report by Yankelovich Partners.

10. Erdem, Tülin, and Swait Joffre, "*Journal of Consumer Research* 31 (2004): 191–198.

11. Kouzes, James M. and Barry Posner, "A prescription for leading in cynical times," Ivey Publishing, Richard Ivey School of Business, The University of Western Ontario, July/August 2004.

12. "Does Q = E?" *Patagonia Catalog*, Fall 1997.

13. "Chopper" was a term derived from the post-World War II era when Harleys that did not run all that well were "chopped up" and retooled into serviceable machines.

14. Phone interview with Aditya Jha, Infosys global brand manager, June 7, 2006.

15. MacLean, Natalie, "Bring on the bling: Rappers give Cristal and Hennessy street cred," special to the *San Francisco Chronicle*, December 16, 2004; and Kortney Stringer, "Only hot products brands make it in songs," *Detroit Free Press*, January 18, 2006.

16. Robertson, Jordan, "How Nike Got Street Cred: The $11 billion company overcame its corporate image to win over the fiercely independent skateboarding market," Business 2.0, May 1, 2004.

17. Stone, Brad, "Nike's Short Game: The swoosh is everywhere. So how does the sports giant market itself as an upstart?" "Think Small," *Newsweek* (online), January 26, 2004.

18. Walker, Rob, "The Brand Underground," *The New York Times Magazine* (online) July 30, 2006.

19. Wayne, Leslie, "Boeing Ethics Woes Take Toll on the Bottom Line," *New York Times* (online), June 30, 2006.

20. Holmes, Stanley, "Into the Wild Blog Yonder: The once-secretive Boeing opens itself up—to employees, customers, and the public," *BusinessWeek*, May 22, 2006, p. 84.

21. "Corporate Responsibility and Investor Confidence Survey" (Executive Summary), conducted by Harris Interactive on behalf of Calvert Group, Ltd., November 18, 2003.

22. Cialdini, Robert B., Petia K. Petrova, and Hoah J. Goldstein, "The Hidden Costs of

Corporate Dishonesty," *MIT Sloan Management Review* 45, 3 (Spring 2004); and Sirota, David, Louis A. Mischkind, and Michael Irwin Meltzer, "Why Your Employees Are Losing Motivation," and "How Management Demotivates," *Harvard Business Review Working Knowledge for Business Leaders* (online), April 10, 2006.

23. Faiola, Anthony, "Safety Scandal Shames Mitsubishi: New Cover-Up Allegations Hobble Japan's Fourth-Largest Automaker," *Washington Post*, July 6, 2004, p. E01.

24. Kher, Unmesh, "Target: Trans Fats: How foodmakers are scrambling to rid their tried-and-true recipes of an artery-clogging fat," *Time*, October 16, 2005.

25. Alexander, Delroy, Jeremy Manier, and Patricia Callahan, "For every fad, another cookie: How science and diet crazes confuse consumers, reshape recipes and fail, ultimately, to reform eating habits," *Chicago Tribune* (online), August 23, 2005.

26. Tischler, Linda, "The Good Brand: Brands are less and less about what we buy, and more and more about who we are. That means your cola can't just taste good. It has to feel good, too," *Fast Company* 85 (August 2004): 47.

27. Results from "The Real Truth About Beauty: A Global Report," a 2004 study in ten countries conducted by StrategyOne, in collaboration with Dr. Nancy Etcoff and the Massachusetts General Hospital/Harvard University, and with the expert consultation of Dr. Susie Orbach of the London School of Economics. For more details, see: www.campaignforrealbeauty.com/press.asp?section = news&id = 110.

28. Prior, Molly, "Dove spreads its wings into new categories," *Drug Store News*, June 21, 2004.

29. Gogoi, Pallavi, "From Reality TV to Reality Ads," *BusinessWeek* (online), August 17, 2005.

30. For further discussion of faux authenticity, see: Olins, Wally, *Wally Olins on B®and* (London: Thames & Hudson, 2004).

Chapter 6

1. "Are Video Late Fees Gone or Just Hiding?" *Associated Press*, December 16, 2004; and Rukmini Callimachi, "Blockbuster settles 'No Late Fees' cases; offers refunds," Associated Press, March 23, 2005

2. Groeller, Greg and Heather Won Tesoriero, "Merck Top Executive Defends Marketing of Vioxx to Doctors," *Wall Street Journal*, September 24, 2005, p. B6.

3. Fonda, Daren and Barbara Kiviat, "Curbing the Drug Marketers: How a clampdown on pitching drugs for unapproved uses is changing the way Big Pharma operates," *Time*, July 5, 2004.

4. "Drug Companies Revisit Ad Campaigns: Voluntarily enforced guidelines have sparked changes in the way products are advertised," from *Associated Press* via *LATimes* (online), March 14, 2006.

5. Staff Report, "Doctors' Group Wants to Halt DTC Drug Ads," *Brandweek.com*, June 16, 2006.

6. Meier, Barry, "Metropolitan Life in Accord For Settlement of Fraud Suits," *New York Times*, August 19, 1999.

7. Carillo, Jose A., "With apologies to the weasel," *Manila Times* (online), May 27, 2003.

8. Gilden, James (The Internet Traveler), "Price guarantees: marketing gimmicks or the real deal?" *latimes.com*, March 5, 2006.

9. "Consumers 50% More Likely to be Influenced by WOM than Radio/TV ads," *Media-BuyerPlanner*, accessed September 11, 2006, based on 2005 Intelliseek Consumer-Generated Media (CGM) and Engagement Study (via MediaPost).

10. Nolan, Hamilton, "Debate on buzz marketing is about more than words," *PR Week USA*, October 31, 2005.

11. Duhigg, Charles, "Taking the Fans' Word for It: Marketing firm M80 harnesses the enthusiasm of devotees to promote products and finds its unusual approach is paying off," *LATimes.com*, March 15, 2006; and Renee Dye, "The Buzz on Buzz," *Harvard Business Review*, November-December 2000.

12. "CMO RealityCheck™ Survey," *CMO Magazine* (online), March 2005.

13. Wipperfurth, Alex, *Brand Hijack: Marketing Without Marketing* (New York: Portfolio, 2005), pp. 239–240.

14. Khermouch, Gerry, "Buzz Marketing: Suddenly This Stealth Strategy Is Hot—but It's Still Fraught with Risk," *BusinessWeek* (online), July 30, 2001.

15. Kaikati, Andrew M. and Jack J. Kaikati, "Stealth Marketing: How to Reach Consumers Surreptitiously," *California Management Review* 46, 4 (August 2, 2004): 6–22.

16. Wells, Melanie, "Kid Nabbing," *Forbes.com* (online), February 2, 2004; and "I Sold It Through the Grapevine, *BusinessWeek*, May 29, 2006.

17. Ibid.

18. Sellers, Patricia, "MySpace Cowboys," *Fortune*, September 4, 2006, p. 68.

19. Hempel, Jessi with Paula Lehman, "The MySpace Generation: They live online. They buy online. They play online. Their power is growing," *BusinessWeek* (online), December 12, 2005.

20. Steel, Emily and Julian Angwin, "MySpace Receives More Pressure to Limit Children's Access to Site," *Wall Street Journal*, June 23, 2006, p. B3.

21. Barbaro, Michael, "Wal-Mart Enlists Bloggers in P.R. Campaign," *New York Times* (online), March 7, 2006.

22. O'Brien, Timothy L., "Spinning Frenzy: P.R.'s Bad Press," *New York Times*, February 13, 2005. *Disclosure Note*: Mr. Williams was hired on behalf of the federal government by Ketchum, a leading public relations firm. Up to mid-1996, this author was an advertising and brand executive working for Ketchum Communications and periodically collaborated with the Ketchum public relations staff.

23. Bandler, James, "Advice for Sale—How Companies Pay TV Experts for on-Air Product Mentions: Plugs Come Amid News Shows and Appear Impartial; Pacts Are Rarely Disclosed; Energizer Gets on 'Today'," *Wall Street Journal*, April 19, 2005, p. A1.

24. Javers, Eamon, "Op-Eds for Sale," *BusinessWeek* (online), December 16, 2005; and "Cato Scholar Resigns, Suspended as Columnist," *Wall Street Journal* (online), December 17, 2005.

25. "Almost 50% of Senior Marketing Executives Said They Have Paid for an Editorial or Broadcast Placement, According to a PRWeek/Manning Selvage & Lee Survey," *Forbes.com* (online) via *BusinessWire*, June 14, 2006.

26. Leonard, Thomas, "Lessons from L.A.: The Wall: A Long History," *Columbia Journalism Review* (online), January/February 2000.

27. This author has a friend who is a former marketing director and now publishes a newspaper in the Midwest. He likes to refer to "The Wall" as "The Cyclone Fence," meaning that reporters and sales execs can pass notes back and forth and talk about news/ad blurring issues, but maintain the integrity of the published product.

28. Hearst Magazines' 2005 Engagement Factor Study, as quoted in "Engagement: Understanding Consumers' Relationships with Media," report from Magazine Publishers of America, 2005.

29. Steinberg, Brian, "Magazine Editors Buck Marketers in New Guidelines, Group Resists Push to Lace Articles with Product Promotions," *Wall Street Journal*, October 17, 2005, p. B3.

30. Bosman, Julie and Katharine Q. Seelye, "Wall Street Journal to Run Ads on Its Front Page," *New York Times* (online), July 18, 2006.

31. Steinberg, Brian, "Take Cover: Magazines Peddle Fronts," *Wall Street Journal*, July 6, 2006, p. B2.

32. Parker, Pamela, "Forecast: Online to Reach 9 Percent Share of Ad Spend in 2011," *ClickZ Network*, July 26, 2006, based on Jupiter Research calculations.

33. Levine, Robert, "Reaching the Unreachables: The most important demographic in advertising—18- to 34-year-old males—is also the most elusive. How do you make them sit up and take notice? By turning away from TV and finding clever new hooks to get their attention," *Business 2.0*, October 2005.

34. "Internet Video Advertising Spending Will Nearly Triple to $640 Million in 2007," *emarketer* press release, November 29, 2005.

35. Grover, Ronald et al., "Mad Ave Is Starry-Eyed Over Net Video," *BusinessWeek* (online), May 23, 2005.

36. Darlin, Damon, "Adviser Urges H.P. to Focus on Ethics Over Legalities," *New York Times*, October 4, 2006, Section C, p.3.

37. Brown, Stephen, "Marketing to Generation ®," *Harvard Business Review* (June 2003): 2.; and www.umbria.com, accessed July 11, 2006.

38. Neuborne, Ellen and Kathleen Kerwin, "Generation Y: Today's teens—the biggest bulge since the boomers—may force marketers to toss their old tricks," *BusinessWeek* (online), February 15, 1999.

39. Creamer, Matthew, "Disclosure Doesn't Hamper Word-of-Mouth Marketing," New study pesented at Orlando WOMMA Conference, *Advertising Age* (online), January 19, 2006.

40. From Patagonia Spring 2006 catalog, p. 3.

41. Staff Report, "Green Technology Innovators," *BusinessWeek* (online), December 12, 2005.

42. Darke, Peter R. and Robin J.B. Ritchie, "The Defensive Consumer: Advertising Deception, Defensive Process, and Distrust," *Journal of Marketing Research*, in press, accessed at www.sauder.ubc.ca/faculty/divisions/marketing/docs/darke-ritchie-jmr-06.pdf., September 22, 2006.

43. Lerner, Preston, "Contenders to the Throne: Ever since Herman Miller's high design aeron chair arrived on the scene, many have tried to depose it, but few have come close," *Los Angeles Times*, September 29, 2002, p. I.47.

44. A story recounted in a memo by Lois Maassen,vice president for marketing communications, technology, and consulting at Herman Miller, July 20, 2006.

45. Teinowitz, Ira, "Food Giants Expand Child-Targeted Advergame Marketing: Study Details Viral World of Campaigns Aimed at Pre-Teens," *Advertising Age* (online), July 19, 2006.

Chapter 7

1. Gibson, Owen, "Shopper's eye view of ads that pass us by: New device helps analyse responses to marketing; Of 3,500 daily messages, 99% have no impact," *Guardian Unlimited (The Guardian* online), November 19, 2005.

2. Stryker, Jeff, "Forehead Billboards," *New York Times.com*, December 11, 2005.

3. Cordle, Ina Paiva, "Bagging new revenue—Airsickness bags will soon become the next advertising medium as airlines explore new ways to boost revenue," *MiamiHerald.com*, July 16, 2006.

4. McCarthy, Michael, "Critics target 'omnipresent' ads: Ad creep is creeping some people out," *USA Today*, July 19, 2002; and Hendo, Brian, "Getting a Head," *BRANDWEEK*, January 2, 2004, p. 14; and Wallach, Todd, "Long-Distance Callers Endure Ads by AT&T," *San Francisco Chronicle*, May 18, 2000, p. B1; and Pfanner, Eric, "In France, Originality Means Using Tabletops to Sell Products," *New York Times*, August 15, 2000.

5. Story, Louise, "Anywhere the Eye Can See, It's Likely to See an Ad," *New York Times* (online), January 15, 2007.

6. Li Yuan and Cassell Bryan-Low, "Coming Soon to Cellphone Screens—More Ads Than Ever," *Wall Street Journal*, August 16, 2006, p. B1.

7. Prado, Mark, "Bridge officials take new look at sponsorship," *Marin Independent Journal* (online), July 28, 2006.

8. Hyman, Mark, "Branding the Course: It doesn't come cheap, but golf tournament sponsorship earns valuable exposure," *BusinessWeek* (online), May 30, 2005.

9. Sanders, Lisa, "Battle for the Streets: Marketers vs. Ad-Weary Consumers: Commercial Messaging Creeps Ever Outward Across City Surfaces," *Advertising Age*, May 31, 2004.

10. Based on public relations release of study findings: "Consumers Say Fewer Commercials Lead to More Radio Listening: According to New Arbitron/Edison Media Research Study Most Listeners Say Commercials Are a 'Fair Price to Pay' for Free Radio," PR *Newswire-First Call*, May 4, 2005, 10:00 A.M.

11. "CC's 'Less is More' Strategy Increases Ad Revenue," *MediaBuyerPlanner.com*, May 3, 2006.

12. McBride, Sarah, "Clear Channel Moves Advertising onto the Table at Food Courts," *Wall Street Journal*, September 18, 2006, p. B4.

13. Flint, Joe, "Marketers Should Learn to Stop Worrying and Love the DVR," *Wall Street Journal* (online), October 26, 2005.

14. Consoli, John, "MindShare Study Contradicts TV Nets' DVR Research," *MediaWeek.com*, December 13, 2005.

15. Vranica, Suzanne, "KFC to Offer Anti-TiVo Ad," *Wall Street Journal* (online), February 22, 2006.

16. Kehaulani, Sara Goo, "Apple Gets a Big Slice of Product-Placement Pie," *Washington Post*, April 15, 2006, p. D1.

17. Manly, Lorne, "On Television, Brands Go from Props to Stars," *New York Times*, October 2, 2005; and Auletta, Ken, "The New Pitch," *New Yorker*, March 28, 2005.

18. Elliott, Stuart, "Pay Attention to the Story, but Please Also," *New York Times* (online), March 13, 2006.

19. Kiley, David, "Rated M for Mad Ave," *BusinessWeek*, February 27, 2006, p. 76.

20. Helm, Burt, "Bet You Can't TiVo Past This," *BusinessWeek*, April 24, 2006, pp. 38–40, and Story, Louise, op. cit.

21. Stuart, Elliott, "NBC and Mazda Jointly Promote New Lineups," *New York Times*, July 21, 2005.

22. Finnie, William, "How Budweiser develops great advertising campaigns," *St. Louis Business Journal*, January 26, 2001.

23. Mucha, Thomas, "The Payoff for Trying Harder: By obsessing over step of the rental

car experience, Avis has built an unmatched record for customer loyalty," *Business 2.0*, July 2002, pp. 85-86.

24. Klaassen, Abbey, "Target Hits Bulls-Eye with Olympics: Move to Skirt IOC by Slapping Logo on Trains Pays Off," Advertisingage.com, February 24, 2006.

25. Stuart Elliott, "JetBlue May Be Big, but It Wants Fliers to Think Small," *New York Times*, March 30, 2006.

26. Rose, Lacey, "America's Most Loved Spokes-Creatures," *Forbes* (online), December 23, 2005.

Chapter 8

1. Capell, Kerry, et al., "IKEA: How the Swedish retailer became a global cult brand," *BusinessWeek* (online), November 14, 2005.

2. "Online Extra: 'Positive Fanatics': IKEA's Credo," *BusinessWeek* (online), November 14, 2005.

3. From www.webflyer.com, based on statistics compiled by Randy Petersen, publisher/editor of *Inside Flyer* magazine, accessed September 6, 2006.

4. Bodow, Steve, "Murthy's Law: Infosys Technologies CEO N.R. Narayana Murthy says he's turning India into an economic powerhouse and dissolving rigid social barriers along the way," *CNN Money.com*, November 2000 issue.

5. "Brand Loyalty High Among American Consumers: New Grocery Manufacturers of America (GMA) survey," GMA press release, June 13, 2002.

6. "The Rise of the Value Retailer: Strategies for Survival in the Era of Value Retailing," Capgemini U.S. LLC white paper, www.us.capgemini.com, April 22, 2005.

7. As reported in a Segway case study by PR agency, Burston-Marsteller, at: www.bm.com/pages/cs/segway, accessed August 22, 2006.

8. Morrison, Mark, "Wal-Mart Fishes Upstream," *BusinessWeek* (online), March 24, 2006.

9. Welles, Edward O., "When Wal-Mart Comes to Town: How one small town reacted to Wal-Mart's opening three stores in the area," *Inc.* magazine, July 1993; and "Store Wars: When Wal-Mart Comes to Town," www.pbs.org/itvs/storewars, accessed January 7, 2006.

10. Zimmerman, Ann and Kris Hudson, "Chasing Upscale Customers Tarnishes Mass-Market Jeweler: Zale Corp.'s Botched Revamp Prompted CEO's Ouster and Merger Bid from Rival—the Allure of $99 Diamonds," *Wall Street Journal*, June 26, 2006, p. A1.

11. McEwen, William J., "Building a Brand Relationship," *Gallup Management Journal*, April 8, 2004.

12. In my MBA classes, I often ask students to provide me with an example of a purchase that involves no emotion, such as the buying of ordinary nails. While that may be an emotionless transaction, the nails are going to be used to build or tack down something, and that door or picture or children's playhouse always involves emotion. If the nail fails to hold, or rusts, there will also be emotion involved. Plus, the hardware store manager will be emotionally tied to the nails if they fail to sell.

13. Capgemini Ernst & Young study, April 23, 2002.

14. "Kmart, Sears Joining Forces," *CBS News* (online), November 17, 2004.

15. Arndt, Michael, "Creativity Overflowing: After its initial efforts stumbled, Whirlpool is reaping big dividends from its push to jump-start innovation," *BusinessWeek*, May 6, 2006, p. 50.

16. For a more detailed explanation of the facets of value, particularly as they relate to the IT industry, see: Sawhney, Mohanbir, "Fundamentals of Value: To achieve a value mind-set, focus relentlessly on customers," *CIO* magazine, July 1, 2003.

17. "Lexus Leads Dependability Study for 11th Year: GM, Ford, Toyota Show Improvements; Kia Comes in Last," *ConsumerAffairs.com,* accessed June 13, 2006; and Welch, David, "How do you turn on the #@!&% Air?" *BusinessWeek,* June 19, 2006, p. 46.

18. "John R. Hoke III: Green Foot Forward: Nike's chief design guru is prodding his designers back to nature and away from plastics," *BusinessWeek* (online), November 28, 2005.

19. Capell, Kerry, with Ariane Sains, et al., "IKEA: How the Swedish Retailer became a global cult brand," *BusinessWeek* (online), November 14, 2005.

20. Magee, David, with Introduction by Robert W. Lane, *The John Deere Way: Performance That Endures* (Hoboken, N.J.: John Wiley & Sons, 2005); and Deere & Company website, www.deere.com, accessed April 8, 2006.

21. "Retailers settle FTC claims: Office Depot, Buy.com, Value America settle charges of misleading ads," *CNNMoney.com,* June 29, 2000.

22. "Wireless Carriers Settle Charges over Misleading Ads," *BRANDWEEK online*, July 22, 2004.

23. Ihlwan Moon, "Camp Samsung: To develop winning products, the Korean giant isolates artists and techies for months on end," *BusinessWeek*, July 3, 2006, pp. 46–48.

24. Maynard, Micheline and Nick Bunkley, "Chrysler's 'Employee Discount' of Next Summer Could Be Revived," *New York Times* (online), June 23, 2006.

25. Myser, Michael, "What Works: Marketing Made Easy," *Business 2.0*, June 2006, pp. 43–44.

26. Hindo, Brian, "The Customer Satisfaction Not Guaranteed," *BusinessWeek*, June 19, 2006, p. 32.

Chapter 9

1. DePree, Max, *Leadership Is an Art* (New York: Doubleday, 1989), pp. 5–6.

2. For a detailed discussion about masterbrands, see: Upshaw, Lynn B. and Earl L. Taylor, *The Masterbrand Mandate: The Management Strategy That Unifies Companies and Multiplies Value* (New York: John Wiley & Sons, 2000).

3. Source: Hoover's online, accessed July 31, 2006.

4. Austin, James E., "The Invisible Side of Leadership," *Leader to Leader* 8 (Spring 1998): 38–46.

5. Source: Hoover's online, accessed July 31, 2006.

6. From www.hope.edu/admin/frost/, the website of The Frost Research Center at Hope College in Holland, Michigan, accessed March 27, 2006.

7. Telephone interview with Rick Ridgeway and Eve Bould, January 27, 2006,

8. Harrison, Laird, "We're All the Boss: Giving workers stock helps a firm only if it also gives them a say in how the place is run," *Time*, April 8, 2002.

9. From company website, www.gore.com, accessed April 5, 2006.

10. Hoovers online, accessed April 5, 2006.

11. Halliday, Jean, "Ford chronicles turnaround efforts in online film series: Automaker explains its 'change or die' mentality," *Advertising Age* (online), June 27, 2006.

12. Bendapudi, Neeli and Venkat Bendapudi, "Creating the Living Brand," *Harvard Business Review*, May 2005.

13. Collins, Jim, *Good to Great: Why Some Companies Make the Leap. . .and Others Don't* (New York: Harper Business, 2001), p. 64.

14. "Guidant Cuts Profit Outlook, Discloses FDA Warning Letter," *Wall Street Journal* (online), December 27, 2005; and Barry Meier, "Files show Guidant foresaw some risks," *New York Times.com,* December 24, 2005; and Barry Meier, "Reviewers cite flaws at Guidant," *New York Times.com*, March 21, 2006; and Mark Jewell, "Guidant letter about risks never sent," latimes.com (Associated Press), June 7, 2006; and Stephen Heuser, "Boston Scientific aims to end Guidant brand," *Boston Globe, boston.com,* May 18, 2006.

15. Staff Report, "Integrity Matters," *Fast Company* 98 (September 2005): 52.

16. Van Lee, Reggie, Lisa Fabish, and Nancy McGaw, "The Value of Corporate Values," *Strategy + Business* 39 (Spring 2005): 5. Reprinted with permission from *strategy + business*, the award-winning management quarterly published by Booz Allen Hamilton, www.strategy-business.com.

17. Wray, Richard, "BP fails to reduce greenhouse gases," *Guardian*, April 12, 2005.

18. News release, *MIT Sloan Management Newsroom*, May 2, 2006.

19. From the Global 100 website, www.global100.org, accessed March 20, 2006.

20. Lagace, Martha, "Going Green Makes Good Business Sense," *Harvard Business School Working Knowledge for Business Leaders* (online), July 15, 2002.

21. Based on phone interview with Dan Henkle, senior vice president, social responsibility, Gap, Inc., March 8, 2006.

22. Based on phone interview with Michele Banks, vice president, compliance, governance, and employment law, Gap, Inc., April 26, 2006.

23. Asmus, Peter, "100 Best Corporate Citizens for 2004," *Business Ethics*, Spring 2004.

24. Phone interview with Aditya Jha, Infosys global brand manager, June 7, 2006.

25. Source: Ethics Resource Center, *The Ethics Resource Center's 2000 National Business Ethics Survey: How Employees Perceive Ethics at Work* (Washington, D.C.: Ethics Resource Center, 2000), p. 38.

26. Kaihla, Paul with Michael V. Copeland, "Best Kept Secrets of the World's Best Companies," *Business 2.0*, April 2006, p. 85.

27. "Things That Matter" (company values publication), Herman Miller, Inc., p. 37.

28. From transcript of CBS Television program *60 Minutes II*, broadcast January 5, 2005.

29. eBay website, accessed December 5, 2005.

30. Hof, Robert D. (interviewer), "Online Extra: Q&A with eBay's Pierre Omidyar," *BusinessWeek*, December 3, 2001.

Chapter 10

1. O'Brien, Timothy, "The Oracle of Omaha's Latest Riddle," *New York Times*, April 10, 2005.

2. As quoted in Pagano, Bob and Tony Siesfeld, "CMOs & ROI: The Critical Connection," *Market2Customer*, Monitor Group, 2005, p. 1.

3. For a thorough discussion of conventional ROMI, see: Lenskold, James D., *Marketing ROI: The Path to Campaign, Customer, and Corporate Profitability* (New York: McGraw-Hill, 2003).

4. For an in-depth discussion of related issues, see: Ambler, Tim, "Is There a Silver Metric for Marketing Accountability?" Marketing NPV.com, based on a London Business School working paper 05-709: "Choosing Marketing Dashboard Metrics" by Tim Ambler and John Roberts.

5. Mucha, Thomas, "In Ads We Trust? Crisis management and the mutual fund industry," *Business 2.0*, November 20, 2003.

6. See Longview Solutions at www.Longview.com.

Chapter 11

1. Hanft, Adam, "Grist: The New Lust for Integrity," *Inc.* magazine 24 (2004): 104.

2. See the W. Edwards Deming Institute website, www.deming.org.

Bibliography

Abate, Tom. "Generation M: Are we so immersed in media brine that it's become an environmental health hazard?" *San Francisco Chronicle Magazine*, January 1, 2006, p. 6.

Berman, Dennis K. and Joseph Pereira. "Timberland Explores Plan to Sell Itself Amid Fashion Shift." *Wall Street Journal*, November 14, 2006, p. A2.

Ceria, Melissa. "Social Studies: Not content to surf the Web solo, serious shoppers are flocking to retail venues that encourage more than just spending." *Time Style & Design*, Fall 2006, p. 30.

Chouinard, Yvon. *Let My People Go Surfing.* New York: Penguin Press, 2005.

Collins, James C. and Jerry I. Porra. *Built to Last: Successful Habits of Visionary Companies.* New York: HarperBusiness (paperback), 1997.

Dupree, Hugh. *Business as Unusual: The People and Principles of Herman Miller.* Zeeland, Mich.: Herman Miller, Inc., 1986.

Dupree, Max. *Leadership Is an Art.* New York: Currency Doubleday, 1989.

Farrell, Christopher. "The Other Side of Adam Smith." *BusinessWeek Online*, November 15, 2002.

Friedman, Thomas. *The World Is Flat: A Brief History of the Twenty-First Century.* New York: Farrar, Straus and Giroux, 2005.

Godin, Seth. *All Marketers Are Liars: The Power of Telling Authentic Stories in a Low-Trust World* (hardcover). New York: Portfolio, 2005.

Golin, Al. *Trust or Consequences: Build Trust Today or Lose Your Market Tomorrow.* New York: AMACOM, 2004.

Gostick, Adrian and Dana Telford. *The Integrity Advantage: How Taking the High Road Creates a Competitive Advantage in Business.* Layton, Utah: Gibbs Smith, 2003.

Ind, Nicolas, ed. *Beyond Branding: How the New Values of Transparency and Integrity Are Changing the World of Brands.* London: Kogan Page, 2003.

Jackson, Ira A. and Jane Nelson. *Profits with Principles: Seven Strategies for Delivering Value with Values.* New York: Currency Doubleday, 2004.

Lenskold, James D. *Marketing ROI: The Path to Campaign, Customer, and Corporate Profitability.* New York: McGraw-Hill, 2003.

Lewis, Len. *The Trader Joe's Adventure: Turning a Unique Approach to Business into a Retail and Cultural Phenomenon.* Chicago: Dearborn Trade Publishing, 2005.

Magee, David and Robert W. Lane. *The John Deere Way: Performance That Endures* (Introduction). Hoboken, N.J.: John Wiley & Sons, 2005.

Murphy, Patrick E. and Gene R. Laczniak. *Marketing Ethics: Cases and Readings.* Upper Saddle River, N.J.: Pearson Prentice-Hall, 2006.

Murphy, Patrick E., et al. *Ethical Marketing: Basic Ethics in Action.* Upper Saddle River, N.J.: Pearson Education, 2005.

Paine, Lynn Sharp. *Value Shift: Why Companies Must Merge Social and Financial Imperatives to Achieve Superior Performance* (paperback). New York: McGraw-Hill, 2003.

Solomon, Robert C. *A Better Way to Think About Business: How Personal Integrity Leads to Corporate Success.* New York: Oxford University Press, 1999.

Wiersema, Fred. *Customer Intimacy: Pick Your Partners, Shape Your Culture, Win Together.* Santa Monica, Calif.: Knowledge Exchange, 1996.

Index

About the Author

Lynn Upshaw is an internationally known brand and marketing consultant based in the San Francisco Bay Area, and a member of the marketing faculty at the Haas School of Business, University of California—Berkeley.

His clients have been leading corporations, mid-size companies, start-ups, and associations in a broad range of industries, including such organizations as Visa International, SBC Communications (now AT&T), 3Com Corp., Well-Point Health Networks, and Bayer Corporation, among many others.

Upshaw has written two previous books on marketing strategy: the pioneering *Building Brand Identity: A Strategy for Success in a Hostile Marketplace*, and *The Masterbrand Mandate: The Management Strategy That Unifies Companies and Multiplies Value*, co-authored with Earl L. Taylor, which won the 2001 WPP Worldwide Atticus Grand Prix Award. He has also authored numerous articles for publications such as *Advertising Age, Brandweek, The Journal of Brand Management (UK), The Design Management Journal,* and *Advertising Express* (India).

Upshaw has been the keynote or featured speaker at industry and client confe6 + rences throughout North America, and in Europe, Asia, South America, and India. In his work at the Haas School of Business, he was awarded the Earl F. Cheit award for teaching excellence, and frequently lectures about marketing and leadership at the Center for Executive Education.

Upshaw received his bachelor's and master's degrees from Northwestern University. He can be reached at upshaw@upshawmarketing.com.